The Complete English
TRADESMAN

DANIEL DEFOE

ALAN SUTTON
1987

ALAN SUTTON PUBLISHING
BRUNSWICK ROAD · GLOUCESTER

First published 1726
This edition first published 1839

First published in paperback 1987

Copyright © in biographical note
Alan Sutton Publishing Limited, 1987

ISBN 0-86299-464-0

Cover picture: Choosing the Wedding Gown *by William Mulready; Victoria and Albert Museum, London. Photograph: The Bridgeman Art Library.*

Typesetting and origination by
Alan Sutton Publishing Limited.
Printed in Great Britain by
The Guernsey Press Company Limited,
Guernsey, Channel Islands.

BIOGRAPHICAL NOTE

DANIEL DEFOE (1660–1731) was a prolific and versatile writer, often engaged on the boundary between journalism and literature, and the author of some 500 works (many of which were published anonymously). These range from his many ephemeral writings as a reporter and pamphleteer to some of the earliest novels in English literature (including the enduringly popular *Robinson Crusoe*), political, economic and ecclesiastical tracts, verse satires, biography and criminal histories, books on trade, traffic and travel, ghost stories and books treating of demonology and the paranormal, of prophecies and occult visions. His own life is as colourful and various as his writings, with careers of enigmatic complexity in the rising world of commerce, in soldiery; espionage and the civil service and misfortunes in piracy, bankruptcy, imprisonment and the pillory, as well as extensive travel and authorship. However dubious his business and political careers, in the last he was an innovative genius, always vigorously creative, curious and concrete; liberal, moral and humane. He has been called 'the founder of modern journalism and of the English novel', as well as 'the first really modern writer'.

Defoe was born in the year of the Restoration, the son of James Foe, a tallow chandler (later a butcher) of Flemish ancestry and moderate prosperity, in the parish of St. Giles, Cripplegate, London. On account of the Act of Uniformity (1662), his parents adopted Presbyterianism and so brought up their son in an atmosphere of bible-reading, and dissenting Nonconformism (which made him ineligible for university education). His mother died when he was eleven and his formal education, beginning at the age of fourteen at the progressive Stoke Newington Presbyterian Academy (*c.* 1674–9) under the Rev. Charles Morton, was probably intended to prepare him for the dissenting ministry. This he decided against, electing instead to pursue a career as a merchant and hosier which enabled him to travel widely in England and Europe. In 1683 he was captured by Algerian pirates between Harwich and Holland. At the time of his marriage in 1684 to Mary Tuffley, who had brought him a substantial dowry, he was already established on his own account in Cornhill as a hose-factor in the wholesale trade.

His interests in trade led him into politics, above all the politics of Dissent, Conformity and trade. At the time of the (unsuccessful) Western Rising of 1685, he fought at a staunch Dissenter in the Rebellion of the Duke of Monmouth against James II. He then joined the army of William of Orange in 1688 and when the Protestant Dutchman became king on the flight of James II to France, he became William III's leading pamphleteer. The first of many political pamphlets by him had appeared in 1683; he published a pamphlet supporting the Revolution of 1688 and then 'The True-Born Englishman' in 1701, a verse satire in defence of William III which made him famous overnight, said to have been the most widely sold poem that had ever been published in English up to that time.

Meanwhile he had diversified his business interests, trading in many kinds of goods, including oysters and wool, but a speculation in marine insurance exacerbated his financial difficulties (he was involved in eight law suits between 1688 and 1694) and he was declared a bankrupt (for £17,000) in 1692. He then became an 'accountant' for the window tax commissioners, a trustee of royal lotteries and added the particle of gentility 'De' to his name. At this time he was developing a successful brick works and was to engage in government business as secret agent to the king.

In 1702 his fortunes again suffered a reversal when the death of the king deferred any political advancement and he published perhaps his most famous (if ill-timed) pamphlet, 'The Shortest Way with the Dissenters'. An ironical parody pleading for the extermination of Dissenters to lampoon the fanatical intolerance of the High Church Tory party, it backfired when it was condemned as a vicious hoax by both Dissenters and High Churchmen. It led to his arrest for libelling the Church, trial, imprisonment at Newgate (an experience which was to provide material for a number of later writings which treat of criminal life) and his exposure in the pillory in 1703 (although the people drank his health and fêted him).

He was released as a popular hero on the intercession of the ministers Godolphin and Robert Harley, Earl of Oxford. His brick works had failed and his family of six children been reduced to poverty during his imprisonment; he had also published the successful mock-Pindaric 'Hymn to the Pillory' (1703), not without a lasting bitterness. He continued to travel and, under the patronage and influence of Harley, he again became a propagandist on behalf of the Government, its secret representative in Scotland during the Union negotiations (which gave him material for a later book on the Union, published in 1709) and established his own periodical, *The Review*, which flourished under him from 1704 to 1713. This he produced eventually thrice weekly, writing nearly all the articles single handed and showing himself as a journalist of genius, adopting a stance of Tory moderation in articles covering trade, current affairs and religion directed at the merchant classes.

When Harley's ministry fell in 1712, a series of three ironically anti-Jacobite pamphlets (ill-judged, as his earlier 'The Shortest Way with the Dissenters' had been), including 'Reasons against the Succession of the House of Hanover' (a satire in support of the Hanoverian cause), led to his prosecution by the Whigs and, after an abortive trial, to a further spell of imprisonment. Again he made his peace with the new ministry, transferring his allegiance in order to resume his activities, although his loyalties were always suspected as a trimmer and hireling renegade. *The Review* had suspended publication on his conviction, and, after his release, Defoe started to edit a new trade journal, *Mercator*. In 1715 he was convicted of libelling Lord Annesley, but escaped prosecution on the intervention of Lord Townshend, the Whig Secretary of State, when he sold his services as a journalist and secret agent.

Against such a background of violent partisanship, surreptitious journalism, cabal and double-dealing, penury and imprisonment, never clear from legal controversy and debt, his career as a creative writer emerged. He had published the first of his 'true' works of fiction, *A True Relation of the Apparition of one Mrs. Veal* (a contemporary ghost story) in 1706. Then, at the age of nearly 60, living in retirement in Stoke Newington, he embarked on a career as a man of letters and novelist to produce the great works by which he is universally known today.

In 1719 he published *Robinson Crusoe*, one of the most famous books ever written, a 'world book' of mythic power whose happily chosen theme of desert island shipwreck has appealed to generations of adults and children alike; it remains the crowning glory of his popular success. There followed in quick succession the approximately eight real and fictitious narratives of his mature achievement on which his reputation continues to rest, bringing together his brilliant talents as a journalist of the 'real' world, informed by common sense middle class values and racy observations, 'transcribing the actual' in a vivid and artless style. He is a writer of fiction of extraordinary power and imagination, completely free of the noble sentiments of belletrist and courtly neo-classicism in a genre virtually untried in English literature.

Daniel Defoe died on April 26, 1731, 'of lethargy' in his lodgings in Ropemakers' Alley, Moorfields.

NICHOLAS MANDER

A NOTE ON THE TEXT

The publishers wish to acknowledge the assistance of Elizabeth Robinson in the preparation of this edition. The text is that published in 1839 by William and Robert Chambers of Edinburgh. For this, the original 1726 text was edited, with some updating of punctuation and spelling and the addition of footnotes; the first edition having been presented in the form of 'letters' rather than chapters.

AUTHOR'S PREFACE

The title of this work is an index of the performance. It is a collection of useful instructions for a young tradesman. The world is grown so wise of late, or (if you will) fancy themselves so, are so *opiniatre*, as the French well express it, so self-wise, that I expect some will tell us beforehand they know every thing already, and want none of my instructions; and to such, indeed, these instructions are not written.

Had I not, in a few years' experience, seen many young tradesmen miscarry, for want of those very cautions which are here given, I should have thought this work needless, and I am sure had never gone about to write it; but as the contrary is manifest, I thought, and think still, the world greatly wanted it.

And be it that those unfortunate creatures that have thus blown themselves up in trade, have miscarried for want of knowing, or for want of practising, what is here offered for their direction, whether for want of wit, or by too much wit, the thing is the same, and the direction is equally needful to both.

An old experienced pilot sometimes loses a ship by his assurance and over confidence of his knowledge, as effectually as a young pilot does by his ignorance and want of experience – this very thing, as I have been informed, was the occasion of the fatal disaster in which Sir Cloudesley Shovel, and so many hundred brave fellows, lost their lives in a moment upon the rocks of Scilly.[1]

He that is above informing himself when he is in danger, is above pity when he miscarries – a young tradesman who sets up thus full of himself, and scorning advice from those who have gone before him, like a horse that rushes into the battle, is only fearless of danger because he does not understand it.

If there is not something extraordinary in the temper and genius of the tradesmen of this age, if there is not something very singular in their customs and methods, their conduct and behaviour in business; also, if there is not something different and more dangerous and fatal in the common road of trading, and tradesmen's management now, than ever was before, what is the reason that there are so many bankrupts and broken tradesmen now among us, more than ever were known before?

1 [October 22, 1707. – Admiral Shovel, with the confederate fleet from the Mediterranean, as he was coming home, apprehended himself near the rocks of Scilly about noon, and the weather being hazy, he brought to and lay by till evening, when he made a signal for sailing. What induced him to be more cautious in the day than in the night is not known; but the fleet had not been long under sail before his own ship, the *Association*, with the *Eagle* and *Romney*, were dashed to pieces upon the rocks called the *Bishop and his Clerks*, and all their men lost; the *Ferdinand* was also cast away, and but twenty-four of her men saved. Admiral Byng, perceiving the misfortune, altered his course, whereby he preserved himself and the rest of the fleet which sailed after him. – *Salmon's Chronological Historian*. London, 1723.]

I make no doubt but there is as much trade now, and as much gotten by trading, as there ever was in this nation, at least in our memory; and if we will allow other people to judge, they will tell us there is much more trade, and trade is much more gainful; what, then, must be the reason that the tradesmen cannot live on their trades, cannot keep open their shops, cannot maintain themselves and families, as well now as they could before? Something extraordinary must be the case.

There must be some failure in the tradesman – it can be nowhere else – either he is less sober and less frugal, less cautious of what he does, whom he trusts, how he lives, and how he behaves, than tradesmen used to be, or he is less industrious, less diligent, and takes less care and pains in his business, or something is the matter; it cannot be but if he had the same gain, and but the same expense which the former ages suffered tradesmen to thrive with, he would certainly thrive as they did. There must be something out of order in the foundation; he must fail in the essential part, or he would not fail in his trade. The same causes would have the same effects in all ages; the same gain, and but the same expense, would just leave him in the same place as it would have left his predecessor in the same shop; and yet we see one grow rich, and the other starve, under the very same circumstances.

The temper of the times explains the case to every body that pleases but to look into it. The expenses of a family are quite different now from what they have been. Tradesmen cannot live as tradesmen in the same class used to live; custom, and the manner of all the tradesmen round them, command a difference; and he that will not do as others do, is esteemed as nobody among them, and the tradesman is doomed to ruin by the fate of the times.

In short, there is a fate upon a tradesman; either he must yield to the snare of the times, or be the jest of the times; the young tradesman cannot resist it; he must live as others do, or lose the credit of living, and be run down as if he were bankrupt. In a word, he must spend more than he can afford to spend, and so be undone; or not spend it, and so be undone.

If he lives as others do, he breaks, because he spends more than he gets; if he does not, he breaks too, because he loses his credit, and that is to lose his trade. What must he do?[2]

The following directions are calculated for this exigency, and to prepare the young tradesman to stem the attacks of those fatal customs, which otherwise, if he yields to them, will inevitably send him the way of all the thoughtless tradesmen that have gone before him.

Here he will be effectually, we hope, encouraged to set out well; to begin wisely and prudently; and to avoid all those rocks which the gay race of tradesmen so frequently suffer shipwreck upon. And here he will have a true plan of his own prosperity drawn out for him, by which, if it be not his own fault, he may square his conduct in an unerring manner, and fear neither bad fortune nor bad friends.

2 [There is much reason for receiving all such complaints as the above with caution. The extravagance of the present, in contrast with the frugality of a past age, has always been a favourite topic of declamation, and appears to have no other foundation than whim. Indeed, it is next to impossible that any great body of men could exist in the circumstances described in the text.]

I had purposed to give a great many other cautions and directions in this work, but it would have spun it out too far, and have made it tedious. I would indeed have discoursed of some branches of home trade, which necessarily embarks the inland tradesman in some parts of foreign business, and so makes a merchant of the shopkeeper almost whether he will or no. For example, almost all the shopkeepers and inland traders in seaport towns, or even in the water-side part of London itself, are necessarily brought in to be owners of ships, and concerned at least in the vessel, if not in the voyage. Some of their trades, perhaps, relate to, or are employed in, the building, or fitting, or furnishing out ships, as is the case at Shoreham, at Ipswich, Yarmouth, Hull, Whitby, Newcastle, and the like. Others are concerned in the cargoes, as in the herring fishery at Yarmouth and the adjacent ports, the colliery at Newcastle, Sunderland, &c., and the like in many other cases.

In this case, the shopkeeper is sometimes a merchant adventurer, whether he will or not, and some of his business runs into sea-adventures, as in the salt trade at Sheffield, in Northumberland, and Durham, and again at Limington; and again in the coal trade, from Whitehaven in Cumberland to Ireland, and the like.

These considerations urged me to direct due cautions to such tradesmen, and such as would be particular to them, especially not to launch out in adventures beyond the compass of their stocks,[3] and withal to manage those things with due wariness. But this work had not room for those things; and as that sort of amphibious tradesmen, for such they are, trading both by water and by land, are not of the kind with those particularly aimed at in these sheets, I thought it was better to leave them quite out than to touch but lightly upon them.

I had also designed one chapter or letter to my inland tradesmen, upon the most important subject of borrowing money upon interest, which is one of the most dangerous things a tradesman is exposed to. It is a pleasant thing to a tradesman to see his credit rise, and men offer him money to trade with, upon so slender a consideration as five per cent. interest, when he gets ten per cent. perhaps twice in the year; but it is a snare of the most dangerous kind in the event, and has been the ruin of so many tradesmen, that, though I had not room for it in the work, I could not let it pass without this notice in the preface.

1. Interest-money eats deep into the tradesman's profits, because it is a payment certain, whether the tradesman gets or loses, and as he may often get double, so sometimes he loses, and then his interest is a double payment; it is a partner with him under this unhappy circumstance, namely, that it goes halves when he gains, but not when he loses.

2. The lender calls for his money when he pleases, and often comes for it when the borrower can ill spare it; and then, having launched out in trade on the supposition of so much in stock, he is left to struggle with the enlarged trade with a contracted stock, and thus he sinks under the weight of it, cannot repay the money, is dishonoured, prosecuted, and at last undone, by the very loan which he took in to help him.

3 [Stock is in this book invariably used for what we express by the term *capital*.]

Interest of money is a dead weight upon the tradesman, and as the interest always keeps him low, the principal sinks him quite down, when that comes to be paid out again. Payment of interest, to a tradesman, is like Cicero bleeding to death in a warm bath;[4] the pleasing warmth of the bath makes him die in a kind of dream, and not feel himself decay, till at last he is exhausted, falls into convulsions, and expires.

A tradesman held up by money at interest, is sure to sink at last by the weight of it, like a man thrown into the sea with a stone tied about his neck, who though he could swim if he was loose, drowns in spite of all his struggle.

Indeed, this article would require not a letter, but a book by itself; and the tragical stories of tradesmen undone by usury are so many, and the variety so great, that they would make a history by themselves. But it must suffice to treat it here only in general, and give the tradesmen a warning of it, as the Trinity-house pilots warn sailors of a sand, by hanging a buoy upon it, or as the Eddystone light-house upon a sunk rock, which, as the poet says, 'Bids men stand off, and live; come near, and die.'

For a tradesman to borrow money upon interest, I take to be like a man going into a house infected with the plague; it is not only likely that he may be infected and die, but next to a miracle if he escapes.

This part being thus hinted at, I think I may say of the following sheets, that they contain all the directions needful to make the tradesman thrive; and if he pleases to listen to them with a temper of mind willing to be directed, he must have some uncommon ill luck if he miscarries.

4 [Cicero is here given by mistake for Seneca, who thus suffered death by order of the tyrant Nero.]

INTRODUCTION

Being to direct this discourse to the tradesmen of this nation, it is needful, in order to make the substance of this work and the subject of it agree together, that I should in a few words explain the terms, and tell the reader who it is we understand by the word tradesman, and how he is to be qualified in order to merit the title of *complete*.

This is necessary, because the said term tradesman is understood by several people, and in several places, in a different manner: for example, in the north of Britain, and likewise in Ireland, when you say a tradesman, you are understood to mean a mechanic, such as a smith, a carpenter, a shoemaker, and the like, such as here we call a handicraftsman. In like manner, abroad they call a tradesman such only as carry goods about from town to town, and from market to market, or from house to house, to sell; these in England we call petty chapmen, in the north pethers, and in our ordinary speech pedlars.

But in England, and especially in London, and the south parts of Britain, we take it in another sense, and in general, all sorts of warehousekeepers, shopkeepers, whether wholesale dealers or retailers of goods, are called tradesmen, or, to explain it by another word, trading men: such are, whether wholesale or retail, our grocers, mercers, linen and woollen drapers, Blackwell-hall factors, tobacconists, haberdashers, whether of hats or small wares, glovers, hosiers, milliners, booksellers, stationers, and all other shopkeepers, who do not actually work upon, make, or manufacture, the goods they sell.

On the other hand, those who make the goods they sell, though they do keep shops to sell them, are not called tradesmen, but handicrafts, such as smiths, shoemakers, founders, joiners, carpenters, carvers, turners, and the like; others, who only make, or cause to be made, goods for other people to sell, are called manufacturers and artists, &c. Thus distinguished, I shall speak of them all as occasion requires, taking this general explication to be sufficient; and I thus mention it to prevent being obliged to frequent and further particular descriptions as I go on.

As there are several degrees of people employed in trade below these, such as workmen, labourers, and servants, so there is a degree of traders above them, which we call merchants; where it is needful to observe, that in other countries, and even in the north of Britain and Ireland, as the handicraftsmen and artists are called tradesmen, so the shopkeepers whom we here call tradesmen, are all called merchants; nay, even the very pedlars are called travelling merchants.[1] But in England the word merchant is understood of none but such as carry on foreign correspondences, importing the goods and growth of other countries, and exporting the growth and manufacture of England to other countries; or, to use a vulgar expression, because I am

1 [This misuse of the term *merchant* continues to exist in Scotland to the present day.]

speaking to and of those who use that expression, such as trade beyond sea. These in England, and these only, are called merchants, by way of honourable distinction; these I am not concerned with in this work, nor is any part of it directed to them.

As the tradesmen are thus distinguished, and their several occupations divided into proper classes, so are the trades. The general commerce of England, as it is the most considerable of any nation in the world, so that part of it which we call the home or inland trade, is equal, if not superior, to that of any other nation, though some of those nations are infinitely greater than England, and more populous also, as France and Germany in particular.

I insist that the trade of England is greater and more considerable than that of any other nation, for these reasons: 1. Because England produces more goods as well for home consumption as for foreign exportation, and those goods all made of its own produce or manufactured by its own inhabitants, than any other nation in the world. 2. Because England consumes within itself more goods of foreign growth, imported from the several countries where they are produced or wrought, than any other nation in the world. And – 3. Because for the doing this England employs more shipping and more seamen than any other nation, and, some think, than all the other nations, of Europe.

Hence, besides the great number of wealthy merchants who carry on this great foreign *negoce* [*negotium* (Latin) business], and who, by their corresponding with all parts of the world, import the growth of all countries hither – I say, besides these, we have a very great number of considerable dealers, whom we call tradesmen, who are properly called warehouse-keepers, who supply the merchants with all the several kinds of manufactures, and other goods of the produce of England, for exportation; and also others who are called wholesalemen, who buy and take off from the merchants all the foreign goods which they import; these, by their corresponding with a like sort of tradesmen in the country, convey and hand forward those goods, and our own also, among those country tradesmen, into every corner of the kingdom, however remote, and by them to the retailers, and by the retailer to the last consumer, which is the last article of all trade. These are the tradesmen understood in this work, and for whose service these sheets are made public.

Having thus described the person whom I understand by the English tradesman, it is then needful to inquire into his qualifications, and what it is that renders him a finished or complete man in his business.

1. That he has a general knowledge of not his own particular trade and business only – that part, indeed, well denominates a handicraftsman to be a complete artist; but our complete tradesman ought to understand all the inland trade of England, so as to be able to turn his hand to any thing, or deal in any thing or every thing of the growth and product of his own country, or the manufacture of the people, as his circumstances in trade or other occasions may require; and may, if he sees occasion, lay down one trade and take up another when he pleases, without serving a new apprenticeship to learn it.

2. That he not only has a knowledge of the species or kinds of goods, but of the places and peculiar countries where those goods, whether product or manufacture, are to be found; that is to say, where produced or where made, and how to come at them or deal in them, at the first hand, and to his best advantage.

3. That he understands perfectly well all the methods of correspondence, returning money or goods for goods, to and from every county in England; in what manner to be done, and in what manner most to advantage; what goods are generally bought by barter and exchange, and what by payment of money; what for present money, and what for time; what are sold by commission from the makers, what bought by factors, and by giving commission to buyers in the country, and what bought by orders to the maker, and the like; what markets are the most proper to buy every thing at, and where and when; and what fairs are proper to go to in order to buy or sell, or meet the country dealer at, such as Sturbridge, Bristol, Chester, Exeter; or what marts, such as Beverly, Lynn, Boston, Gainsborough, and the like.

In order to complete the English tradesman in this manner, the first thing to be done is lay down such general maxims of trade as are fit for his instruction, and then to describe the English or British product, being the fund of its inland trade, whether we mean its produce as the growth of the country, or its manufactures, as the labour of her people; then to acquaint the tradesman with the manner of the circulation where those things are found, how and by what methods all those goods are brought to London, and from London again conveyed into the country; where they are principally bought at best hand, and most to the advantage of the buyer, and where the proper markets are to dispose of them again when bought.

These are the degrees by which the complete tradesman is brought up, and by which he is instructed in the principles and methods of his commerce, by which he is made acquainted with business, and is capable of carrying it on with success, after which there is not a man in the universe deserves the title of a complete tradesman, like the English shopkeeper.

CHAPTER I

THE TRADESMAN IN HIS PREPARATIONS WHILE AN APPRENTICE

The first part of a trader's beginning is ordinarily when he is very young, I mean, when he goes as an apprentice, and the notions of trade are scarcely got into his head; for boys go apprentices while they are but boys; to talk to them in their first three or four years signifies nothing; they are rather then to be taught submission to families, and subjection to their masters, and dutiful attendance in their shops or warehouses; and this is not our present business.

But after they have entered the fifth or sixth year, they may then be entertained with discourses of another nature; and as they begin then to look forward beyond the time of their servitude, and think of setting up and being for themselves, I think then is the time to put them upon useful preparations for the work, and to instruct them in such things as may qualify them best to enter upon the world, and act for themselves when they are so entered.

The first thing a youth in the latter part of his time is to do, is to endeavour to gain a good judgment in the wares of all kinds that he is likely to deal in – as, for example, if a draper, the quality of cloths; if a stationer, the quality of papers; if a grocer, the quality of sugars, teas, &c.; and so on with all other trades. During the first years of a young man's time, he of course learns to weigh and measure either liquids or solids, to pack up and make bales, trusses, packages, &c., and to do the coarser and laborious part of business; but all that gives him little knowledge in the species and quality of the goods, much less a nice judgment in their value and sorts, which however is one of the principal things that belong to trade.

It is supposed that, by this time, if his master is a man of considerable business, his man is become the eldest apprentice, and is taken from the counter, and from sweeping the warehouse, into the counting-house, where he, among other things, sees the bills of parcels of goods bought, and thereby knows what every thing costs at first hand, what gain is made of them, and if a miscarriage happens, he knows what loss too; by which he is led of course to look into the goodness of the goods, and see the reason of things: if the goods are not to expectation, and consequently do not answer the price, he sees the reason of that loss, and he looks into the goods, and sees where and how far they are deficient, and in what; this, if he be careful to make his observations, brings him naturally to have a good judgment in the goods.

If a young man neglects this part, and passes over the season for such improvement, he very rarely ever recovers it; for this part has its season, and that more remarkable than in many other cases, and that season lost, never comes again; a judgment in goods taken in early, is never lost, and a judgment taken in late is seldom good.

If the youth slips this occasion, and, not minding what is before him, goes out of his time without obtaining such a skill as this in the goods he is to deal in, he enters into trade without his most useful tools, and must use spectacles before his time.

For want of this knowledge of the goods, he is at a loss in the buying part, and is liable to be cheated and imposed upon in the most notorious manner by the sharp-sighted world, for his want of judgment is a thing that cannot be hid; the merchants or manufacturers of whom he buys, presently discover him; the very boys in the wholesalemen's warehouses, and in merchant's warehouses, will play upon him, sell him one thing for another, show him a worse sort when he calls for a better, and, asking a higher price for it, persuade him it is better; and when they have thus bubbled him, they triumph over his ignorance when he is gone, and expose him to the last degree.

Besides, for want of judgment in the goods he is to buy, he often runs a hazard of being cheated to a very great degree, and perhaps some time or other a tradesman may be ruined by it, or at least ruin his reputation.

When I lived abroad, I had once a commission sent me from a merchant in London, to buy a large parcel of brandy: the goods were something out of my way, having never bought any in that country before. However, it happened that I had frequently bought and imported brandies in England, and had some judgment in them, so much that I ventured to buy without taking a cooper with me, which was not usual in that place. The first parcel of brandy I saw was very good, and I bought freely to the value of about £600, and shipped them for England, where they gave very good satisfaction to my employer. But I could not complete my commission to my mind in that parcel. Some days after, some merchants, who had seen me buy the other, and thought me a novice in the business, and that I took no cooper to taste the brandy, laid a plot for me, which indeed was such a plot as I was not in the least aware of; and had not the little judgment which I had in the commodity prevented, I had been notoriously abused. The case was thus: – They gave me notice by the same person who helped me to the sight of the first brandy, that there was a cellar of extraordinary good brandy at such a place, and invited me to see it. Accordingly I went in an afternoon, and tasted the brandy, being a large parcel, amounting to about £460.

I liked the goods very well; but the merchant, as they called him, that is to say, the knave appointed to cheat the poor stranger, was cunningly out of the way, so that no bargain was to be made that night. But as I had said that I liked the brandy, the same person who brought me an account of them, comes to my lodgings to treat with me about the price. We did not make many words: I bade him the current price which I had bought for some days before, and after a few struggles for five crowns a-tun more, he came to my price, and his next word was to let me know the gage of the cask; and as I had seen the goods already, he thought there was nothing to do but to make a bargain, and order the goods to be delivered.

But young as I was, I was too old for that too; and told him, I could not tell positively how many I should take, but that I would come in the afternoon, and taste them again, and mark out what I wanted. He seemed uneasy at that, and pretended he had two merchants waiting to see them, and he could sell them immediately, and I might do him a prejudice if I made him wait and put them off, who perhaps might buy in the mean time.

I answered him coldly, I would not hinder him selling them by any means if he could have a better chapman, that I could not come sooner, and that I would not be obliged to take the whole parcel, nor would I buy any of them without tasting them again: he argued much to have me buy them, seeing, as he said, I had tasted them before, and liked them very well.

'I did so,' said I, 'but I love to have my palate confirm one day what it approved the day before.' 'Perhaps,' says he, 'you would have some other person's judgment of them, and you are welcome to do so, sir, with all my heart; send any body you please:' but still he urged for a bargain, when the person sent should make his report; and then he had his agents ready, I understood afterwards, to manage the persons I should send.

I answered him frankly, I had no great judgment, but that, such as it was, I ventured to trust to it; I thought I had honest men to deal with, and that I should bring nobody to taste them for me but myself.

This pleased him, and was what he secretly wished; and now, instead of desiring me to come immediately, he told me, that seeing I would not buy without seeing the goods again, and would not go just then, he could not be in the way in the afternoon, and so desired I would defer it till next morning, which I readily agreed to.

In the morning I went, but not so soon as I had appointed; upon which, when I came, he seemed offended, and said I had hindered him

– that he could have sold the whole parcel, &c. I told him I could not have hindered him, for that I had told him he should not wait for me, but sell them to the first good customer he found. He told me he had indeed sold two or three casks, but he would not disoblige me so much as to sell the whole parcel before I came. This I mention, because he made it a kind of a bite upon me, that I should not be alarmed at seeing the casks displaced in the cellar.

When I came to taste the brandy, I began to be surprised. I saw the very same casks which I had touched with the marking-iron when I was there before, but I did not like the brandy by any means, but did not yet suspect the least foul play.

I went round the whole cellar, and I could not mark above three casks which I durst venture to buy; the rest apparently showed themselves to be mixed, at least I thought so. I marked out the three casks, and told him my palate had deceived me, that the rest of the brandy was not for my turn.

I saw the man surprised, and turn pale, and at first seemed to be very angry, that I should, as he called it, disparage the goods – that sure I did not understand brandy, and the like – and that I should have brought somebody with me that did understand it. I answered coldly, that if I ventured my money upon my own judgment, the hazard was not to the seller, but to the buyer, and nobody had to do with that; if I did not like his goods, another, whose judgment was better, might like them, and so there was no harm done: in a word, he would not let me have the three casks I had marked, unless I took more, and I would take no more – so we parted, but with no satisfaction on his side; and I afterwards came to hear that he had sat up all the night with his coopers, mixing spirits in every cask, whence he drew off a quantity of the right brandy, and corrupted it, concluding, that as I had no judgment to choose by but my own, I could not discover it; and it came out by his quarrelling with the person who brought me to him, for telling him I did not understand the goods, upon which presumption he ventured to spoil the whole parcel.

I give you this story as a just caution to a young tradesman, and to show how necessary it is that a tradesman should have judgment in the goods he buys, and how easily he may be imposed upon and abused, if he offers to buy upon his own judgment, when really it is defective. I could enlarge this article with many like examples, but I think this may suffice.

The next thing I recommend to an apprentice at the conclusion of his time, is to acquaint himself with his master's chapmen;[1] I mean of both kinds, as well those he sells to, as those he buys of, and, if he is a

1 [Individuals dealt with.]

factor, with his master's employers. But what I aim at now is the chapmen and customers whom his master chiefly sells to. I need not explain myself not to mean by this the chance customers of a retailer's shop, for there can be no acquaintance, or very little, made with them; I mean the country shopkeepers, or others, who buy in parcels, and who buy to sell again, or export as merchants. If the young man comes from his master, and has formed no acquaintance or interest among the customers whom his master dealt with, he has, in short, slipt or lost one of the principal ends and reasons of his being an apprentice, in which he has spent seven years, and perhaps his friends given a considerable sum of money.

For a young man coming out of his time to have his shop or warehouse stocked with goods, and his customers all to seek, will make his beginning infinitely more difficult to him than it would otherwise be; and he not only has new customers to seek, but has their characters to seek also, and knows not who is good and who not, till he buys that knowledge by his experience, and perhaps sometimes pays too dear for it.

It was an odd circumstance of a tradesman in this city a few years ago, who, being out of his time, and going to solicit one of his master's customers to trade with him, the chapman did not so much as know him, or remember that he had ever heard his name, except as he had heard his master call his apprentice Jacob. I know some masters diligently watch to prevent their apprentices speaking to their customers, and to keep them from acquainting themselves with the buyers, that when they come out of their times they may not carry the trade away with them.

To hinder an apprentice from an acquaintance with the dealers of both sorts, is somewhat like Laban's usage of Jacob, namely, keeping back the beloved Rachel, whom he served his seven years' time for, and putting him off with a blear-eyed Leah in her stead; it is, indeed, a kind of robbing him, taking from him the advantage which he served his time for, and sending him into the world like a man out of a ship set on shore among savages, who, instead of feeding him, are indeed more ready to eat him up and devour him.[2]

An apprentice who has served out his time faithfully and diligently, ought to claim it as a debt to his indentures, that his master should let him into an open acquaintance with his customers; he does not else perform his promise to teach him the art and mystery of his trade; he does not make

2 [It would be hard to doubt that Defore was sincere in this pleading of the rights of the apprentice; but its morality is certainly far from clear. The master may have gained customers with difficulty, by the exercise of much ingenuity, patience, and industry, or through some peculiar merit of his own. Indeed, it is always to be presumed that a tradesman's customers are attached to him from some of these causes. Of course, it would be hard if his apprentices, instead of collecting customers for themselves by the same means, seduced away those of his master. The true and direct object of an apprenticeshop is to acquire a trade, not to acquire customers.]

him master of his business, or enable him as he ought to set up in the world; for, as buying is indeed the first, so selling is the last end of trade, and the faithful apprentice ought to be fully made acquainted with them both.

Next to being acquainted with his master's customers and chapmen, the apprentice, when his time is near expiring, ought to acquaint himself with the books, that is to say, to see and learn his master's method of book-keeping, that he may follow it, if the method is good, and may learn a better method in time, if it is not.

The tradesman should not be at a loss how to keep his books, when he is to begin his trade; that would be to put him to school when he is just come from school; his apprenticeship is, and ought in justice to be, a school to him, where he ought to learn every thing that should qualify him for his business, at least every thing that his master can teach him; and if he finds his master either backward or unwilling to teach him, he should complain in time to his own friends, that they may some how or other supply the defect.

A tradesman's books are his repeating clock, which upon all occasions are to tell him how he goes on, and how things stand with him in the world: there he will know when it is time to go on, or when it is time to give over; and upon his regular keeping, and fully acquainting himself with his books, depends at least the comfort of his trade, if not the very trade itself. If they are not duly posted, and if every thing is not carefully entered in them, the debtor's accounts kept even, the cash constantly balanced, and the credits all stated, the tradesman is like a ship at sea, steered without a helm; he is all in confusion, and knows not what he does, or where he is; he may be a rich man, or a bankrupt – for, in a word, he can give no account of himself to himself, much less to any body else.

His books being so essential to his trade, he that comes out of his time without a perfect knowledge of the method of book-keeping, like a bride undrest, is not fit to be married; he knows not what to do, or what step to take; he may indeed have served his time, but he has not learned his trade, nor is he fit to set up; and be the fault in himself for not learning, or in his master for not teaching him, he ought not to set up till he has gotten some skilful person to put him in a way to do it, and make him fully to understand it.

It is true, there is not a great deal of difficulty in keeping a tradesman's books, especially if he be a retailer only; but yet, even in the meanest trades, they ought to know how to keep books. But the advice is directed to those who are above the retailer, as well as to them; if the book-keeping be small, it is the sooner learned, and the apprentice is the more to blame if he neglects it. Besides, the objection is much more trifling than the advice. The tradesman cannot carry on any considerable trade without books; and he must, during his apprenticeship, prepare himself for business by acquainting himself with every thing needful for his going on with his trade, among which that of book-keeping is absolutely necessary.

The last article, and in itself essential to a young tradesman, is to know how to buy; if his master is kind and generous, he will consider the justice of this part, and let him into the secret of it of his own free will, and that before his time is fully expired; but if that should not happen, as often it does not, let the apprentice know, that it is one of the most needful things to him that can belong to his apprenticeship, and that he ought not to let his time run over his head, without getting as much insight into it as possible; that therefore he ought to lose no opportunity to get into it, even whether his master approves of it or no; for as it is a debt due to him from his master to instruct him in it, it is highly just he should use all proper means to come at it.

Indeed, the affair in this age between masters and their apprentices, stands in a different view from what the same thing was a few years past; the state of our apprenticeship is not a state of servitude now, and hardly of subjection, and their behaviour is accordingly more like gentlemen than tradesmen; more like companions to their masters, than like servants. On the other hand, the masters seem to have made over their authority to their apprentices for a sum of money, the money taken now with apprentices being most exorbitantly great, compared to what it was in former times.

Now, though this does not at all exempt the servant or apprentice from taking care of himself, and to qualify himself for business while he is an apprentice, yet it is evident that it is no furtherance to apprentices; the liberties they take towards the conclusion of their time, are so much employed to worse purposes, that apprentices do not come out of their times better finished for business and trade than they did formerly, but much the worse: and though it is not the proper business and design of this work to enlarge on the injustice done both to master and servant by this change of custom, yet to bring it to my present purpose, it carries this force with it, namely, that the advice to apprentices to endeavour to finish themselves for business during the time of the indenture, is so much the more needful and seasonable.

Nor is this advice for the service of the master, but of the apprentice; for if the apprentice neglects this advice, if he omits to qualify himself for business as above, if he neither will acquaint himself with the customers, nor the books, nor with the buying part, nor gain judgment in the wares he is to deal in, the loss is his own, not his master's – and, indeed, he may be said to have served not himself, but his master – and both his money and his seven years are all thrown away.

CHAPTER II

THE TRADESMAN'S WRITING LETTERS

As plainness, and a free unconstrained way of speaking, is the beauty and excellence of speech, so an easy free concise way of writing is the best style for a tradesman. He that affects a rumbling and bombast style, and fills his letters with long harangues, compliments, and flourishes, should turn poet instead of tradesman, and set up for a wit, not a shopkeeper. Hark how such a young tradesman writes, out of the country, to his wholesaleman in London, upon his first setting up.

'SIR – The destinies having so appointed it, and my dark stars concurring, that I, who by nature was framed for better things, should be put out to a trade, and the gods having been so propitious to me in the time of my servitude, that at length the days are expired, and I am launched forth into the great ocean of business, I thought fit to acquaint you, that last month I received my fortune, which, by my father's will, had been my due two years past, at which time I arrived to man's estate, and became major, whereupon I have taken a house in one of the principal streets of the town of ——, where I am entered upon my business, and hereby let you know that I shall have occasion for the goods hereafter mentioned, which you may send to me by the carrier.'

This fine flourish, and which, no doubt, the young fellow dressed up with much application, and thought was very well done, put his correspondent in London into a fit of laughter, and instead of sending him the goods he wrote for, put him either first upon writing down into the country to inquire after his character, and whether he was worth dealing with, or else it obtained to be filed up among such letters as deserved no answer.

The same tradesman in London received by the post another letter, from a young shopkeeper in the country, to the purpose following:–

'Being obliged, Sir, by my late master's decease, to enter immediately upon his business, and consequently open my shop without coming up to London to furnish myself with such goods as at present I want, I have here sent you a small order, as underwritten. I hope you will think yourself obliged to use me well, and particularly that the goods may be good of the sorts, though I cannot be at London to look them out myself. I have enclosed a bill of exchange for £75, on Messrs A. B. and Company, payable to you, or your order, at one-and-twenty days' sight; be pleased to get it accepted, and if the goods amount to more than that sum, I shall, when I have your bill of parcels, send you the remainder. I repeat my desire, that you will send me the goods well sorted, and well chosen, and as cheap as possible, that I may be encouraged to a further correspondence. I am, your humble servant,

C.K.'

This was writing like a man that understood what he was doing; and his correpondent in London would presently say – 'This young man writes like a man of business; pray let us take care to use him well, for in all probability he will be a very good chapman.'

The sum of the matter is this: a tradesman's letters should be plain, concise, and to the purpose; no quaint expressions, no book-phrases, no flourishes, and yet they must be full and sufficient to express what he means, so as not to be doubtful, much less unintelligible. I can by no means approve of studied abbreviations, and leaving out the needful copulatives of speech in trading letters; they are to an extreme affected; no beauty to the style, but, on the contrary, a deformity of the grossest nature. They are affected to the last degree, and with this aggravation, that it is an affectation of the grossest nature; for, in a word, it is affecting to be thought a man of more than ordinary sense by writing extraordinary nonsense; and affecting to be a man of business, by giving orders and expressing your meaning in terms which a man of business may not think himself bound by. For example, a tradesman at Hull writes to his correspondent at London the following letter:–

'SIR, yours received, have at present little to reply. Last post you had bills of loading, with invoice of what had loaden for your account in Hamburgh factor bound for said port. What have farther orders for, shall be dispatched with expedition. Markets slacken much on this side; cannot sell the iron for more than 37s. Wish had your orders if shall part with it at that rate. No ships since the 11th. London fleet may be in the roads before the late storm, so hope they are safe: if have not insured, please omit the same till hear farther; the weather proving good, hope the danger is over.

My last transmitted three bills exchange, import £315; please signify if are come to hand, and accepted, and give credit in account current to your humble servant.'

I pretend to say there is nothing in all this letter, though appearing to have the face of a considerable dealer, but what may be taken any way, *pro* or *con*. The Hamburgh factor may be a ship, or a horse – be bound to Hamburgh or London. What shall be dispatched may be one thing, or any thing, or every thing, in a former letter. No ships since the 11th, may be no ships come in, or no ships gone out. The London fleet being in the roads, it may be the London fleet from Hull to London, or from London to Hull, both being often at sea together. The roads may be Yarmouth roads, or Grimsby, or, indeed, any where.

By such a way of writing, no orders can be binding to him that gives them, or to him they are given to. A merchant writes to his factor at Lisbon:–

'Please to send, per first ship, 150 chests best Seville, and 200 pipes best Lisbon white. May value yourself per exchange £1250 sterling, for the account of above orders. Suppose you can send the sloop to Seville for the ordered chests, &c. I am.'

Here is the order to send a cargo, with a *please to send*; so the factor may let it alone if he does not please.[1] The order is 150 chests Seville; it is supposed he means oranges, but it may be 150 chests orange-trees as well, or chests of oil, or any thing. Lisbon white, may be wine or any thing else, though it is supposed to be wine. He may draw £1250, but he may refuse to accept it if he pleases, for any thing such an order as that obliges him.

On the contrary, orders ought to be plain and explicit; and he ought to have assured him, that on his drawing on him, his bills should be honoured – that is, accepted and paid.

I know this affectation of style is accounted very grand, looks modish, and has a kind of majestic greatness in it; but the best merchants in the world are come off from it, and now choose to write plain and intelligibly: much less should country tradesmen, citizens, and shopkeepers, whose business is plainness and mere trade, make use of it.

I have mentioned this in the beginning of this work, because, indeed, it is the beginning of a tradesman's business. When a tradesman takes an apprentice, the first thing he does for him, after he takes him from behind his counter, after he lets him into his counting-house and his books, and after trusting him with his more private business – I say, the first thing is to let him write letters to his dealers, and correspond with his friends; and this he does in his master's name, subscribing his letters thus:–

I am, for my master, A. B. and Company, your
humble servant, C. D.

1 [The practice of trade now sanctions courteous expressions of this kind.]

And beginning thus:–

Sir, I am ordered by my master A. B. to advise you that ——

Or thus:–

Sir, By my master's order, I am to signify to you that——

Orders for goods ought to be very explicit and particular, that the dealer may not mistake, especially if it be orders from a tradesman to a manufacturer to make goods, or to buy goods, either of such a quality, or to such a pattern; in which, if the goods are made to the colours, and of a marketable goodness, and within the time limited, the person ordering them cannot refuse to receive them, and make himself debtor to the maker. On the contrary, if the goods are not of a marketable goodness, or not to the patterns, or are not sent within the time, the maker ought not to expect they should be received. For example–

The tradesman, or warehouseman, or what else we may call him, writes to his correspondent at Devizes, in Wiltshire, thus:–

'SIR – The goods you sent me last week are not at all for my purpose, being of a sort which I am at present full of: however, if you are willing they should lie here, I will take all opportunities to sell them for your account; otherwise, on your first orders, they shall be delivered to whoever you shall direct: and as you had no orders from me for such sorts of goods, you cannot take this ill. But I have here enclosed sent you five patterns as under, marked 1 to 5; if you think fit to make me fifty pieces of druggets of the same weight and goodness with the fifty pieces, No. A.B., which I had from you last October, and mixed as exactly as you can to the enclosed patterns, ten to each pattern, and can have the same to be delivered here any time in February next, I shall take them at the same price which I gave you for the last; and one month after the delivery you may draw upon me for the money, which shall be paid to your content. Your friend and servant.

P.S. Let me have your return per next post, intimating that you can or cannot answer this order, that I may govern myself accordingly.
To Mr H. G., clothier, Devizes.'

The clothier, accordingly, gives him an answer the next post, as follows:–

'SIR – I have the favour of yours of the 22d past, with your order for fifty fine druggets, to be made of the like weight and goodness with the two packs, No. A.B., which I made for you and sent last October, as also the five patterns enclosed, marked 1 to 5, for my direction in the mixture. I give you this trouble, according to your order, to let you know I have already put the said fifty pieces in hand; and as I am always willing to serve you to the best of my power, and am thankful for your favours, you may depend upon them within the time, that is to say, some time in February next, and that they shall be of the like fineness and substance with the other, and as near to the patterns as possible. But in regard our poor are very craving, and money at this time very scarce, I beg you will give me leave (twenty or thirty pieces of them being finished and delivered to you at any time before the remainder), to draw fifty pounds on you for present occasion; for which I shall think myself greatly obliged, and shall give you any security you please that the rest shall follow within the time.

As to the pack of goods in your hands, which were sent up without your order, I am content they remain in your hands for sale on my account, and desire you will sell them as soon as you can, for my best advantage. I am,' &c.

Here is a harmony of business, and every thing exact; the order is given plain and express; the clothier answers directly to every point; here can be no defect in the correspondence; the diligent clothier applies immediately to the work, sorts and dyes his wool, mixes his colours to the patterns, puts the wool to the spinners, sends his yarn to the weavers, has the pieces brought home, then has them to the thicking or fulling-mill, dresses them in his own workhouse, and sends them up punctually by the time; perhaps by the middle of the month. Having sent up twenty pieces five weeks before, the warehouse-keeper, to oblige him, pays his bill of £50, and a month after the rest are sent in, he draws for the rest of the money, and his bills are punctually paid. The consequence of this exact writing and answering is this–

The warehouse-keeper having the order from his merchant, is furnished in time, and obliges his customer; then says he to his servant, 'Well, this H. G. of Devizes is a clever workman, understands his business, and may be depended on: I see if I have an order to give that requires any exactness and honest usage, he is my man; he understands orders when they are sent, goes to work immediately, and answers them punctually.'

Again, the clothier at Devizes says to his head man, or perhaps his son, 'This Mr H. is a very good employer, and is worth obliging; his orders are so plain and so direct, that a man cannot mistake, and if the goods are made honestly and to his time, there's one's money; bills are cheerfully accepted, and punctually paid; I'll never disappoint him; whoever goes without goods, he shall not.'

On the contrary, when orders are darkly given, they are doubtfully observed; and when the goods come to town, the merchant dislikes them, the warehouseman shuffles them back upon the clothier, to lie for his account, pretending they are not made to his order; the clothier is discouraged, and for want of his money discredited, and all their correspondence is confusion, and ends in loss both of money and credit.

CHAPTER III

THE TRADING STYLE

In the last chapter I gave my thoughts for the instruction of young tradesmen in writing letters with orders, and answering orders, and especially about the proper style of a tradesman's letters, which I hinted should be plain and easy, free in language, and direct to the purpose intended. Give me leave to go on with the subject a little farther, as I think it is useful in another part of the tradesman's correspondence.

I might have made some apology for urging tradesmen to write a plain and easy style; let me add, that the tradesmen need not be offended at my condemning them, as it were, to a plain and homely style – easy, plain, and familiar language is the beauty of speech in general, and is the excellency of all writing, on whatever subject, or to whatever persons they are we write or speak. The end of speech is that men might understand one another's meaning; certainly that speech, or that way of speaking, which is most easily understood, is the best way of speaking. If any man were to ask me, which would be supposed to be a perfect style, or language, I would answer, that in which a man speaking to five hundred people, of all common and various capacities, idiots or lunatics excepted, should be understood by them all in the same manner with one another, and in the same sense which the speaker intended to be understood – this would certainly be a most perfect style.

All exotic sayings, dark and ambiguous speakings, affected words, and, as I said in the last chapter, abridgement, or words cut off, as they are foolish and improper in business, so, indeed, are they in any other things; hard words, and affectation of style in business, is like bombast in poetry, a kind of rumbling nonsense, and nothing of the kind can be more ridiculous.

The nicety of writing in business consists chiefly in giving every species of goods their trading names, for there are certain peculiarities in the trading language, which are to be observed as the greatest proprieties, and without which the language your letters are written in would be obscure, and the tradesmen you write to would not understand you – for example, if you write to your factor at Lisbon, or at Cadiz, to make you returns in hardware, he understands you, and sends you so many bags of pieces of eight. So, if a merchant comes to me to hire a small ship of me, and tells me it is for the pipin trade, or to buy a vessel, and tells me he intends to make a pipiner of her, the meaning is, that she is to run to Seville for oranges, or to Malaga for lemons. If he says he intends to send her for a lading of fruit, the meaning is, she is to go to Alicant, Denia, or Xevia, on the coast of Spain, for raisins of the sun, or to Malaga for Malaga raisins. Thus, in the home trade in England: if in Kent a man tells me he is to go among the night-riders, his meaning is, he is to go a-carrying wool to the sea-shore – the people that usually run the wool off in boats, are called owlers – those that steal customs, smugglers, and the like. In a word, there is a kind of slang in trade, which a tradesman ought to know, as the beggars and strollers know the gipsy cant, which none can speak but themselves; and this in letters of business is allowable, and, indeed, they cannot understand one another without it.

A brickmaker being hired by a brewer to make some bricks for him at his country-house, wrote to the brewer that he could not go forward unless he had two or three loads of *spanish*, and that otherwise his bricks would cost him six or seven chaldrons of coals extraordinary, and the bricks would not be so good and hard neither by a great deal, when they were burnt.

The brewer sends him an answer, that he should go on as well as he could for three or four days, and then the *spanish* should be sent him: accordingly, the following week, the brewer sends him down two carts loaded with about twelve hogsheads or casks of molasses, which frighted the brickmaker almost out of his senses. The case was this:-The brewers formerly mixed molasses with their ale to sweeten it, and abate the quantity of malt, molasses, being, at that time, much cheaper in proportion, and this they called *spanish*, not being willing that people should know it. Again, the brickmakers all about London, do mix sea-coal ashes, or laystal-stuff, as we call it, with the clay of which they make bricks, and by that shift save eight chaldrons of coals out of eleven, in proportion to what other people use to burn them with, and these ashes they call *spanish*.

Thus the received terms of art, in every particular business, are to be observed, of which I shall speak to you in its turn: I name them here to intimate, that when I am speaking of plain writing in matters of business, it must be understood with an allowance for all these things – and a tradesman must be not only allowed to use them in his style, but cannot write properly without them – it is a particular excellence in a tradesman to be able to know all the terms of art in every separate business, so as to be able to speak or write to any particular handicraft or manufacturer in his own dialect, and it is as necessary as it is for a seaman to understand the names of all the several things belonging to a ship.

This, therefore, is not to be understood when I say, that a tradesman should write plain and explicit, for these things belong to, and are part of, the language of trade.

But even these terms of art, or customary expressions, are not to be used with affectation, and with a needless repetition, where they are not called for.

Nor should a tradesman write those out-of-the-way words, though it is in the way of the business he writes about, to any other person, who he knows, or has reason to believe, does not understand them – I say, he ought not to write in those terms to such, because it shows a kind of ostentation, and a triumph over the ignorance of the person they are written to, unless at the very same time you add an explanation of the terms, so as to make them assuredly intelligible at the place, and to the person to whom they are sent.

A tradesman, in such cases, like a parson, should suit his language to his auditory; and it would be as ridiculous for a tradesman to write a letter filled with the peculiarities of this or that particular trade, which trade he knows the person he writes to is ignorant of, and the terms whereof he is unacquainted with, as it would be for a minister to quote the Chrysostome and St Austin, and repeat at large all their sayings in the Greek and the Latin, in a country church, among a parcel of ploughmen and farmers. Thus a sailor, writing a letter to a surgeon, told him he had a swelling on the north-east side of his face – that his windward leg being hurt by a bruise, it so put him out of trim, that he always heeled to starboard when he made fresh way, and so run to leeward, till he was often forced aground ; then he desired him to give him some directions how to put himself into a sailing posture again. Of all which the surgeon understood little more than that he had a swelling on his face, and a bruise in his leg.

It would be a very happy thing, if tradesmen had all their *lexicon technicum* at their fingers' ends; I mean (for pray, remember, that I observe my own rule, not to use a hard word without explaining it), that every tradesman would study so the terms of art of other trades, that he might be able to speak to every manufacturer or artist in his own language, and understand them when they talked one to another; this would make trade be a kind of universal language, and the particular marks they are obliged to, would be like the notes of music, an universal character, in which all the tradesmen in England might write to one another in the language and characters of their several trades, and be as intelligible to one another as the minister is to his people, and perhaps much more.

I therefore recommend it to every young tradesman to take all occasions to converse with mechanics of every kind, and to learn the particular language of their business; not the names of their tools only, and the way of working with their instruments as well as hands, but the very cant of their trade, for every trade has its *nostrums*, and its little made words, which they often pride themselves in, and which yet are useful to them on some occasion or other.

There are many advantages to a tradesman in thus having a general knowledge of the terms of art, and the cant, as I call it, of every business; and particularly this, that they could not be imposed upon so easily by other tradesmen, when they came to deal with them.

If you come to deal with a tradesman or handicraft man, and talk his own language to him, he presently supposes you understand his business; that you know what you come about; that you have judgment in his goods, or in his art, and cannot easily be imposed upon; accordingly, he treats you like a man that is not to be cheated, comes close to the point, and does not crowd you with words and rattling talk to set out his wares, and to cover their defects; he finds you know where to look or feel for the defect of things, and how to judge their worth. For example:–

What trade has more hard words and peculiar ways attending it, than that of a jockey, or horse-courser, as we call them! They have all the parts of the horse, and all the diseases attending him, necessary to be mentioned in the market, upon every occasion of buying or bargaining. A jockey will know you at first sight, when you do but go round a horse, or at the first word you say about him, whether you are a dealer, as they call themselves, or a stranger. If you begin well, if you take up the horse's foot right, if you handle him in the proper places, if you bid his servant open his mouth, or go about it yourself like a workman, if you speak of his shapes or goings in the proper words – 'Oh!' says the jockey to his fellow, 'he understands a horse, he speaks the language:' then he knows you are not to be cheated, or, at least, not so easily; but if you go awkwardly to work, whisper to your man you bring with you to ask every thing for you, cannot handle the horse yourself, or speak the language of the trade, he falls upon you with his flourishes, and with a flux of horse rhetoric imposes upon you with oaths and asseverations, and, in a word, conquers you with the mere clamour of his trade.

Thus, if you go to a garden to buy flowers, plants, trees, and greens, if you know what you go about, know the names of flowers, or simples, or greens; know the particular beauties of them, when they are fit to remove, and when to slip and draw, and when not; what colour is ordinary, and what rare; when a flower is rare, and when ordinary – the gardener presently talks to you as to a man of art, tells you that you are a lover of art, a friend to a florist, shows you his exotics, his green-house, and his stores; what he has set out, and what he has budded or enarched, and the like; but if he finds you have none of the terms of art, know little or nothing of the names of plants, or the nature of planting, he picks your pocket instantly, shows you a fine trimmed fuz-bush for a juniper, sells you common pinks for painted ladies, an ordinary tulip for a rarity, and the like. Thus I saw a gardener sell a gentleman a large yellow auricula, that is to say, a *running away*, for a curious flower, and take a great price. It seems, the gentleman was a lover of a good yellow; and it is known, that when nature in the auricula is exhausted, and has spent her strengh in showing a fine flower, perhaps some years upon the same root, she faints at last, and then turns into a yellow, which yellow shall be bright and pleasant the first year, and look very well to one that knows nothing of it, though another year it turns pale, and at length almost white. This the gardeners call a *run flower*, and this they put upon the gentleman for a rarity, only because he discovered at his coming that he knew nothing of the matter. The same gardener sold another person a root of white painted thyme for the right *Marum Syriacum*; and thus they do every day.

A person goes into a brickmaker's field to view his clamp, and buy a load of bricks; he resolves to see them loaded, because he would have good ones; but not understanding the goods, and seeing the workmen loading them where they were hard and well burnt, but looked white and grey, which, to be sure, were the best of the bricks, and which perhaps they would not have done if he had not been there to look at them, they supposing he understood which were the best; but he, in the abundance of his ignorance, finds fault with them, because they were not a good colour, and did not look red; the brickmaker's men took the hint immediately, and telling the buyer they would give him red bricks to oblige him, turned their hands from the grey hard well-burnt bricks to the soft *sammel*[1] half-burnt bricks, which they were glad to dispose of, and which nobody that had understood them would have taken off their hands.

I mention these lower things, because I would suit my writing to the understanding of the meanest people, and speak of frauds used in the most ordinary trades; but it is the like in almost all the goods a tradesman can deal in. If you go to Warwickshire to buy cheese, you demand the cheese 'of the first make,' because that is the best. If you go to Suffolk to buy butter, you refuse the butter of the first make, because that is not the best, but you bargain for 'the right rowing butter,' which is the butter that is made when the cows are turned into the grounds where the grass has been mowed, and the hay carried off, and grown again: and so in many other cases. These things demon-

1 [*Sammel* is a term of art the brickmakers use for those bricks which are not well burnt, and which generally look of a pale red colour, and as fair as the other, but are soft.]

strate the advantages there are to a tradesman, in his being thoroughly informed of the terms of art, and the peculiarities belonging to every particular business, which, therefore, I call the language of trade.

As a merchant should understand all languages, at least the languages of those countries which he trades to, or corresponds with, and the customs and usages of those countries as to their commerce, so an English tradesman ought to understand all the languages of trade, within the circumference of his own country, at least, and particularly of such as he may, by any of the consequences of his commerce, come to be any way concerned with.

Especially, it is his business to acquaint himself with the terms and trading style, as I call it, of those trades which he buys of, as to those he sells to; supposing he sells to those who sell again, it is their business to understand him, not his to understand them: and if he finds they do not understand him, he will not fail to make their ignorance be his advantage, unless he is honester and more conscientious in his dealings than most of the tradesmen of this age seem to be.

CHAPTER IV

OF THE TRADESMAN ACQUAINTING HIMSELF WITH ALL BUSINESS IN GENERAL

It is the judgment of some experienced tradesmen, that no man ought to go from one business to another, and launch out of the trade or employment he was bred to: *Tractent fabrilia fabri* – 'Every man to his own business;' and, they tell us, men never thrive when they do so.

I will not enter into that dispute here. I know some good and encouraging examples of the contrary, and which stand as remarkable instances, or as exceptions to the general rule: but let that be as it will, sometimes providence eminently calls upon men out of one employ into another, out of a shop into a warehouse, out of a warehouse into a shop, out of a single hand into a partnership, and the like; and they trade one time here, another time there, and with very good success too. But I say, be that as it will, a tradesman ought so far to acquaint himself with business, that he should not be at a loss to turn his hand to this or that trade, as occasion presents, whether in or out of the way of his ordinary dealing, as we have often seen done in London and other places, and sometimes with good success.

This acquainting himself with business does not intimate that he should learn every trade, or enter into the mystery of every employment. That cannot well be; but that he should have a true notion of business in general, and a knowledge how and in what manner it is carried on; that he should know where every manufacture is made, and how bought at first hand; that he should know which are the proper markets, and what the particular kinds of goods to exchange at those markets; that he should know the manner how every manufacture is managed, and the method of their sale.

It cannot be expected that he should have judgment in the choice of all kinds of goods, though in a great many he may have judgment too: but there is a general understanding in trade, which every tradesman both may and ought to arrive to; and this perfectly qualifies him to engage in any new undertaking, and to embark with other persons better qualified than himself in any new trade, which he was not in before; in which, though he may not have a particular knowledge and judgment in the goods they are to deal in or to make, yet, having the benefit of the knowledge his new partner is master of, and being himself apt to take in all additional lights, he soon becomes experienced, and the knowledge of all the other parts of business qualifies him to be a sufficient partner. For example – A.B. was bred a dry-salter, and he goes in partner with with C.D., a scarlet-dyer, called a bow-dyer, at Wandsworth.

As a salter, A.B. has had experience enough in the materials for dyeing, as well scarlets as all other colours, and understands very well the buying of cochineal, indigo, galls, shumach, logwood, fustick, madder, and the like; so that he does his part very well. C.D. is an experienced scarlet-dyer; but now, doubling their stock, they fall into a larger work, and they dye bays and stuffs, and other goods, into differing colours, as occasion requires; and this brings them to an equality in the business, and by hiring good experienced servants, they go on very well together.

The like happens often when a tradesman turns his hand from one trade to another; and when he embarks, either in partnership or out of it, in any new business, it is supposed he seldom changes hands in such a manner without some such suitable person to join with, or that he has some experienced head workman to direct him, which, if that workman proves honest, is as well as a partner. On the other hand, his own application and indefatigable industry supply the want of judgment. Thus, I have known several tradesmen turn their hands from one business to another, or from one trade entirely to another, and very often with good success. For example, I have seen a confectioner turn a sugar-baker; another a distiller; an apothecary turn chemist, and not a few turn physicians, and prove very good physicians too; but that is a step beyond what I am speaking of.

But my argument turns upon this – that a tradesman ought to be able to turn his hand to any thing; that is to say, to lay down one trade and take up another, if occasion leads him to it, and if he sees an evident view of profit and advantage in it; and this is only done by his having a general knowledge of trade, so as to have a capacity of judging: and by but just looking upon what is offered or proposed, he sees as much at first view as others do by long inquiry, and with the judgment of many advisers.

When I am thus speaking of the tradesman's being capable of making judgment of things, it occurs, with a force not to be resisted, that I should add, he is hereby fenced against bubbles and projects, and against those fatal people called projectors, who are, indeed, among tradesmen, as birds of prey are among the innocent fowls – devourers and destroyers. A tradesman cannot be too well armed, nor too much cautioned, against those sort of people; they are constantly surrounded with them, and are as much in jeopardy from them, as a man in a crowd is of having his pocket picked – nay, almost as a man is when in a crowd of pickpockets.

Nothing secures the tradesman against those men so well as his being thoroughly knowing in business, having a judgment to weigh all the delusive schemes and the fine promises of the wheedling projector, and to see which are likely to answer, or which not; to examine all his specious pretences, his calculations and figures, and see whether they are as likely to answer the end as he takes upon him to say they will; to make allowances for all his fine flourishes and outsides, and then to judge for himself. A projector is to a tradesman a kind of incendiary; he is in a constant plot to blow him up, or set fire to him; for projects are generally as fatal to a tradesman as fire in a magazine of gunpowder.

The honest tradesman is always in danger, and cannot be too wary; and therefore to fortify his judgment, that he may be able to guard against such people as these, is one of the most necessary things I can do for him.

In order, then, to direct the tradesman how to furnish himself thus with a needful stock of trading knowledge, first, I shall propose to him to converse with tradesmen chiefly: he that will be a tradesman should confine himself within his own sphere: never was the Gazette so full of the advertisements of commissions of bankrupt as since our shopkeepers are so much engaged in parties, formed into clubs to hear news, and read journals and politics; in short, when tradesmen turn statesmen, they should either shut up their shops, or hire somebody else to look after them.

The known story of the upholsterer is very instructive,[1] who, in his abundant concern for the public, ran himself out of his business into a jail; and even when he was in prison, could not sleep for the concern he had for the liberties of his dear country: the man was a good patriot, but a bad shopkeeper; and, indeed, should rather have shut up his shop, and got a commission in the army, and then he had served his country in the way of his calling. But I may speak to this more in its turn.

My present subject is not the negative, what he should not do, but the affirmative, what he should do; I say, he should take all occasions to converse within the circuit of his own sphere, that is, dwell upon the subject of trade in his conversation, and sort with and converse among tradesmen as much as he can; as writing teaches to write – *scribendo discis scribere* – so conversing among tradesmen will make him a tradesman. I need not explain this so critically as to tell you I do not mean he should confine or restrain himself entirely from all manner of conversation but among his own class: I shall speak to that in its place

1 [The story of the political upholsterer forms the subject of several amusing papers by Addison in the *Tatler*.]

also. A tradesman may on occasion keep company with gentlemen as well as other people; nor is a trading man, if he is a man of sense, unsuitable or unprofitable for a gentleman to converse with, as occasion requires; and you will often find, that not private gentlemen only, but even ministers of state, privy-councillors, members of parliament, and persons of all ranks in the government, find it for their purpose to converse with tradesmen, and are not ashamed to acknowledge, that a tradesman is sometimes qualified to inform them in the most difficult and intricate, as well as the most urgent, affairs of government; and this has been the reason why so many tradesmen have been advanced to honours and dignities above their ordinary rank, as Sir Charles Duncombe, a goldsmith; Sir Henry Furnese, who was originally a retail hosier; Sir Charles Cook, late one of the board of trade, a merchant; Sir Josiah Child, originally a very mean tradesman; the late Mr Lowndes, bred a scrivener; and many others, too many to name.

But these are instances of men called out of their lower sphere for their eminent usefulness, and their known capacities, being first known to be diligent and industrious men in their private and lower spheres; such advancements make good the words of the wise man – 'Seest thou a man diligent in his calling, he shall stand before kings; he shall not stand before mean men.'[2]

In the mean time, the tradesman's proper business is in his shop or warehouse, and among his own class or rank of people; there he sees how other men go on, and there he learns how to go on himself; there he sees how other men thrive, and learns to thrive himself; there he hears all the trading news – as for state news and politics, it is none of his business; there he learns how to buy, and there he gets oftentimes opportunities to sell; there he hears of all the disasters in trade, who breaks, and why; what brought such and such a man to misfortunes and disasters; and sees the various ways how men go down in the world, as well as the arts and management, by which others from nothing arise to wealth and estates.

Here he sees the Scripture itself thwarted, and his neighbour tradesman, a wholesale haberdasher, in spite of a good understanding, in spite of a good beginning, and in spite of the most indefatigable industry, sink in his circumstances, lose his credit, then his stock, and then break and become bankrupt, while the man takes more pains to be poor than others do to grow rich.

There, on the other hand, he sees G.D., a plodding, weak-headed, but laborious wretch, of a confined genius, and that cannot look a

2 [To stand in the presence of a prince is the highest mark of honour in the east, as to sit is with us.]

quarter of a mile from his shop-door into the world, and beginning with little or nothing, yet rises apace in the mere road of business, in which he goes on like the miller's horse, who, being tied to the post, is turned round by the very wheel which he turns round himself; and this fellow shall get money insensibly, and grow rich even he knows not how, and no body else knows why.

Here he sees F.M. ruined by too much trade, and there he sees M.F. starved for want of trade; and from all these observations he may learn something useful to himself, and fit to guide his own measures, that he may not fall into the same mischiefs which he sees others sink under, and that he may take the advantage of that prudence which others rise by.

All these things will naturally occur to him, in his conversing among his fellow-tradesmen. A settled little society of trading people, who understand business, and are carrying on trade in the same manner with himself, no matter whether they are of the very same trades or no, and perhaps better not of the same – such a society, I say, shall, if due observations are made from it, teach the tradesman more than his apprenticeship; for there he learned the operation, here he learns the progression; his apprenticeship is his grammar-school, this is his university; behind his master's counter, or in his warehouse, he learned the first rudiments of trade, but here he learns the trading sciences; here he comes to learn the *arcana*, speak the language, understand the meaning of every thing, of which before he only learned the beginning: the apprenticeship inducts him, and leads him as the nurse the child; this finishes him; there he learned the beginning of trade, here he sees it in its full extent; in a word, there he learned to trade, here he is made a complete tradesman.

Let no young tradesman object, that, in the conversation I speak of, there are so many gross things said, and so many ridiculous things argued upon, there being always a great many weak empty heads among the shop-keeping trading world: this may be granted without any impeachment of what I have advanced – for where shall a man converse, and find no fools in the society? – and where shall he hear the weightiest things debated, and not a great many empty weak things offered, out of which nothing can be learned, and from which nothing can be deduced? – for 'out of nothing, nothing can come.'

But, notwithstanding, let me still insist upon it to the tradesman to keep company with tradesmen; let the fool run on in his own way; let the talkative green-apron rattle in his own way; let the manufacturer and his factor squabble and brangle; the grave self-conceited puppy, who was born a boy, and will die before he is a man, chatter and say a great deal of nothing, and talk his neighbours to death – out of every one you will learn something – they are all tradesmen, and there is always something for a young tradesman to learn from them.

If, understanding but a little French, you were to converse every day a little among some Frenchmen in your neighbourhood, and suppose those Frenchmen, you thus kept company with, were every one of them fools, mere ignorant, empty, foolish fellows, there might be nothing learnt from their sense, but you would still learn French from them, if it was no more than the tone and accent, and the ordinary words usual in conversation.

Thus, among your silly empty tradesmen, let them be as foolish and empty other ways as you can suggest, though you can learn no philosophy from them, you may learn many things in trade from them, and something from every one; for though it is not absolutely necessary that every tradesman should be a philosopher, yet every tradesman, in his way, knows something that even a philosopher may learn from.

I knew a philosopher that was excellently skilled in the noble science or study of astronomy, who told me he had some years studied for some simile, or proper allusion, to explain to his scholars the phenomena of the sun's motion round its own axis, and could never happen upon one to his mind, till by accident he saw his maid Betty trundling her mop: surprised with the exactness of the motion to describe the thing he wanted, he goes into his study, calls his pupils about him, and tells them that Betty, who herself knew nothing of the matter, could show them the sun revolving about itself in a more lively manner than ever he could. Accordingly, Betty was called, and bidden bring out her mop, when, placing his scholars in a due-position, opposite not to the face of the maid, but to her left side, so that they could see the end of the mop, when it whirled round upon her arm. They took it immediately – there was the broad-headed nail in the centre, which was as the body of the sun, and the thrums whisking round, flinging the water about every way by innumerable little streams, describing exactly the rays of the sun, darting light from the centre to the whole system.

If ignorant Betty, by the natural consequences of her operation, instructed the astronomer, why may not the meanest shoemaker or pedlar, by the ordinary sagacity of his trading wit, though it may be indeed very ordinary, coarse, and unlooked for, communicate something, give some useful hint, dart some sudden thought into the mind of the observing tradesman, which he shall make his use of, and apply to his own advantage in trade, when, at the same time, he that gives such hint shall himself, like Betty and her mop, know nothing of the matter?

Every tradesman is supposed to manage his business his own way, and, generally speaking, most tradesmen have some ways peculiar and particular to themselves, which they either derived from the masters who taught them, or from the experience of things, or from something in the course of their business, which had not happened to them before.

And those little *nostrums* are oftentime very properly and with advantage communicated from one to another; one tradesman finds out a nearer way of buying than another, another finds a vent for what is bought beyond what his neighbour knows of, and these, in time, come to be learned of them by their ordinary conversation.

I am not for confining the tradesman from keeping better company, as occasion and leisure requires; I allow the tradesman to act the gentleman sometimes, and that even for conversation, at least if his understanding and capacity make him suitable company to them, but still his business is among those of his own rank. The conversation of gentlemen, and what they call keeping good company, may be used as a diversion, or as an excursion, but his stated society must be with his neighbours, and people in trade; men of business are companions for men of business; with gentlemen he may converse pleasantly, but here he converses profitably; tradesmen are always profitable to one another; as they always gain by trading together, so they never lose by conversing together; if they do not get money, they gain knowledge in business, improve their experience, and see farther and farther into the world.

A man of but an ordinary penetration will improve himself by conversing in matters of trade with men of trade; by the experience of the old tradesmen they learn caution and prudence, and by the rashness and the miscarriages of the young, they learn what are the mischiefs that themselves may be exposed to.

Again, in conversing with men of trade, they get trade; men first talk together, then deal together – many a good bargain is made, and many a pound gained, where nothing was expected, by mere casual coming to talk together, without knowing any thing of the matter before they met. The tradesmen's meetings are like the merchants' exchange, where they manage, negociate, and, indeed, beget business with one another.

Let no tradesman mistake me in this part; I am not encouraging them to leave their shops and warehouses, to go to taverns and ale-houses, and spend their time there in unnecessary prattle, which, indeed, is nothing but sotting and drinking; this is not meeting to do business, but to neglect business. Of which I shall speak fully afterwards.

But the tradesmen conversing with one another, which I mean, is the taking suitable occasions to discourse with their fellow tradesmen, meeting them in the way of their business, and improving their spare hours together. To leave their shops, and quit their counters, in the proper seasons for their attendance there, would be a preposterous negligence, would be going out of business to gain business, and would be cheating themselves, instead of improving themselves. The proper hours of business are sacred to the shop and the warehouse. He that goes out of the order of trade, let the pretence of business be what it will, loses his business, not increases it; and will, if continued, lose the credit of his conduct in business also.

CHAPTER V

DILIGENCE AND APPLICATION IN BUSINESS

Solomon was certainly a friend to men of business, as it appears by his frequent good advice to them. In Prov. xviii. 9, he says, 'He that is slothful in business, is brother to him that is a great waster:' and in another place, 'The sluggard shall be clothed in rags,' (Prov. xxiii. 1), or to that purpose. On the contrary, the same wise man, by way of encouragement, tells them, 'The diligent hand maketh rich,' (Prov. x. 4), and, 'The diligent shall bear rule, but the slothful shall be under tribute.'

Nothing can give a greater prospect of thriving to a young tradesman, than his own diligence; it fills himself with hope, and gives him credit with all who know him; without application, nothing in this world goes forward as it should do: let the man have the most perfect knowledge of his trade, and the best situation for his shop, yet without application nothing will go on. What is the shop without the master? what the books without the book-keeper? what the credit without the man? Hark how the people talk of such conduct as the slothful negligent trader discovers in his way.

'Such a shop,' says the customer, 'stands well, and there is a good stock of goods in it, but there is nobody to serve but a 'prentice-boy or two, and an idle journeyman: one finds them always at play together, rather than looking out for customers; and when you come to buy, they look as if they did not care whether they showed you any thing or no. One never sees a master in the shop, if we go twenty times, nor anything that bears the face of authority. Then, it is a shop always exposed, it is perfectly haunted with thieves and shop-lifters; they see nobody but raw boys in it, that mind nothing, and the diligent devils never fail to haunt them, so that there are more outcries of 'Stop thief!' at their door, and more constables fetched to that shop, than to all the shops in the row. There was a brave trade at that shop in Mr —'s time; he was a true shopkeeper; like the quack doctor, you never missed him from seven in the morning till twelve, and from two till nine at night, and he throve accordingly – he left a good estate behind him. But I don't know what these people are; they say there are two partners of them, but there had as good be none, for they are never at home, nor in their shop: one wears a long wig and a sword, I hear, and you see him often in the Mall and at court, but very seldom in his shop, or waiting on his customers; and the other, they say, lies a-bed till eleven o'clock every day, just comes into the shop and shows himself, then stalks about to the tavern to take a whet, then to Child's coffee-house to hear the news, comes home to dinner at one, takes a long sleep in his chair after it, and about four o'clock comes into the shop for half an hour, or thereabouts, then to the tavern, where he stays till two in the morning, gets drunk, and is led home by the watch, and so lies till eleven again; and thus he walks round like the hand of a dial. And what will it all come to? – they'll certainly break, that you may be sure of; they can't hold it long.'

'This is the town's way of talking, where they see an example of it in the manner as is described; nor are the inferences unjust, any more than the description is unlike, for such certainly is the end of such management, and no shop thus neglected ever made a tradesman rich.

On the contrary, customers love to see the master's face in the shop, and to go to a shop where they are sure to find him at home. When he does not sell, or cannot take the price offered, yet the customers are not disobliged, and if they do not deal now, they may another time: if they do deal, the master generally gets a better price for his goods than a servant can, besides that he gives better content; and yet the customers always think they buy cheaper of the master too.

I seem to be talking now of the mercer or draper, as if my discourse were wholly bent and directed to them; but it is quite contrary, for it concerns every tradesman – the advice is general, and every tradesman claims a share in it; the nature of trade requires it. It is an old Anglicism, 'Such a man drives a trade;' the allusion is to a carter, that with his voice, his hands, his whip, and his constant attendance, keeps the team always going, helps himself, lifts at the wheel in every slough, doubles his application upon every difficulty, and, in a word, to complete the simile, if he is not always with his horses, either the wagon is set in a hole, or the team stands still, or, which is worst of all, the load is spoiled by the waggon overthrowing.

It is therefore no improper speech to say, such a man drives his trade; for, in short, if trade is not driven, it will not go.

Trade is like a hand-mill, it must always be turned about by the diligent hand of the master; or, if you will, like the pump-house at Amsterdam, where they put offenders in for petty matters, especially beggars; if they will work and keep pumping, they sit well, and dry and safe, and if they work very hard one hour or two, they may rest, perhaps, a quarter of an hour afterwards; but if they oversleep themselves, or grow lazy, the water comes in upon them and wets them, and they have no dry place to stand in, much less to sit down in; and, in short, if they continue obstinately idle, they must sink; so that it is nothing but *pump* or *drown*, and they may choose which they like best.

He that engages in trade, and does not resolve to work at it, is *felo de se*; it is downright murdering himself; that is to say, in his trading capacity, he murders his credit, he murders his stock, and he starves, which is as bad as murdering, his family.

Trade must not be entered into as a thing of light concern; it is called business very properly, for it is a business *for* life, and ought to be followed as one of the great businesses *of* life – I do not say the chief, but one of the great businesses of life it certainly is – trade must, I say, be worked at, not played with; he that trades in jest, will certainly break in earnest; and this is one reason indeed why so many tradesmen come to so hasty a conclusion of their affairs.

There was another old English saying to this purpose, which shows how much our old fathers were sensible of the duty of a shopkeeper: speaking of the tradesman as just opening his shop, and beginning a dialogue with it; the result of which is, that the shop replies to the tradesman thus: 'Keep me, and I will keep thee.' It is the same with driving the trade; if the shopkeeper will not keep, that is, diligently attend to his shop, the shop will not keep, that is, maintain him: and in the other sense it is harsher to him, if he will not drive his trade, the trade will drive him; that is, drive him out of the shop, drive him away.

All these old sayings have this monitory substance in them; namely, they all concur to fill a young tradesman with true notions of what he is going about; and that the undertaking of a trade is not a sport or game, in which he is to meet with diversions only, and entertainment, and not to be in the least troubled or disturbed: trade is a daily employment, and must be followed as such, with the full attention of the mind, and full attendance of the person; nothing but what are to be called the necessary duties of life are to intervene; and even these are to be limited so as not to be prejudicial to business.

And now I am speaking of the necessary things which may intervene, and which may divide the time with our business or trade, I shall state the manner in a few words, that the tradesman may neither give too much, nor take away too much, to or from any respective part of what may be called his proper employment, but keep as due a balance of his time as he should of his books or cash.

The life of man is, or should be, a measure of allotted time; as his time is measured out to him, so the measure is limited, must end, and the end of it is appointed.

The purposes for which time is given, and life bestowed, are very momentous; no time is given uselessly, and for nothing; time is no more to be unemployed, than it is to be ill employed. Three things are chiefly before us in the appointment of our time: 1. Necessaries of nature. 2. Duties of religion, or things relating to a future life. 3. Duties of the present life, namely, business and calling.

I. Necessities of nature, such as eating and drinking; rest, or sleep; and in case of disease, a recess from business; all which have two limitations on them, and no more; namely, that they be

1. Referred to their proper seasons.
2. Used with moderation.

Both these might give me subject to write many letters upon; but I study brevity, and desire rather to hint than dwell upon things which are serious and grave, because I would not tire you.

II. Duties of religion: these may be called necessities too in their kind, and that of the sublimest nature; and they ought not to be thrust at all out of their place, and yet they ought to be kept in their place too.

III. Duties of life, that is to say, business, or employment, or calling, which are divided into three kinds:

1. Labour, or servitude.
2. Employment.
3. Trade.

By labour, I mean the poor manualist, whom we properly call the labouring man, who works for himself indeed in one respect, but sometimes serves and works for wages, as a servant, or workman.

By employment, I mean men in business, which yet is not properly called trade, such as lawyers, physicians, surgeons, scriveners, clerks, secretaries, and such like: and

By trade I mean merchants and inland-traders, such as are already described in the introduction to this work.

To speak of time, it is divided among these; even in them all there is a just equality of circumstances to be preserved, and as diligence is required in one, and necessity to be obeyed in another, so duty is to be observed in the third; and yet all these with such a due regard to one another, as that one duty may not jostle out another; and every thing going on with an equality and just regard to the nature of the thing, the tradesman may go on with a glad heart and a quiet conscience.

This article is very nice, as I intend to speak to it; and it is a dangerous thing indeed to speak to, lest young tradesmen, treading on the brink of duty on one side, and duty on the other side, should pretend to neglect their duty to heaven, on pretence that I say they must not neglect their shops. But let them do me justice, and they will do themselves no injury; nor do I fear that my arguing on this point should give them any just cause to go wrong; if they will go wrong, and plead my argument for their excuse, it must be by their abusing my directions, and taking them in pieces, misplacing the words, and disjointing the sense, and by the same method they may make blasphemy of the Scripture.

The duties of life, I say, must not interfere with one another, must not jostle one another out of the place, or so break in as to be prejudicial to one another. It is certainly the duty of every Christian to worship God, to pay his homage morning and evening to his Maker, and at all other proper seasons to behave as becomes a sincere worshipper of God; nor must any avocation, either of business or nature, however necessary, interfere with this duty, either in public or in private. This is plainly asserting the necessity of the duty, so no man can pretend to evade that.

But the duties of nature and religion also have such particular seasons, and those seasons so proper to themselves, and so stated, as not to break in or trench upon one another, that we are really without excuse, if we let any one be pleaded for the neglect of the other. Food, sleep, rest, and the necessities of nature, are either reserved for the night, which is appointed for man to rest, or take up so little room in the day, that they can never be pleaded in bar of either religion or employment.

He, indeed, who will sleep when he should work, and perhaps drink when he should sleep, turns nature bottom upwards, inverts the appointment of providence, and must account to himself, and afterwards to a higher judge, for the neglect.

The devil – if it be the devil that tempts, for I would not wrong Satan himself – plays our duties often one against another; and to bring us, if possible, into confusion in our conduct, subtly throws religion out of its place, to put it in our way, and to urge us to a breach of what we ought to do: besides this subtle tempter – for, as above, I won't charge it all upon the devil – we have a great hand in it ourselves; but let it be who it will, I say, this subtle tempter hurries the well-meaning tradesman to act in all manner of irregularity, that he may confound religion and business, and in the end may destroy both.

When the tradesman well inclined rises early in the morning, and is moved, as in duty to his Maker he ought, to pay his morning vows to him either in his closet, or at the church, where he hears the six o'clock bell ring to call his neighbours to the same duty – then the secret hint comes across his happy intention, that he must go to such or such a place, that he may be back time enough for such other business as has been appointed over-night, and both perhaps may be both lawful and necessary; so his diligence oppresses his religion, and away he runs to transact his business, and neglects his morning sacrifice to his Maker.

On the other hand, and at another time, being in his shop, or his counting-house, or warehouse, a vast throng of business upon his hands, and the world in his head, when it is highly his duty to attend it, and shall be to his prejudice to absent himself – then the same deceiver presses him earnestly to go to his closet, or to the church to prayers, during which time his customer goes to another place, the neighbours miss him in his shop, his business is lost, his reputation suffers; and by this turned into a practice, the man may say his prayers so long and so unseasonably till he is undone, and not a creditor he has (I may give it him from experience) will use him the better, or show him the more favour, when a commission of bankrupt comes out against him.

Thus, I knew once a zealous, pious, religious tradesman, who would almost shut up his shop every day about nine or ten o'clock to call all his family together to prayers; and yet he was no presbyterian, I assure you; I say, he would almost shut up his shop, for he would suffer none of his servants to be absent from his family worship.

This man had certainly been right, had he made all his family get up by six o'clock in the morning, and called them to prayers before he had opened his shop; but instead of that, he first suffered sleep to interfere with religion, and lying a-bed to postpone and jostle out his prayers – and then, to make God Almighty amends upon himself, wounds his family by making his prayers interfere with his trade, and shuts his customers out of his shop; the end of which was, the poor good man deceived himself, and lost his business.

Another tradesman, whom I knew personally well, was raised in the morning very early, by the outcries of his wife, to go and fetch a midwife. It was necessary, in his way, to go by a church, where there was always, on that day of the week, a morning sermon early, for the supplying the devotion of such early Christians as he; so the honest man, seeing the door open, steps in, and seeing the minister just gone up into the pulpit, sits down, joins in the prayers, hears the sermon, and goes very gravely home again; in short, his earnestness in the worship, and attention to what he had heard, quite put the errand he was sent about out of his head; and the poor woman in travail, after having waited long for the return of her husband with the midwife, was obliged (having run an extreme hazard by depending on his expedition) to dispatch other messengers, who fetched the midwife, and she was come, and the work over, long before the sermon was done, or that any body heard of the husband: at last, he was met coming gravely home from the church, when being upbraided with his negligence, in a dreadful surprise he struck his hands together, and cried out, 'How is my wife? I profess I forgot it!'

What shall we say now to this ill-timed devotion, and who must tempt the poor man to this neglect? Certainly, had he gone for the midwife, it had been much more his duty, than to go to hear a sermon at that time.

I knew also another tradesman, who was such a sermon-hunter, and, as there are lectures and sermons preached in London, either in the churches or meeting-houses, almost every day in the week, used so assiduously to hunt out these occasions, that whether it was in a church or meeting-house, or both, he was always abroad to hear a sermon, at least once every day, and sometimes more; and the consequence was, that the man lost his trade, his shop was entirely neglected, the time which was proper for him to apply to his business was misapplied, his trade fell off, and the man broke.

Now it is true, and I ought to take notice of it also, that, though these things happen, and may wrong a tradesman, yet it is oftener, ten times for once, that tradesmen neglect their shop and business to follow the track of their vices and extravagence – some by taverns, others to the gaming-houses, others to balls and masquerades, plays, harlequins, and operas, very few by too much religion.

But my inference is still sound, and the more effectually so as to that part; for if our business and trades are not to be neglected, no, not for the extraordinary excursions of religion, and religious duties, much less are they to be neglected for vices and extravagances.

This is an age of gallantry and gaiety, and never was the city transposed to the court as it is now; the play-houses and balls are now filled with citizens and young tradesmen, instead of gentlemen and families of distinction; the shopkeepers wear a differing garb now, and are seen with their long wigs and swords, rather than with aprons on, as was formerly the figure they made.

But what is the difference in the consequences? You did not see in those days acts of grace for the relief of insolvent debtors almost every session of parliament, and yet the jails filled with insolvents before the next year, though ten or twelve thousand have been released at a time by those acts.

Nor did you hear of so many commissions of bankrupt every week in the Gazette, as is now the case; in a word, whether you take the lower sort of tradesman, or the higher, where there were twenty that failed in those days, I believe I speak within compass if I say that five hundred turn insolvent now; it is, as I said above, an age of pleasure, and as the wise man said long ago, 'He that loves pleasure shall be a poor man' – so it is now; it is an age of drunkenness and extravagance, and thousands ruin themselves by that; it is an age of luxurious and expensive living, and thousands more undo themselves by that; but, among all our vices, nothing ruins a tradesman so effectually as the neglect of his business: it is true, all those things prompt men to neglect their business, but the more seasonable is the advice; either enter upon no trade, undertake no business, or, having undertaken it, pursue it diligently: drive your trade, that the world may not drive you out of trade, and ruin and undo you.

Without diligence a man can never thoroughly understand his business and how should a man thrive, when he does not perfectly know what he is doing, or how to do it? Application to his trade teaches him how to carry it on, as much as his going apprentice taught him how to set it up. Certainly, that man shall never improve in his trading knowledge, that does not know his business, or how to carry it on: the diligent tradesman is always the knowing and complete tradesman.

Now, in order to have a man apply heartily, and pursue earnestly, the business he is engaged in, there is yet another thing necessary, namely, that he should delight in it: to follow a trade, and not to love and delight in it, is a slavery, a bondage, not a business: the shop is a bridewell, and the warehouse a house of correction to the tradesman, if he does not delight in his trade. While he is bound, as we say, to keep his shop, he is like the galley-slave chained down to the oar; he tugs and labours indeed, and exerts the utmost of his strength, for fear of the strapado, and because he is obliged to do it; but when he is on shore, and is out from the bank, he abhors the labour, and hates to come to it again.

To delight in business is making business pleasant and agreeable; and such a tradesman cannot but be diligent in it, which, according to Solomon, makes him certainly rich, and in time raises him above the world and able to instruct and encourage those who come after him.

CHAPTER VI

OVER-TRADING

It is an observation, indeed, of my own, but I believe it will hold true almost in all the chief trading towns in England, that there are more tradesmen undone by having too much trade, than for want of trade. Over-trading is among tradesmen as over-lifting is among strong men: such people, vain of the strengh, and their pride prompting them to put it to the utmost trial, at last lift at something too heavy for them, over-strain their sinews, break some of nature's bands, and are cripples ever after.

I take over-trading to be to a shopkeeper as ambition is to a prince. The late king of France, the great king Louis, ambition led him to invade the dominions of his neighbours; and while upon the empire here, or the states-general there, or the Spanish Netherlands on another quarter, he was an over-match for every one, and, in their single capacity, he gained from them all; but at last pride made him think himself a match for them all together, and he entered into a declared war against the emperor and the empire, the kings of Spain and Great Britain, and the states of Holland, all at once. And what was the consequence? They reduced him to the utmost distress, he lost all his conquests, was obliged, by a dishonourable peace, to quit what he had got by encroachment, to demolish his invincible towns, such as Pignerol, Dunkirk, &c., the two strongest fortresses in Europe; and, in a word, like a bankrupt monarch, he may, in many cases, be said to have died a beggar.

Thus the strong man in the fable, who by main strength used to rive a tree, undertook one at last which was too strong for him, and it closed upon his fingers, and held him till the wild beasts came and devoured him. Though the story is a fable, the moral is good to my present purpose, and is not at all above my subject; I mean that of a tradesman, who should be warned against over-trading, as earnestly, and with as much passion, as I would warn a dealer in gunpowder to be wary of fire, or a distiller or rectifier of spirits to moderate his furnace, lest the heads of his stills fly off, and he should be scalded to death.

For a young tradesman to over-trade himself, is like a young swimmer going out of his depth, when, if help does not come immediately, it is a thousand to one but he sinks, and is drowned.

All rash adventures are condemned by the prudent part of mankind; but it is as hard to restrain youth in trade, as it is in any other thing, where the advantage stands in view, and the danger out of sight; the profits of trade are baits to the avaricious shopkeeper, and he is forward to reckon them up to himself, but does not perhaps cast up the difficulty which there may be to compass it, or the unhappy consequences of a miscarriage.

For want of this consideration, the tradesman often-times drowns, as I may call it, even within his depth – that is, he sinks when he has really the substance at bottom to keep him up – and this is all owing to an adventurous bold spirit in trade, joined with too great a gust of gain. Avarice is the ruin of many people besides tradesmen; and I might give the late South Sea calamity for an example in which the longest heads were most overreached, not so much by the wit or cunning of those they had to deal with as by the secret promptings of their own avarice; wherein they abundantly verified an old proverbial speech or saying, namely, 'All covet, all lose;' so it was there indeed, and the cunningest, wisest, sharpest, men lost the most money.

There are two things which may be properly called over-trading, in a young beginner; and by both which tradesmen are often overthrown.

1. Trading beyond their stock.
2. Giving too large credit.

A tradesman ought to consider and measure well the extent of his own strengh; his stock of money, and credit, is properly his beginning; for credit is a stock as well as money. He that takes too much credit is really in as much danger as he that gives too much credit; and the danger lies particularly in this, if the tradesman over-buys himself, that is, buys faster than he can sell, buying upon credit, the payments perhaps become due too soon for him; the goods not being sold, he must answer the bills upon the strength of his proper stock – that is, pay for them out of his own cash; if that should not hold out, he is obliged to put off his bills after they are due, or suffer the impertinence of being dunned by the creditor, and perhaps by servants and apprentices, and that with the usual indecencies of such kind of people.

This impairs his credit, and if he comes to deal with the same merchant, or clothier, or other tradesman again, he is treated like one that is but an indifferent paymaster; and though they may give him credit as before, yet depending that if he bargains for six months, he will take eight or nine in the payment, they consider it in the price, and use him accordingly; and this impairs his gain, so that loss of credit is indeed loss of money, and this weakens him both ways.

A tradesman, therefore, especially at his beginning, ought to be very wary of taking too much credit; he had much better slip the occasion of buying now and then a bargain to his advantage, for that is usually the temptation, than buying a greater quantity of goods than he can pay for, run into debt, and be insulted, and at last ruined. Merchants, and wholesale dealers, to put off their goods, are very apt to prompt young shopkeepers and young tradesmen to buy great quantities of goods, and take large credit at first; but it is a snare that many a young beginner has fallen into, and been ruined in the very bud; for if the young beginner does not find a vent for the quantity, he is undone; for at the time of payment the merchant expects his money, whether the goods are sold or not; and if he cannot pay, he is gone at once.

The tradesman that buys warily, always pays surely, and every young beginner ought to buy cautiously; if he has money to pay, he need never fear goods to be had; the merchants' warehouses are always open, and he may supply himself upon all occasions, as he wants, and as his customers call.

It may pass for a kind of an objection here, that there are some goods which a tradesman may deal in, which are to be bought at such and such markets only, and at such and such fairs only, that is to say, are chiefly bought there; as the cheesemongers buy their stocks of cheese and of butter, the cheese at several fairs in Warwickshire, as at Atherston fair in particular, or at —— fair in Gloucestershire, and at Sturbridge fair, near Cambridge; and their butter at Ipswich fair, in Suffolk; and so of many other things; but the answer is plain: those things which are generally bought thus, are ready money goods, and the tradesman has a sure rule for buying, namely, his cash. But as I am speaking of taking credit, so I must be necessarily supposed to speak of such goods as are bought upon credit, as the linen-draper buys of the Hamburgh and Dutch merchants, the woollen-draper of the Blackwell-hall men, the haberdasher of the thread merchants, the mercer of the weavers and Italian merchants, the silk-man of the Turkey merchants, and the like; here they are under no necessity of running deep into debt, but may buy sparingly, and recruit again as they sell off.

I know some tradesmen are very fond of seeing their shops well stocked, and their warehouses full of goods, and this is a snare to them, and brings them to buy in more goods than they want; but this is a great error, either in their judgment or their vanity; for, except in retailers' shops, and that in some trades where they must have a great choice of goods, or else may want a trade, otherwise a well-experienced tradesman had rather see his warehouse too empty than too full: if it be too empty, he can fill it when he pleases, if his credit be good, or his cash strong; but a thronged warehouse is a sign of a want of customers, and of a bad market; whereas, an empty warehouse is a sign of a nimble demand.[1]

Let no young tradesman value himself upon having a very great throng of goods in hand, having just a necessary supply to produce a choice of new and fashionable goods – nay, though he be a mercer, for they are the most under the necessity of a large stock of goods; but I say, supposing even the mercer to have a tolerable show and choice of fashionable goods, that gives his shop a reputation, he derives no credit at all from a throng of old shopkeepers, as they call them, namely, out-of-fashion things: but in other trades it is much more a needful caution; a few goods, and a quick sale, is the beauty of a tradesman's warehouse, or shop either; and it is his wisdom to keep himself in that posture that his payments may come in on his front as fast as they go out in his rear; that he may be able to answer the demands of his merchants or dealers, and, if possible, let no man come twice for his money.

The reason of this is plain, and leads me back to where I began; credit is stock, and, if well supported, is as good as a stock, and will be as durable. A tradesman whose credit is good, untouched, unspotted, and who, as above, has maintained it with care, shall in many cases buy his goods as cheap at three or four months' time of payment, as another man shall with ready money – I say in some cases, and in goods which are ordinarily sold for time, as all our manufactures, the bay trade excepted, generally are.

He, then, that keeps his credit unshaken, has a double stock – I mean, it is an addition to his real stock, and often superior to it: nay, I have known several considerable tradesmen in this city who have traded with great success, and to a very considerable degree, and yet have not had at bottom one shilling real stock; but by the strength of their reputation, being sober and diligent, and having with care preserved the character of honest men, and the credit of their business, by cautious dealing and punctual payments, they have gone on till the gain of their trade has effectually established them, and they have raised estates out of nothing.

But to return to the dark side, namely, over-trading; the second danger is the giving too much credit. He that takes credit may give credit, but he must be exceedingly watchful; for it is the most

1 [The keeping of a half empty shop will not suit the necessities of trade in modern times. Instead of following the advice of Defoe, therefore, the young tradesman is recommended to keep a sufficient stock of every kind of goods in which he professes to deal. A shopkeeper can hardly commit a greater blunder than allow himself to *be out* of any article of his trade. One of his chief duties ought to consist in keeping up a *fresh stock* of every article which there is a chance of being sought for, and, while avoiding the imprudence of keeping too large a stock of goods – which comes nearest to Defoe's meaning – it is certain that, by having on hand an abundant choice, the shop gains a name, and has the best chance of securing a concourse of customers.]

dangerous state of life that a tradesman can live in, for he is in as much jeopardy as a seaman upon a lee-shore.

If the people he trusts fail, or fail but of a punctual compliance with him, he can never support his own credit, unless by the caution I am now giving; that is, to be very sure not to give so much credit as he takes.

By the word *so much*, I must be understood thus – either he must sell for shorter time than he takes, or in less quantity; the last is the safest, namely, that he should be sure not to trust out so much as he is trusted with. If he has a real stock, indeed, besides the credit he takes, that, indeed, makes the case differ; and a man that can pay his own debts, whether other people pay him or no, that man is out of the question – he is past danger, and cannot be hurt; but if he trusts beyond the extent of his stock and credit, even *he* may be over-thrown too.

There were many sad examples of this in the time of the late war,[2] and in the days when the public credit was in a more precarious condition that it has been since – I say, sad examples, namely, when tradesmen in flourishing circumstances, and who had indeed good estates at bottom, and were in full credit themselves, trusted the public with too great sums; which, not coming in at the time expected, either by the deficiency of the funds given by parliament, and the parliament themselves not soon making good those deficiencies, or by other disasters of those times; I say, their money not coming in to answer their demands, they were ruined, at least their credit wounded, and some quite undone, who yet, had they been paid, could have paid all their own debts, and had good sums of money left.

Others, who had ability to afford it, were obliged to sell their tallies and orders at forty or fifty per cent. loss; from whence proceeded that black trade of buying and selling navy and victualling bills and transport debts, by which the brokers and usurers got estates, and many thousands of tradesmen were brought to nothing; even those that stood it, lost great sums of money by selling their tallies: but credit cannot be bought too dear; and the throwing away one half to save the other, was much better than sinking under the burden; like sailors in a storm, who, to lighten the ship wallowing in the trough of the sea, will throw the choicest goods overboard, even to half the cargo, in order to keep the ship above water, and save their lives.

These were terrible examples of over-trading indeed; the men were tempted by the high price which the government gave for their goods, and which they were obliged to give, because of the badness of the public credit at that time; but this was not sufficient to make good the loss sustained in the sale of the tallies, so that even they that sold and

2 [The war of the Spanish succession, concluded by the treaty of Utrecht, 1713.]

were able to stand without ruin, were yet great sufferers, and had enough to do to keep up their credit.

This was the effect of giving over-much credit; for though it was the government itself which they trusted, yet neither could the government itself keep up the sinking credit of those whom it was indebted to; and, indeed, how should it, when it was not able to support its own credit? But that by the way. I return to the young tradesman, whom we are now speaking about.

It is his greatest prudence, therefore, after he has considered his own fund, and the stock he has to rest upon – I say, his next business is to take care of his credit, and, next to limiting his buying-liberty, let him be sure to limit his selling. Could the tradesman buy all upon credit, and sell all for ready money, he might turn usurer, and put his own stock out to interest, or buy land with it, for he would have no occasion for one shilling of it; but since that is not expected, nor can be done, it is his business to act with prudence in both parts – I mean of taking and giving credit – and the best rule to be given him for it is, never to give so much credit as he takes, by at least one-third part.

By giving credit, I do not mean, that even all the goods which he buys upon credit, may not be sold upon credit; perhaps they are goods which are usually sold so, and no otherwise; but the alternative is before him thus – either he must not give so much credit in quantity of goods, or not so long credit in relation to time – for example:

Suppose the young tradesman buys ten thousand pounds' value of goods on credit, and this ten thousand pounds are sold for eleven thousand pounds likewise on credit; if the time given be the same, the man is in a state of apparent destruction, and it is a hundred to one but he is blown up: perhaps he owes the ten thousand pounds to twenty men, perhaps the eleven thousand pounds is owing to him by two hundred men – it is scarce possible that these two hundred petty customers of his, should all so punctually comply with their payments as to enable him to comply with his; and if two or three thousand pounds fall short, the poor tradesman, unless he has a fund to support the deficiency, must be undone.

But if the man had bought ten thousand pounds at six or eight months' credit, and had sold them all again as above to his two hundred customers, at three months' and four months' credit, then it might be supposed all, or the greatest part of them, would have paid time enough to make his payments good; if not, all would be lost still.

But, on the other hand, suppose he had sold but three thousand pounds' worth of the ten for ready money, and had sold the rest for six months' credit, it might be supposed that the three thousand pounds in cash, and what else the two hundred debtors might pay in time, might stop the months of the tradesman's creditors till the difference might be made good.

So easy a thing is it for a tradesman to lose his credit in trade, and so hard is it, once upon such a blow, to retrieve it again. What need, then, is there for the tradesman to guard himself against running too far into debt, or letting other people run too far into debt to him; for if they do not pay him, he cannot pay others, and the next thing is a commission of bankrupt, and so the tradesman may be undone, though he has eleven thousand pounds to pay ten with?

It is true, it is not possible in a country where there is such an infinite extent of trade as we see managed in this kingdom, that either on one hand or another it can be carried on, without a reciprocal credit both taken and given; but it is so nice an article, that I am of opinion as many tradesmen break with giving too much credit, as break with taking it. The danger, indeed, is mutual, and very great. Whatever, then, the young tradesman omits, let him guard against both his giving and taking too much credit.

But there are divers ways of over-trading, besides this of taking and giving too much credit; and one of these is the running out into projects and heavy undertakings, either out of the common road which the tradesman is already engaged in, or grasping at too many undertakings at once, and having, as it is vulgarly expressed, too many irons in the fire at a time; in both which cases the tradesman is often wounded, and that deeply, sometimes too deep to recover.

The consequences of those adventures are generally such as these: first, that they stock-starve the tradesman, and impoverish him in his ordinary business, which is the main support of his family; they lessen his strength, and while his trade is not lessened, yet his stock is lessened; and as they very rarely add to his credit, so, if they lessen the man's stock, they weaken him in the main, and he must at last faint under it.

Secondly, as they lessen his stock, so they draw from it in the most sensible part – they wound him in the tenderest and most nervous part, for they always draw away his ready money; and what follows? The money, which was before the sinews of his business, the life of his trade, maintained his shop, and kept up his credit in the full extent of it, being drawn off, like the blood let out of the veins, his trade languishes, his credit, by degrees, flags and goes off, and the tradesman falls under the weight.

Thus I have seen many a flourishing tradesman sensibly decay; his credit has first a little suffered, then for want of that credit trade has declined – that is to say, he has been obliged to trade for less and less, till at last he is wasted and reduced: if he has been wise enough and wary enough to draw out betimes, and avoid breaking, he has yet come out of trade, like an old invalid soldier out of the wars, maimed, bruised, sick, reduced, and fitter for an hospital than a shop – such miserable havoc has launching out into projects and remote undertakings made among tradesmen.

But the safe tradesman is he, that avoiding all such remote excursions, keeps close within the verge of his own affairs, minds his shop or warehouse, and confining himself to what belongs to him there, goes on in the road of his business without launching into unknown oceans; and content with the gain of his own trade, is neither led by ambition or avarice, and neither covets to be greater nor richer by such uncertain and hazardous attempts.

CHAPTER VII

OF THE TRADESMAN IN DISTRESS, AND BECOMING BANKRUPT

In former times it was a dismal and calamitous thing for a tradesman to break. Where it befell a family, it put all into confusion and distraction; the man, in the utmost terror, fright, and distress, ran away with what goods he could get off, as if the house were on fire, to get into the Friars[1] or the Mint; the family fled, one one way, and one another, like people in desperation; the wife to her father and mother, if she had any, and the children, some to one relation, some to another. A statute (so they vulgarly call a commission of bankrupt) came and swept away all, and oftentimes consumed it too, and left little or nothing, either to pay the creditors or relieve the bankrupt. This made the bankrupt desperate, and made him fly to those places of shelter with his goods, where, hardened by the cruelty of the creditors, he chose to spend all the effects which should have paid the creditors, and at last perished in misery.

But now the case is altered; men make so little of breaking, that many times the family scarce removes for it. A commission of bankrupt is so familiar a thing, that the debtor oftentimes causes it to be taken out in his favour, that he may sooner be effectually delivered from all his creditors at once, the law obliging him only to give a full account of himself upon oath to the commissioners, who, when they see his integrity, may effectually deliver him from all further molestation, give him a part even of the creditors' estate; and so he may push into the world again, and try whether he cannot retrieve his fortunes by a better management, or with better success for the future.

Some have said, this law is too favourable to the bankrupt; that it makes tradesmen careless; that they value not breaking at all, but run on at all hazards, venturing without forecast and without consideration, knowing they may come off again so cheap and so easy, if they miscarry. But though I cannot enter here into a long debate upon that subject, yet I may have room to say, that I differ from those people very much; for, though the terror of the commission is in some

1 [Whitefriars, in the neighbourhood of the Temple, London. This and the Mint were sanctuaries for debtors.]

measure abated, as indeed it ought to be, because it was before exorbitant and unreasonable, yet the terror of ruining a man's family, sinking his fortunes, blasting his credit, and throwing him out of business, and into the worst of disgrace that a tradesman can fall into, this is not taken away, or abated at all; and this, to an honest trading man, is as bad as all the rest ever was or could be.

Nor can a man be supposed, in the rupture of his affairs, to receive any comfort, or to see through his disasters into the little relief which he may, and at the same time cannot be sure he shall, receive, at the end of his troubles, from the mercy of the commission.

These are poor things, and very trifling for a tradesman to entertain thoughts of a breach from, especially with any prospect of satisfaction; nor can any tradesman with the least shadow of principle entertain any thought of breaking, but with the utmost aversion, and even abhorrence; for the circumstances of it are attended with so many mortifications, and so many shocking things, contrary to all the views and expectations that a tradesman can begin the world with, that he cannot think of it, but as we do of the grave, with a chillness upon the blood, and a tremor in the spirits. Breaking is the death of a tradesman; he is mortally stabbed, or, as we may say, shot through the head, in his trading capacity; his shop is shut up, as it is when a man is buried; his credit, the life and blood of his trade, is stagnated; and his attendance, which was the pulse of his business, is stopped, and beats no more; in a word, his fame, and even name, as to trade is buried, and the commissioners, that act upon him, and all their proceedings, are but like the executors of the defunct, dividing the ruins of his fortune, and at last, his certificate is a kind of performing the obsequies for the dead, and praying him out of purgatory.

Did ever tradesman set up on purpose to break? Did ever a man build himself a house on purpose to have it burnt down? I can by no means grant that any tradesman, at least in his senses, can entertain the least satisfaction in his trading, or abate any thing of his diligence in trade, from the easiness of breaking, or the abated severities of the bankrupt act.

I could argue it from the nature of the act itself, which, indeed, was made, and is effectual, chiefly for the relief of creditors, not debtors; to secure the bankrupt's effects for the use of those to whom it of right belongs, and to prevent the extravagant expenses of the commission, which before were such as often devoured all, ruining both the bankrupt and his creditors too. This the present law has providently put a stop to; and the creditors now are secure in this point, that what is to be had, what the poor tradesman has left, they are sure to have preserved for, and divided among them, which, indeed, before they were not. The case is so well known, and so recent in every tradesman's memory, that I need not take up any more of your time about it.

As to the encouragements in the act for the bankrupt, they are only these – namely, that, upon his honest and faithful surrender of his affairs, he shall be set at liberty; and if they see cause, they, the creditors, may give him back a small gratification for his discovering his effects, and assisting to the recovery of them; and all this, which amounts to very little, is upon his being, as I have said, entirely honest, and having run through all possible examinations and purgations, and that it is at the peril of his life if he prevaricates.

Are these encouragements to tradesmen to be negligent and careless of the event of things? Will any man in his wits fail in his trade, break his credit, and shut up his shop, for these prospects? Or will he comfort himself in case he is forced to fail – I say, will he comfort himself with these little benefits, and make the matter easy to himself on that account? He must have a very mean spirit that can do this, and must act upon very mean principles in life, who can fall with satisfaction, on purpose to rise no higher than this; it is like a man going to bed on purpose to rise naked, pleasing himself with the thoughts that, though he shall have no clothes to put on, yet he shall have the liberty to get out of bed and shift for himself.

On these accounts, and some others, too long to mention here, I think it is out of doubt, that the easiness of the proceedings on commissions of bankrupt can be no encouragement to any tradesman to break, or so much as to entertain the thoughts of it, with less horror and aversion than he would have done before this law was made.

But I must come now to speak of the tradesman in his real state of mortification, and under the inevitable necessity of a blow upon his affairs. He has had losses in his business, such as are too heavy for his stock to support; he has, perhaps, launched out in trade beyond his reach: either he has so many bad debts, that he cannot find by his books he has enough left to pay his creditors, or his debts lie out of his reach, and he cannot get them in, which in one respect is as bad; he has more bills running against him than he knows how to pay, and creditors dunning him, whom it is hard for him to comply with; and this, by degrees, sinks his credit.

Now, could the poor unhappy tradesman take good advice, now would be his time to prevent his utter ruin, and let his case be better or worse, his way is clear.

If it be only that he has overshot himself in trade, taken too much credit, and is loaded with goods; or given too much credit, and cannot get his debts in; but that, upon casting up his books, he finds his circumstances good at bottom, though his credit has suffered by his effects being out of his hands; let him endeavour to retrench, let him check his career in trade – immediately take some extraordinary measures to get in his debts, or some extraordinary measures, if he can, to raise money in the meantime, till those debts come in, that he may stop the crowd of present demands. If this will not do, let him treat with some of his principal creditors, showing them a true and faithful state of his affairs, and giving them the best assurances he can of payment, that they may be easy with him till he can get in his debts; and then, with the utmost care, draw in his trade within the due compass of his stock, and be sure never to run out again farther than he is able to answer, let the prospect of advantage be what it will; and by this method he may perhaps recover his credit again, at least he may prevent his ruin. But this is always supposing the man has a firm bottom, that he is sound in the main, and that his stock is at least sufficient to pay all his debts.

But the difficulty which I am proposing to speak of, is when the poor tradesman, distressed as above in point of credit, looking into his affairs, finds that his stock is diminished, or perhaps entirely sunk – that, in short, he has such losses and such disappointments in his business, that he is not sound at bottom; that he has run too far, and that his own stock being wasted or sunk, he has not really sufficient to pay his debts; what is this man's business? – and what course shall he take?

I know the ordinary course with such tradesmen is this: – 'It is true,' says the poor man, 'I am running down, and I have lost so much in such a place, and so much by such a chapman that broke, and, in short, so much, that I am worse than nothing; but come, I have such a thing before me, or I have undertaken such a project, or I have such an adventure abroad, if it suceeds, I may recover again; I'll try my utmost; I'll never drown while I can swim; I'll never fall while I can stand; who knows but I may get over it?' In a word, the poor man is loth to come to the fatal day; loth to have his name in the Gazette, and see his wife and family turned out of doors, and the like; who can blame him? or who is not, in the like case, apt to take the like measures? – for it is natural to us all to put the evil day far from us, at least to put it as far off as we can. Though the criminal believes he shall be executed at last, yet he accepts of every reprieve, as it puts him within the possibility of an escape, and that as long as there is life there is hope; but at last the dead warrant comes down, then he sees death unavoidable, and gives himself up to despair.

Indeed, the malefactor was in the right to accept, as I say, of every reprieve, but it is quite otherwise in the tradesman's case; and if I may give him a rule, safe, and in its end comfortable, in proportion to his circumstances, but, to be sure, out of question, just, honest, and prudent, it is this:–

When he perceives his case as above, and knows that if his new adventures or projects should fail, he cannot by any means stand or support himself, I not only give it as my advice to all tradesmen, as their interest, but insist upon it, as they are honest men, they should break, that is, stop in time: fear not to do that which necessity obliges you to do; but, above all, fear not to do that early, which, if omitted, necessity will oblige you to do late.

First, let me argue upon the honesty of it, and next upon the prudence of it. Certainly, honesty obliges every man, when he sees that his stock is gone, that he is below the level, and eating into the estate of other men, to put a stop to it, and to do it in time, while something is left. It has been a fault, without doubt, to break in upon other men's estates at all; but perhaps a plea may be made that it was ignorantly done, and they did not think they were run so far as to be worse than nothing; or some sudden disaster may have occasioned it, which they did not expect, and, it may be, could not foresee; both which may indeed happen to a tradesman, though the former can hardly happen without his fault, because he ought to be always acquainting himself with his books, stating his expenses and his profits, and casting things up frequently, at least in his head, so as always to know whether he goes backward or forward. The latter, namely, sudden disaster, may happen so to any tradesman as that he may be undone, and it may not be his fault; for ruin sometimes falls as suddenly as unavoidably upon a tradesman, though there are but very few incidents of that kind which may not be accounted for in such a manner as to charge it upon his prudence.

Some cases may indeed happen, some disasters may befall a tradesman, which it was not possible he should foresee, as fire, floods of water, thieves, and many such – and in those cases the disaster is visible, the plea is open, every body allows it, the man can have no blame. A prodigious tide from the sea, joined with a great fresh or flood in the river Dee, destroyed the new wharf below the Roodee at West Chester, and tore down the merchants' warehouses there, and drove away not only all the goods, but even the buildings and altogether, into the sea. Now, if a poor shopkeeper in Chester had a large parcel of goods lying there, perhaps newly landed in order to be brought up to the city, but were all swept away, if, I say, the poor tradesman were ruined by the loss of those goods on that occasion, the creditors would see reason in it that they should every one take a share in the loss; the tradesman was not to blame.

Likewise in the distress of the late fire which began in Thames Street, near Bear Quay, a grocer might have had a quantity of goods in a warehouse thereabouts, or his shop might be there, and the goods perhaps might be sugars, or currants, or tobacco, or any other goods in his way, which could not be easily removed; this fire was a surprise, it was a blast of powder, it was at noonday, when no person coud foresee it. The man may have been undone and be in no fault himself, one way or other; no man can reasonably say to him, why did you keep so many goods upon your hands, or in such a place? for it was his proper business both to have a stock of goods, and to have them in such a place; every thing was in the right position, and in the order which the nature of his trade required.

On the other hand, if it was the breaking of a particular chapman, or an adventure by sea, the creditors would perhaps reflect on his prudence; why should any man trust a single chapman so much, or adventure so much in one single bottom, and uninsured, as that the loss of it would be his undoing?

But there are other cases, however, which may happen to a tradesman, and by which he may be at once reduced below his proper stock, and have nothing left to trade on but his credit, that is to say, the estates of his creditors. In such a case, I question whether it can be honest for any man to continue trading; for, first, it is making his creditors run an unjust hazard, without their consent; indeed, if he discovers his condition to one or two of them, who are men of capital stocks, and will support him, they giving him leave to pay others off, and go on at their risks, that alters the case; or if he has a ready money trade, that will apparently raise him again, and he runs no more hazards, but is sure he shall at least run out no farther; in these two cases, and I do not know another, he may with honesty continue.

On the contrary, when he sees himself evidently running out, and declining, and has only a shift here and a shift there, to lay hold on, as sinking men generally do; and knows, that unless something extraordinary happen, which, perhaps, also is not probable, he must fall, for such a man to go on, and trade in the ordinary way, notwithstanding losses, and hazards – in such a case, I affirm, he cannot act the honest man, he cannot go on with justice to his creditors, or his family; he ought to call his creditors together, lay his circumstances honestly before them, and pay as far as it will go. If his creditors will do any thing generously for him, to enable him to go on again, well and good, but he cannot honestly oblige them to run the risk of his unfortunate progress, and to venture their estates on his bottom, after his bottom is really nothing at all but their money.

But I pass from the honesty to the prudence of it – from what regards his creditors, to what regards himself – and I affirm, nothing can be more imprudent and impolite, as it regards himself and his family, than to go on after he sees his circumstances irrecoverable. If he has any consideration for himself, or his future happiness, he will stop in time, and not be afraid of meeting the mischief which he sees follows too fast for him to escape; be not so afraid of breaking, as not to break till necessity forces you, and that you have nothing left. In a word, I speak it to every declining tradesman, if you love yourself, your family, or your reputation, and would ever hope to look the world in the face again, *break* in time.

By breaking in time you will first obtain the character of an honest, though unfortunate man; it is owing to the contrary course, which is indeed the ordinary practice of tradesmen, namely, not to break till they run the bottom quite out, and have little or nothing left to pay; I say, it is owing to this, that some people think all men that break are knaves. The censure, it is true, is unjust, but the cause is owing to the indiscretion, to call it no worse, of the poor tradesmen, who putting the mischief as far from them as they can, trade on to the last gasp, till a throng of creditors coming on them together, or being arrested, and not able to get bail, or by some such public blow to their credit, they are brought to a stop or breach of course, like a man fighting to the last gasp who is knocked down, and laid on the ground, and then his resistance is at an end; for indeed a tradesman pushing on under irresistable misfortunes is but fighting with the world to the last drop, and with such unequal odds, that like the soldier surrounded with enemies, he must be killed; so the debtor must sink, it cannot be prevented.

It is true, also, the man that thus struggles to the last, brings upon him an universal reproach, and a censure, that is not only unavoidable, but just, which is worse; but when a man breaks in time, he may hold up his face to his creditors, and tell them, that he could have gone on a considerable while longer, but that he should have had less left to pay them with, and that he has chosen to stop while he may be able to give them so considerable a sum as may convince them of his integrity.

We have a great clamour among us of the cruelty of creditors, and it is a popular clamour, that goes a great way with some people; but let them tell us when ever creditors were cruel, when the debtor came thus to them with fifteen shillings in the pound in his offer. Perhaps when the debtor has run to the utmost, and there appears to be little or nothing left, he has been used roughly; and it is enough to provoke a creditor, indeed, to be offered a shilling or half-a-crown in the pound for a large debt, when, had the debtor been honest, and broke in time, he might have received perhaps two-thirds of his debt, and the debtor been in better condition too.

Break then in time, young tradesman, if you see you are going down, and that the hazard of going on is doubtful; you will certainly be received by your creditors with compassion, and with a generous treatment; and, whatever happens, you will be able to begin the world again with the title of an honest man – even the same creditors will embark with you again, and be more forward to give you credit than before.

It is true, most tradesmen that break merit the name of knave or dishonest man, but it is not so with all; the reason of the difference lies chiefly in the manner of their breaking – namely, whether sooner or later. It is possible, he may be an honest man who cannot, but he can never be honest that can, and will not pay his debts. Now he, that, being able to pay fifteen shillings in the pound, will struggle on till he sees he shall not be able to pay half-a-crown in the pound, this man was able to pay, but would not, and, therefore, as above, cannot be an honest man.

In the next place, what shall we say to the peace and satisfaction of mind in breaking, which the tradesman will always have when he acts the honest part, and breaks betimes, compared to that guilt and chagrin of the mind, occasioned by a running on, as I said, to the last gasp, when they have little to pay? Then, indeed, the tradesman can expect no quarter from his creditors, and will have no quiet in himself.

I might instance here the miserable, anxious, perplexed life, which the poor tradesman lives under; the distresses and extremities of his declining state; how harassed and tormented for money; what shifts he is driven to for supporting himself; how many little, mean, and even wicked things, will even the religious tradesman stoop to in his distress, to deliver himself – even such things as his very soul would abhor at another time, and for which he goes perhaps with a wounded conscience all his life after!

By giving up early, all this, which is the most dreadful part of all the rest, would be prevented. I have heard many an honest unfortunate man confess this, and repent, even with tears, that they had not learned to despair in trade some years sooner than they did, by which they had avoided falling into many foul and foolish actions, which they afterwards had been driven to by the extremity of their affairs.

CHAPTER VIII

THE ORDINARY OCCASIONS OF THE RUIN OF TRADESMEN

Since I have given advice to tradesmen, when they fell into difficulties, and find they are run behind-hand, to break in time, before they run on too far, and thereby prevent the consequences of a fatal running on to extremity, it is but just I should give them some needful directions, to avoid, if possible, breaking at all.

In order to this, I will briefly inquire what are the ordinary originals of a tradesman's ruin in business. To say it is negligence, when I have already pressed to a close application and diligence; that it is launching into, and grasping at, more business than their stock, or, perhaps, their understandings, are able to manage, when I have already spoken of the fatal consequences of over-trading; to say it is trusting carelessly people unable to pay, and running too rashly into debt, when I have already spoken of taking and giving too much credit – this would all be but saying the same thing over again – and I am too full of particulars, in this important case, to have any need of tautologies and repetitions; but there are a great many ways by which tradesmen precipitate themselves into ruin besides those, and some that need explaining and enlarging upon.

1. Some, especially retailers, ruin themselves by fixing their shops in such places as are improper for their business. In most towns, but particularly in the city of London, there are places as it were appropriated to particular trades, and where the trades which are placed there succeed very well, but would do very ill any where else, or any other trades in the same places; as the orange-merchants and wet-salters about Billingsgate, and in Thames Street; the costermongers at the Three Cranes; the wholesale cheesemongers in Thames Street; the mercers and drapers in the high streets, such as Cheapside, Ludgate Street, Cornhill, Round Court, and Grace-church Street, &c.

Pray what would a bookseller make of his business at Billingsgate, or a mercer in Tower Street, or near the Custom-house, or a draper in Thames Street, or about Queen-hithe? Many trades have their peculiar streets, and proper places for the sale of their goods, where people expect to find such shops, and consequently, when they want such goods, they go thither for them; as the booksellers in St Paul's churchyard, about the Exchange, Temple, and the Strand, &c., the mercers on both sides Ludgate, in Round Court, and Grace-church and Lombard Streets; the shoemakers in St Martins le Grand, and Shoemaker Row; the coach-makers in Long-acre, Queen Street, and Bishopsgate; butchers in Eastcheap; and such like.

For a tradesman to open his shop in a place unresorted to, or in a place where his trade is not agreeable, and where it is not expected, it is no wonder if he has no trade. What retail trade would a milliner have among the fishmongers' shops on Fishstreet-hill, or a toyman about Queen-hithe? When a shop is ill chosen, the tradesman starves; he is out of the way, and business will not follow him that runs away from it: suppose a ship-chandler should set up in Holborn, or a block-maker in Whitecross Street, an anchor-smith at Moorgate, or a coachmaker in Redriff, and the like!

It is true, we have seen a kind of fate attend the very streets and rows where such trades have been gathered together; and a street, famous some years ago, shall, in a few years after, be quite forsaken; as Paternoster Row for mercers, St Paul's Churchyard for woollen-drapers; both the Eastcheaps for butchers; and now you see hardly any of those trades left in those places.

I mention it for this reason, and this makes it to my purpose in an extraordinary manner, that whenever the principal shopkeepers remove from such a street, or settled place, where the principal trade used to be, the rest soon follow – knowing, that if the fame of the trade is not there, the customers will not resort thither: and that a tradesman's business is to follow wherever the trade leads. For a mercer to set up now in Paternoster Row, or a woollen-draper in St Paul's Churchyard, the one among the sempstresses, and the other among the chair-makers, would be the same thing as for a country shopkeeper not to set up in or near the market-place.[1]

The place, therefore, is to be prudently chosen by the retailer, when he first begins his business, that he may put himself in the way of business; and then, with God's blessing, and his own care, he may expect his share of trade with his neighbours.

2. He must take an especial care to have his shop not so much crowded with a large bulk of goods, as with a well-sorted and well-chosen quantity proper for his business, and to give credit to his beginning. In order to this, his buying part requires not only a good judgment in the wares he is to deal in, but a perfect government of his judgment by his understanding to suit and sort his quantities and

1 [Paternoster Row has long been the chief seat of the bookselling and publishing trade in London; and there are now some splendid shops of mercers or haberdashers in St Paul's Churchyard, also in Ludgate hill adjoining.]

proportions, as well to his shop as to the particular place where his shop is situated; for example, a particular trade is not only proper for such or such a part of the town, but a particular assortment of goods, even in the same way, suits one part of the town, or one town and not another; as he that sets up in the Strand, or near the Exchange, is likely to sell more rich silks, more fine Hollands, more fine broad-cloths, more fine toys and trinkets, than one of the same trade setting up in the skirts of the town, or at Ratcliff, or Wapping, or Redriff; and he that sets up in the capital city of a county, than he that is placed in a private market-town, in the same county; and he that is placed in a market-town, than he that is placed in a country village. A tradesman in a sea-port town sorts himself different from one of the same trade in an inland town, though larger and more populous; and this the tradesman must weigh very maturely before he lays out his stock.

Sometimes it happens a tradesman serves his apprenticeship in one town, and sets up in another; and sometimes circumstances altering, he removes from one town to another; the change is very important to him, for the goods, which he is to sell in the town he removes to, are sometimes so different from the sorts of goods which he sold in the place he removed from, though in the same way of trade, that he is at a great loss both in changing his hand, and in the judgment of buying. This made me insist, in a former chapter, that a tradesman should take all occasions to extend his knowledge in every kind of goods, that which way soever he may turn his hand, he may have judgment in every thing.

In thus changing his circumstances of trade, he must learn, as well as he can, how to furnish his shop suitable to the place he is to trade in, and to sort his goods to the demand which he is like to have there; otherwise he will not only lose the customers for want of proper goods, but will very much lose by the goods which he lays in for sale, there being no demand for them where he is going.

When merchants send adventures to our British colonies, it is usual with them to make up to each factor what they call a *sortable cargo*; that is to say, they want something of every thing that may furnish the tradesmen there with parcels fit to fill their shops, and invite their customers; and if they fail, and do not thus sort their cargoes, the factors there not only complain, as being ill sorted, but the cargo lies by unsold, because there is not a sufficient quantity of sorts to answer the demand, and make them all marketable together.

It is the same thing here: if the tradesman's shop is not well sorted, it is not suitably furnished, or fitted to supply his customers; and nothing dishonours him more than to have people come to buy things usual to be had in such shops, and go away without them. The next thing they say to one another is, 'I went to that shop, but I could not be furnished; they are not stocked there for a trade; one seldom finds any thing there that is new or fashionable:' and so they go away to another shop; and not only go away themselves, but carry others away with them – for it is observable, that the buyers or retail customers, especially the ladies, follow one another as sheep follow the flock; and if one buys a beautiful silk, or a cheap piece of Holland, or a new-fashioned thing of any kind, the next inquiry is, where it was bought; and the shop is presently recommended for a shop well sorted, and for a place where things are to be had not only cheap and good, but of the newest fashion, and where they have always great choice to please the curious, and to supply whatever is called for. And thus the trade runs away insensibly to the shops which are best sorted.

3. The retail tradesman in especial, but even every tradesman in his station, must furnish himself with a competent stock of patience; I mean, that patience which is needful to bear with all sorts of impertinence, and the most provoking curiosity, that it is possible to imagine the buyers, even the worst of them, are or can be guilty of. A tradesman behind his counter must have no flesh and blood about him, no passions, no resentment. He must never be angry; no, not so much as seem to be so. If a customer tumbles him five hundred pounds' worth of goods, and scarce bids money for any thing – nay, though they really come to his shop with no intent to buy, as many do, only to see what is to be sold, and if they cannot be better pleased than they are at some other shop where they intend to buy, it is all one, the tradesman must take it, and place it to the account of his calling, that it is his business to be ill used, and resent nothing; and so must answer as obligingly to those that give him an hour or two's trouble and buy nothing, as he does to those who in half the time lay out ten or twenty pounds. The case is plain: it is his business to get money, to sell and please; and if some do give him trouble and do not buy, others make him amends, and do buy; and as for the trouble, it is the business of his shop.

I have heard that some ladies, and those, too, persons of good note, have taken their coaches and spent a whole afternoon in Ludgate Street or Covent Garden, only to divert themselves in going from one mercer's shop to another, to look upon their fine silks, and to rattle and banter the journeymen and shopkeepers, and have not so much as the least occasion, much less intention, to buy any thing; nay, not so much as carrying any money out with them to buy anything if they fancied it: yet this the mercers who understand themselves know their business too well to resent; nor if they really knew it, would they take the least notice of it, but perhaps tell the ladies they were welcome to look upon their goods; that it was their business to show them; and that if they did not come to buy now, they might perhaps see they were furnished to please them when they might have occasion.

On the other hand, I have been told that sometimes those sorts of ladies have been caught in their own snare; that is to say, have been so engaged by the good usage of the shopkeeper, and so unexpectedly surprised with some fine thing or other that has been shown them, that they have been drawn in by their fancy against their design, to lay out money, whether they had it or no; that is to say, to buy, and send home for money to pay for it.

But let it be how and which way it will, whether mercer or draper, or what trade you please, the man that stands behind the counter must be all courtesy, civility, and good manners; he must not be affronted, or any way moved, by any manner of usage, whether owing to casualty or design; if he sees himself ill used, he must wink, and not see it – he must at least not appear to see it, nor any way show dislike or distaste; if he does, he reproaches not only himself but his shop, and puts an ill name upon the general usuage of customers in it; and it is not to be imagined how, in this gossiping, tea-drinking age, the scandal will run, even among people who have had no knowledge of the person first complaining. 'Such a shop!' says a certain lady to a citizen's wife in conversation, as they were going to buy clothes; 'I am resolved I won't go to it; the fellow that keeps it is saucy and rude: if I lay out my money, I expect to be well used; if I don't lay it out, I expect to be well treated.'

'Why, Madam,' says the citizen, 'did the man of the shop use your ladyship ill?'

Lady. – No, I can't say he used me ill, for I never was in his shop.

Cit. – How does your ladyship know he does so then?

Lady. – Why, I know he used another lady saucily, because she gave him a great deal of trouble, as he called it, and did not buy.

Cit. – Was it the lady that told you so herself, Madam?

Lady. – I don't know, really, I have forgot who it was; but I have such a notion in my head, and I don't care to try, for I hate the sauciness of shopkeepers when they don't understand themselves.

Cit. – Well; but, Madam, perhaps it may be a mistake – and the lady that told you was not the person neither?

Lady. – Oh, Madam, I remember now who told me; it was my Lady Tattle, when I was at Mrs Whymsy's on a visiting day; it was the talk of the whole circle, and all the ladies took notice of it, and said they would take care to shun that shop.

Cit. – Sure, Madam, the lady was strangely used; did she tell any of the particulars?

Lady. – No; I did not understand that she told the particulars, for it seems it was not to her, but to some other lady, a friend of hers; but it was all one; the company took as much notice of it as if it had been to her, and resented it as much, I assure you.

Cit. – Yet, and without examining the truth of the fact.

Lady. – We did not doubt the story.

Cit. – But had no other proof of it, Madam, than her relation?

Lady. – Why, that's true; nobody asked for a proof; it was enough to tell the story.

Cit. – What! though perhaps the lady did not know the person, or whether it was true or no, and perhaps had it from a third or fourth hand – your ladyship knows any body's credit may be blasted at that rate.

Lady. – We don't inquire so nicely, you know, into the truth of stories at a tea-table.

Cit. – No, Madam, that's true; but when reputation is at stake, we should be a little careful too.

Lady. – Why, that's true too. But why are you so concerned about it, Madam? do you know the man that keeps the shop?

Cit. – No otherwise, Madam, than that I have often bought there, and I always found them the most civil, obliging people in the world.

Lady. – It may be they know you, Madam.

Cit. – I am persuaded they don't, for I seldom went but I saw new faces, for they have a great many servants and journeymen in the shop.

Lady. – It may be you are easy to be pleased; you are good-humoured yourself, and cannot put their patience to any trial.

Cit. – Indeed, Madam, just the contrary; I believe I made them tumble two or three hundred pounds' worth of goods one day, and bought nothing; and yet it was all one; they used me as well as if I had laid out twenty pounds.

Lady. – Why, so they ought.

Cit. – Yes, Madam, but then it is a token they do as they ought, and understand themselves.

Lady. – Well, I don't know much of it indeed, but thus I was told.

Cit. – Well, but if your ladyship would know the truth of it, you would do a piece of justice to go and try them.

Lady. – Not I; besides, I have a mercer of my acquaintance.

Cit. – Well, Madam, I'll wait on your ladyship to your own mercer, and if you can't find any thing to your liking, will you go and try the other shop?

Lady. – Oh! I am sure I shall deal if I go to my mercer.

Cit. – Well, but if you should, let us go for a frolic, and give the other as much trouble as we can for nothing, and see how he'll behave, for I want to be satisfied; if I find them as your ladyship has been told, I'll never go there any more.

Lady. – Upon that condition I agree – I will go with you; but I will go and lay out my money at my own mercer's first, because I wont be tempted.

Cit. – Well, Madam, I'll wait on your ladyship till you have laid out your money.

After this discourse they drove away to the mercer's shop where the lady used to buy; and when they came there, the lady was surprised – the shop was shut up, and nobody to be seen. The next door was a laceman's, and the journeyman being at the door, the lady sent her servant to desire him to speak a word or two to her; and when he came, says the lady to him,

Pray, how long has Mr —'s shop been shut up?

Laceman. – About a month, madam.

Lady. – What! is Mr — dead?

Laceman. – No, madam, he is not dead.

Lady. – What then, pray?

Laceman. – Something worse, madam; he has had some misfortunes.

Lady. – I am very sorry to hear it, indeed. So her ladyship made her bow, and her coachman drove away.

The short of the story was, her mercer was broke; upon which the city lady prevailed upon her ladyship to go to the other shop, which she did, but declared beforehand she would buy nothing, but give the mercer all the trouble she could; and so said the other. And to make the thing more sure, she would have them go into the shop single, because she fancied the mercer knew the city lady, and therefore would behave more civilly to them both on that account, the other having laid out her money there several times. Well, they went in, and the lady asked for such and such rich things, and had them shown her, to a variety that she was surprised at; but not the best or richest things they could show her gave her any satisfaction – either she did not like the pattern, or the colours did not suit her fancy, or they were too dear; and so she prepares to leave the shop, her coach standing at a distance, which she ordered, that they might not guess at her quality.

But she was quite deceived in her expectation; for the mercer, far from treating her in the manner as she had heard, used her with the utmost civility and good manners. She treated him, on the contrary, as she said herself, even with a forced rudeness; she gave him all the impertinent trouble she was able, as above; and, pretending to like nothing he showed, turned away with an air of contempt, intimating that his shop was ill furnished, and that she should be easily served, she doubted not, at another.

He told her he was very unhappy in not having any thing that suited her fancy – that, if she knew what particular things would please her, he would have them in two hours' time for her, if all the French and Italian merchants' warehouses in London, or all the weavers' looms in Spitalfields, could furnish them. But when that would not do, she comes forward from his back shop, where she had plagued him about an hour and a half; and makes him the slight compliment of (in a kind of a scornful tone too), 'I am sorry I have given you so much trouble.'

'The trouble, madam, is nothing; it is my misfortune not to please you; but, as to trouble, my business is to oblige the ladies, my customers; if I show my goods, I may sell them; if I do not show them, I cannot; if it is not a trouble to you, I'll show you every piece of goods in my shop; if you do not buy now, you may perhaps buy another time.' And thus, in short, he pursued her with all the good words in the world, and waited on her towards the door.

As she comes forward, there she spied the city lady, who had just used the partner as the lady had used the chief master; and there, as if it had been by mere chance, she salutes her with, 'Your servant, cousin; pray, what brought you here?' The cousin answers, 'Madam, I am mighty glad to see your ladyship here; I have been haggling here a good while, but this gentleman and I cannot bargain, and I was just going away.'

'Why, then,' says the lady, 'you have been just such another customer as I, for I have troubled the gentleman mercer this two hours, and I cannot meet with any thing to my mind.' So away they go together to the door; and the lady gets the mercer to send one of his servants to bid her coachman drive to the door, showing him where the fellow stood.

While the boy was gone, she takes the city lady aside, and talking softly, the mercer and his partner, seeing them talk together, withdrew, but waited at a distance to be ready to hand them to the coach. So they began a new discourse, as follows:-

Lady. – Well, I am satisfied this man has been ill used in the world.

Cit. – Why, Madam, how does your ladyship find him?

Lady. – Only the most obliging, most gentleman-like man of a tradesman that ever I met with in my life.

Cit. – But did your ladyship try him as you said you would?

Lady. – Try him! I believe he has tumbled three thousand pounds' worth of goods for me.

Cit. – Did you oblige him to do so?

Lady. – I forced him to it, indeed, for I liked nothing.

Cit. – Is he well stocked with goods?

Lady. – I told him his shop was ill furnished.

Cit. – What did he say to that?

Lady. – Say! why he carried me into another inner shop, or warehouse, where he had goods to a surprising quantity and value, I confess.

Cit. – And what could you say, then?

Lady. – Say! in truth I was ashamed to say any more, but still was resolved not to be pleased, and so came away, as you see.

Cit. – And he has not disobliged you at all, has he?

Lady. – Just the contrary, indeed. (Here she repeated the words the mercer had said to her, and the modesty and civility he had treated her with.)

Cit. – Well, Madam, I assure you I have been faithful to my promise, for you cannot have used him so ill as I have used his partner – for I have perfectly abused him for having nothing to please me – I did as good as tell him I believed he was going to break, and that he had no choice.

Lady. – And how did he treat you?

Cit. – Just in the same manner as his partner did your ladyship, all mild and mannerly, smiling, and in perfect temper; for my part, if I was a young wench again, I should be in love with such a man.

Lady. – Well, but what shall we do now?

Cit. – Why, be gone. I think we have teazed them enough; it would be cruel to bear-bait them any more.

Lady. – No, I am not for teazing them any more; but shall we really go away, and buy nothing?

Cit. – Nay, that shall be just as your ladyship pleases – you know I promised you I would not buy; that is to say, unless you discharge me of that obligation.

Lady. – I cannot, for shame, go out of this shop, and lay out nothing.

Cit. – Did your ladyship see any thing that pleased you?

Lady. – I only saw some of the finest things in England – I don't think all the city of Paris can outdo him.

Cit. – Well, madam, if you resolve to buy, let us go and look again.

Lady. – 'Come, then.' And upon that the lady, turning to the mercer – 'Come, sir,' says she, 'I think I will look upon that piece of brocade again; I cannot find in my heart to give you all this trouble for nothing.'

'Madam,' says the mercer, 'I shall be very glad if I can be so happy as to please you; but, I beseech your ladyship, don't speak of the trouble, for that is the duty of our trade; we must never think our business a trouble.'

Upon this the ladies went back with him into his inner shop, and laid out between sixty and seventy pounds, for they both bought rich suits of clothes, and used his shop for many years after.

The short inference from this long discourse is this: That here you see, and I could give many examples very like this, how, and in what manner, a shopkeeper is to behave himself in the way of his business – what impertinences, what taunts, flouts, and ridiculous things, he must bear in his business, and must not show the least return, or the least signal of disgust – he must have no passions, no fire in his temper – he must be all soft and smooth: nay, if his real temper be naturally fiery and hot, he must show none of it in his shop – he must be a perfect complete hypocrite, if he will be a complete tradesman.[2]

It is true, natural tempers are not to be always counterfeited – the man cannot easily be a lamb in his shop, and a lion in himself; but let it be easy or hard, it must be done, and it is done. There are men who have, by custom and usage, brought themselves to it, that nothing could be meeker and milder than they, when behind the counter, and yet nothing be more furious and raging in every other part of life – nay, the provocations they have met with in their shops have so irritated their rage, that they would go upstairs from their shop, and fall into phrensies, and a kind of madness, and beat their heads against the wall, and mischief themselves, if not prevented, till the violence of it had gotten vent, and the passions abate and cool. Nay, I heard once

2 [The necessity here insisted on seems a hard one, and scarcely consistent with a just morality. Yet, if the tradesman takes a right view of his situation, he will scarcely doubt the propriety of Defoe's advice. He must consider, that, in his shop, he is, as it were, acting a part. He performs a certain character in the drama of our social arrangements, one which requires all the civility and forbearance above insisted on. He is not called upon, in such circumstances, to feel, speak, and act, as he would find himself in honour required to do in his private or absolutely personal capacity – in his own house, for instance, or in any public place where he mingled on a footing of equality with his fellow-citizens. Accordingly, there is such a general sense of the justifiableness of his conducting himself in this submissive spirit, that no one would think of imputing it to him as a fault; but he would be more apt to be censured or ridiculed if he had so little sense as to take offence, in his capacity of tradesman, at any thing which it would only concern him to resent if it were offered to him in his capacity as a private citizen.

An incident, somewhat like that so dramatically related by Defoe, occurred a few years ago in the northern capital. A lady had, through whim, pestered a mercer in the manner related in the text, turning over all his goods, and only treating him with rudeness in return. When she finally turned to leave the shop, to inquire, as she said, for better and cheaper goods elsewhere, she found that a shower was falling, against which she had no protection. The tradesman, who had politely shown her to the door, observing her hesitate on the threshold at sight of the rain, requested her to wait a moment, and, stepping backwards for his umbrella, instantly returned, and, in the kindest accents, requested her to accept the loan of it. She took it, and went away, but in a few minutes returned it, in a totally different frame of spirit, and not only purchased extensively on this occasion, but became a constant customer for the future.

Another tradesman in the same city was so remarkable for his imperturbable civility, that it became the subject of a bet – an individual undertaking to irritate him, or, if he failed, to forfeit a certain sum. He went to the shop, and caused an immense quantity of the finest silks to be turned over, after which he coolly asked for a pennyworth of a certain splendid piece of satin. 'By all means,' said the discreet trader; 'allow me, Sir, to have your penny.' The coin was handed to him, and, taking up the piece of satin, and placing the penny on the end of it, he cut round with his scissors, thus detaching a little bit of exactly the size and shape of the piece of money which was to purchase it. This, with the most polite air imaginable, he handed to his customer, whose confusion may be imagined.]

of a shopkeeper that behaved himself thus to such an extreme, that, when he was provoked by the impertinence of the customers, beyond what his temper could bear, he would go upstairs and beat his wife, kick his children about like dogs, and be as furious for two or three minutes as a man chained down in Bedlam, and when the heat was over, would sit down and cry faster then the children he had abused; and after the fit was over he would go down into his shop again, and be as humble, as courteous, and as calm as any man whatever – so absolute a government of his passions had he in the shop, and so little out of it; in the shop a soul-less animal that can resent nothing, and in the family a madman; in the shop meek like the lamb, but in the family outrageous like a Lybian lion.

The sum of the matter is this: it is necessary for a tradesman to subject himself, by all the ways possible, to his business; his customers are to be his idols: so far as he may worship idols by allowance, he is to bow down to them and worship them;[3] at least, he is not any way to displease them, or show any disgust or distaste at any thing they say or do. The bottom of it all is, that he is intending to get money by them; and it is not for him that gets money by them to offer the least inconvenience to them by whom he gets it; but he is to consider, that, as Solomon says, 'The borrower is servant to the lender,' so the seller is servant to the buyer.

When a tradesman has thus conquered all his passions, and can stand before the storm of impertinence, he is said to be fitted up for the main article, namely, the inside of the counter.

On the other hand, we see that the contrary temper, nay, but the very suggestion of it, hurries people on to ruin their trade, to disoblige the customers, to quarrel with them, and drive them away. We see by the lady above, after having seen the ways she had taken to put this man out of temper – I say, we see it conquered her temper, and brought her to lay out her money cheefully, and be his customer ever after.

A sour, morose, dogmatic temper would have sent these ladies both away with their money in their pockets; but the man's patience and temper drove the lady back to lay out her money, and engaged her entirely.

3 [It appears to the editor that the case is here somewhat over-stated. While imperterbable good temper and civility are indispensible in the shop-keeper, it is not impossible that he may also err in displaying a *too great obsequiousness* of *manner*. This, by disgusting the common sense and good taste of customers, may do as much harm as want of civility. A too *pressing* manner, likewise, does harm, by causing the customer to feel as if he were *obliged* to purchase. The medium of an easy, obliging, and good-humoured manner, is perhaps what suits best. But here, as in many other things, it is not easy to lay down any general rule. Much must be left to the goos sense and *tact* of the trader.]

CHAPTER IX

OF OTHER REASONS FOR THE TRADESMAN'S DISASTERS: AND, FIRST, OF INNOCENT DIVERSIONS

A few directions seasonably given, and wisely received, will be sufficient to guide a tradesman in a right management of his business, so as that, if he observes them, he may secure his prosperity and success: but it requires a long and serious caveat to warn him of the dangers he meets with in his way. Trade is a straight and direct way, if they will but keep in it with a steady foot, and not wander, and launch out here and there, as a loose head and giddy fancy will prompt them to do.

The road, I say, is straight and direct; but there are many turnings and openings in it, both to the right hand and to the left, in which, if a tradesman but once ventures to step awry, it is ten thousand to one but he loses himself, and very rarely finds his way back again; at least if he does, it is like a man that has been lost in a wood; he comes out with a scratched face, and torn clothes, tired and spent, and does not recover himself in a long while after.

In a word, one steady motion carries him up, but many things assist to pull him down; there are many ways open to his ruin, but few to his rising: and though employment is said to be the best fence against temptations, and he that is busy heartily in his business, temptations to idleness and negligence will not be so busy about him, yet tradesmen are as often drawn from their business as other men; and when they are so, it is more fatal to them a great deal, than it is to gentlemen and persons whose employments do not call for their personal attendance so much as a shop does.

Among the many turnings and bye-lanes, which, as I say, are to be met with in the straight road of trade, there are two as dangerous and fatal to their prosperity as the worst, though they both carry an appearance of good, and promise contrary to what they perform; these are –

I. Pleasures and diversions, especially such as they will have us call innocent diversions.

II. Projects and adventures, and especially such as promise mountains of profit *in nubibus* [in the clouds], and are therefore the more likely to ensnare the poor eager avaricious tradesman.

1. I am now to speak of the first, namely, pleasures and diversions. I cannot allow any pleasures to be innocent, when they turn away either the body or the mind of a tradesman from the one needful thing which his calling makes necessary, and that necessity makes his duty – I mean, the application both of his hands and head to his business. Those pleasures and diversions may be innocent in themselves, which are not so to him: there are very few things in the world that are simply evil, but things are made circumstantially evil when they are not so in themselves: killing a man is not simply sinful; on the contrary, it is not lawful only, but a duty, when justice and the laws of God or man require it; but when done maliciously, from any corrupt principle, or to any corrupted end, is murder, and the worst of crimes.

Pleasures and diversions are thus made criminal, when a man is engaged in duty to a full attendance upon such business as those pleasures and diversions necessarily interfere with and interrupt; those pleasures, though innocent in themselves, become a fault in him, because his legal avocations demand his attendance in another place. Thus those pleasures may be lawful to another man, which are not so to him, because another man has not the same obligation to a calling, the same necessity to apply to it, the same cry of a family, whose bread may depend upon his diligence, as a tradesman has.

Solomon, the royal patron of industry, tells us, 'He that is a lover of pleasure, shall be a poor man.' I must not doubt but Solomon is to be understood of tradesmen and working men, such as I am writing of, whose time and application is due to their business, and who, in pursuit of their pleasures, are sure to neglect their shops, or employments, and I therefore render the words thus, to the present purpose – 'The tradesman that is a lover of pleasure, shall be a poor man.' I hope I do not wrest the Scripture in my interpretation of it; I am sure it agrees with the whole tenor of the wise man's other discourses.

When I see young shopkeepers keep horses, ride a-hunting, learn dog-language, and keep the sportsmen's brogue upon their tongues, I will not say I read their destiny, for I am no fortune-teller, but I do say, I am always afraid for them; especially when I know that either their fortunes and beginnings are below it, or that their trades are such as in a particular manner to require their constant attendance. As to see a barber abroad on a Saturday, a corn-factor abroad on a Wednesday and Friday, or a Blackwell-hall man on a Thursday, you may as well say a country shopkeeper should go a-hunting on a market-day, or go a-feasting at the fair day of the town where he lives; and yet riding and hunting are otherwise lawful diversions, and in their kind very good for exercise and health.

I am not for making a galley-slave of a shopkeeper, and have him chained down to the oar; but if he be a wise, a prudent, and a diligent tradesman, he will allow himself as few excursions as possible.

Business neglected is business lost; it is true, there are some businesses which require less attendance than others, and give a man less occasion of application; but, in general, that tradesman who can satisfy himself to be absent from his business, must not expect success; if he is above the character of a diligent tradesman, he must then be above the business too, and should leave it to somebody, that, having more need of it, will think it worth his while to mind it better.

Nor, indeed, is it possible a tradesman should be master of any of the qualifications which I have set down to denominate him complete, if he neglects his shop and his time, following his pleasures and diversions.

I will allow that the man is not vicious and wicked, that he is not addicted to drunkenness, to women, to gaming, or any such things as those, for those are not woundings, but murder, downright killing. A man may wound and hurt himself sometimes, in the rage of an ungoverned passion, or in a phrensy or fever, and intend no more; but if he shoots himself through the head, or hangs himself, we are sure then he intended to kill and destroy himself, and he dies inevitably.

For a tradesman to follow his pleasures, which indeed is generally attended with a slighting of his business, leaving his shop to servants or others, it is evident to me that he is indifferent whether it thrives or no; and, above all, it is evident that his heart is not in his business; that he does not delight in it, or look on it with pleasure. To a complete tradesman there is no pleasure equal to that of being in his business, no delight equal to that of seeing himself thrive, to see trade flow in upon him, and to be satisfied that he goes on prosperously. He will never thrive, that cares not whether he thrives or no. As trade is the chief employment of his life, and is therefore called, by way of eminence, *his business*, so it should be made the chief delight of his life. The tradesman that does not love his business, will never give it due attendance.

Pleasure is a bait to the mind, and the mind will attract the body: where the heart is, the object shall always have the body's company. The great objection I meet with from young tradesmen against this argument is, they follow no unlawful pleasures; they do not spend their time in taverns, and drinking to excess; they do not spend their money in gaming, and so stock-starve their business, and rob the shop to supply the extravagant losses of play; or they do not spend their hours in ill company and debaucheries; all they do, is a little innocent diversion in riding abroad now and then for the air, and for their health, and to ease their thoughts of the throng of other affairs which are heavy upon them, &c.

These, I say, are the excuses of young tradesmen; and, indeed, they are young excuses, and, I may say truly, have nothing in them. It is perhaps true, or I may grant it so for the present purpose, that the pleasure the tradesman takes is, as he says, not unlawful, and that he follows only a little innocent diversion; but let me tell him, the words are ill put together, and the diversion is rather recommended from the word *little*, than from the word *innocent*: if it be, indeed, but little, it may be innocent; but the case is quite altered by the extent of the thing; and the innocence lies here, not in the nature of the thing, not in the diversion or pleasure that is taken, but in the time it takes; for if the man spends the time in it which should be spent in his shop or warehouse, and his business suffers by his absence, as it must do, if the absence is long at a time, or often practised – the diversion so taken becomes criminal to him, though the same diversion might be innocent in another.

Thus I have heard a young tradesman, who loved his bottle, excuse himself, and say, 'It is true, I have been at the tavern, but I was treated, it cost me nothing.' And this, he thinks, clears him of all blame; not considering that when he spends no money, yet he spends five times the value of the money in time. Another says, 'Why, indeed, I was at the tavern yesterday all the afternoon, but I could not help it, and I spent but sixpence.' But at the same time perhaps it might be said he spent five pounds' worth of time, his business being neglected, his shop unattended, his books not posted, his letters not written, and the like – for all those things are works necessary to a tradesman, as well as the attendance on his shop, and infinitely above the pleasure of being treated at the expense of his time. All manner of pleasures should buckle and be subservient to business: he that makes his pleasure be his business, will never make his business be a pleasure. Innocent pleasures become sinful, when they are used to excess, and so it is here; the most innocent diversion becomes criminal, when it breaks in upon that which is the due and just employment of the man's life. Pleasures rob the tradesman, and how, then, can he call them innocent diversions? They are downright thieves; they rob his shop of his attendance, and of the time which he ought to bestow there; they rob his family of their due support, by the man's neglecting that business by which they are to be supported and maintained; and they oftentimes rob the creditors of their just debts, the tradesman sinking by the inordinate use of those innocent diversions, as he calls them, as well by the expense attending them, as the loss of his time, and neglect of his business, by which he is at last reduced to the necessity of shutting up shop in earnest, which was indeed as good as shut before. A shop without a master is like the same shop on a middling holiday, half shut up, and he that keeps it long so, need not doubt but he may in a little time more shut it quite up.

In short, pleasure is a thief to business; how any man can call it innocent, let him answer that does so; it robs him every way, as I have said above: and if the tradesman be a Christian, and has any regard to religion and his duty, I must tell him, that when upon his disasters he shall reflect, and see that he has ruined himself and his family, by following too much those diversions and pleasures which he thought innocent, and which perhaps in themselves were really so, he will find great cause to repent of that which he insisted on as innocent; he will find himself lost, by doing lawful things, and that he made those innocent things sinful, and those lawful things unlawful to him. Thus, as they robbed his family and creditors before of their just debts – for maintenance is a tradesman's just debt to his family, and a wife and children are as much a tradesman's real creditors as those who trusted him with their goods – I say, as his innocent pleasures robbed his family and creditors before, they will rob him now of his peace, and of all that calm of soul which an honest, industrious, though unfortunate, tradesman meets with under his disasters.

I am asked here, perhaps, how much pleasure an honest-meaning tradesman may be allowed to take? for it cannot be supposed I should insist that all pleasure is forbidden him, that he must have no diversion, no spare hours, no intervals from hurry and fatigue; that would be to pin him down to the very floor of his shop, as John Sheppard was locked down to the floor of his prison.

The answer to this question every prudent tradesman may make for himself: if his pleasure is in his shop, and in his business, there is no danger of him; but if he has an itch after exotic diversions – I mean such as are foreign to his shop, and to his business, and which I therefore call *exotic* – let him honestly and fairly state the case between his shop and his diversions, and judge impartially for himself. So much pleasure, and no more, may be innocently taken, as does not interfere with, or do the least damage to his business, by taking him away from it.

Every moment that his trade wants him in his shop or warehouse, it is his duty to be there; it is not enough to say, I believe I shall not be wanted; or I believe I shall suffer no loss by my absence. He must come to a point and not deceive himself; if he does, the cheat is all his own. If he will not judge sincerely at first, he will reproach himself sincerely at last; for there is no fraud against his own reflections: a man is very rarely a hypocrite to himself.

The rule may be, in a few words, thus: those pleasures or diversions, and those only, can be innocent, which the man may or does use, or allow himself to use, without hindrance of, or injury to, his business and reputation.

Let the diversions or pleasures in question be what they will, and how innocent soever they are in themselves, they are not so to him, because they interrupt or interfere with his business, which is his immediate duty. I have mentioned the circumstance which touches this part too, namely, that there may be a time when even the needful duties of religion may become faults, and unseasonable, when another more needful attendance calls for us to apply to it; much more, then, those things which are only barely lawful. There is a visible difference between the things which we may do, and the things which we must do. Pleasures at certain seasons are allowed, and we may give ourselves some loose to them; but business, I mean to the man of business, is that needful thing, of which it is not to be said it *may*, but it *must* be done.

Again, those pleasures which may not only be lawful in themselves, but which may be lawful to other men, yet are criminal and unlawful to him. To gentlemen of fortunes and estates, who being born to large possessions, and have no avocations of this kind, it is certainly lawful to spend their spare hours on horseback, with their hounds or hawks, pursuing their game; or, on foot, with their gun and their net, and their dogs to kill the hares or birds, &c. – all which we call sport. These are the men that can, with a particular satisfaction, when they come home, say they have only taken an innocent diversion; and yet even in these, there are not wanting some excesses which take away the innocence of them, and consequently the satisfaction in their reflection, and therefore it was I said it was lawful to them to spend their spare hours – by which I am to be understood, those hours which are not due to more solemn and weighty occasions, such as the duties of religion in particular. But as this is not my present subject, I proceed; for I am not talking to gentlemen now, but to tradesmen.

The prudent tradesman will, in time, consider what he ought or ought not to do, in his own particular case, as to his pleasures – not what another man may or may not do. In short, nothing of pleasure or diversion can be innocent to him, whatever it may be to another, if it injures his business, if it takes either his time, or his mind, or his delight, or his attendance, from his business; nor can all the little excuses, of its being for his health, and for the needful unbending the bow of the mind, from the constant application of business, for all these must stoop to the great article of his shop and business; though I might add, that the bare taking the air for health, and for a recess to the mind, is not the thing I am talking of – it is the taking an immoderate liberty, and spending an immoderate length of time, and that at unseasonable and improper hours, so as to make his pleasures and diversions be prejudicial to his business – this is the evil I object to, and this is too much the ruin of the tradesmen of this age; and thus any man who calmly reads these papers will see I ought to be understood.

Nor do I confine this discourse to the innocent diversions of a horse, and riding abroad to take the air; things which, as above, are made hurtful and unlawful to him, only as they are hindrances to his business, and are more or less so, as they rob his shop or warehouse, or business, or his attendance and time, and cause him to draw his affections off from his calling.

But we see other and new pleasures daily crowding in upon the tradesman, and some which no age before this have been in danger of – I mean, not to such an excess as is now the case, and consequently there were fewer tradesmen drawn into the practice.

The present age is a time of gallantry and gaiety; nothing of the present pride and vanity was known, or but very little of it, in former times: the baits which are every where laid for the corruption of youth, and for the ruin of their fortunes, were never so many and so mischievous as they are now.

We scarce now see a tradesman's apprentice come to his fifth year, but he gets a long wig and a sword, and a set of companions suitable; and this wig and sword, being left at proper and convenient places, are put on at night after the shop is shut, or when they can slip out to go a-raking in, and when they never fail of company ready to lead them into all manner of wickedness and debauchery; and from this cause it is principally that so many apprentices are ruined, and run away from their masters before they come out of their times – more, I am persuaded, now, than ever were to be found before.

Nor, as I said before, will I charge the devil with having any hand in the ruin of these young fellows – indeed, he needs not trouble himself about them, they are his own by early choice – they anticipate temptation, and are as forward as the devil can desire them to be. These may be truly said to be drawn aside of their own lusts, and enticed – they need no tempter.

But of these I may also say, they seldom trouble the tradesmen's class; they get ruined early, and finish the tradesman before they begin, so my discourse is not at present directed much to them; indeed, they are past advice before they come in my way.

Indeed, I knew one of these sort of gentlemen-apprentices make an attempt to begin, and set up his trade – he was a dealer in what they call Crooked-lane wares: he got about £300 from his father, an honest plain countryman, to set him up, and his said honest father exerted himself to the utmost to send him up so much money.

When he had gotten the money, he took a shop near the place where he had served his time, and entering upon the shop, he had it painted, and fitted up, and some goods he bought in order to furnish it; but before that, he was obliged to pay about £70 of the money to little debts, which he had contracted in his apprenticeship, at two or three ale-houses, for drink and eatables, treats, and junketings; and at the barber's for long perukes, at the sempstress's for fine Holland-shirts, turn-overs, white gloves, &c., to make a beau of him, and at several other places.

When he came to dip into this, and found that it wanted still £30 or £40 to equip him for the company which he had learned to keep, he took care to do this first; and being delighted with his new dress, and how like a gentleman he looked, he was resolved, before he opened a shop, to take his swing a little in the town; so away he went, with two of his neighbour's apprentices, to the play-house, thence to the tavern, not far from his dwelling, and there they fell to cards, and sat up all night – and thus they spent about a fortnight; the rest just creeping into their masters' houses, by the connivance of their fellow-servants, and he getting a bed in the tavern, where what he spent, to be sure, made them willing enough to oblige him – that is to say, to encourage him to ruin himself.

They then changed their course, indeed, and went to the ball, and that necessarily kept them out the most part of the night, always having their supper dressed at the tavern at their return; and thus, in a few words, he went on till he made way through all the remaining money he had left, and was obliged to call his creditors together, and break before he so much as opened his shop – I say, his creditors, for great part of the goods which he had furnished his shop with were unpaid for; perhaps some few might be bought with ready money.

This man, indeed, is the only tradesman that ever I met with, that set up and broke before his shop was open; others I have indeed known make very quick work of it.

But this part rather belongs to another head. I am at present not talking of madmen, as I hope, indeed, I am not writing to madmen, but I am talking of tradesmen undone by lawful things, by what they call innocent and harmless things – such as riding abroad, or walking abroad to take the air, and to divert themselves, dogs, gun, country-sport, and city-recreation. These things are certainly lawful, and in themselves very innocent; nay, they may be needful for health, and to give some relaxation to the mind, hurried with too much business; but the needfulness of them is so much made an excuse, and the excess of them is so injurious to the tradesman's business and to his time, which should be set apart for his shop and his trade, that there are not a few tradesmen thus lawfully ruined, as I may call it – in a word, lawful or unlawful, their shop is neglected, their business goes behind-hand, and it is all one to the subject of breaking, and to the creditor, whether the man was undone by being a knave, or by being a fool; it is all one whether he lost his trade by scandalous immoral negligence, or by sober or religious negligence.

In a word, business languishes, while the tradesman is absent, and neglects it, be it for his health or for his pleasure, be it in good company or in bad, be it from a good or an ill design; and if the business languishes, the tradesman will not be long before he languishes too; for nothing can support the tradesman but his supporting his trade by a due attendance and application.[1]

1 [In the above admirable series of plain-spoken advices, the author has omitted one weighty reason why young tradesmen should not spend their evenings in frivolous, or otherwise improper company. The actual loss of time and of money incurred by such courses of conduct, is generally of less consequence than the losses arising from habitual distraction of mind, and the acquisition of an acquaintanceship with a set of idle or silly companions. It is of the utmost importance that young tradesmen should spend their leisure hours in a way calculated to soothe the feelings, and enlarge the mind; and in the present day, from the prevalance of literature, and other rational means for amusement, they have ample opportunities of doing so.]

CHAPTER X

OF EXTRAVAGANT AND EXPENSIVE LIVING; ANOTHER STEP TO A TRADESMAN'S DISASTER

Hitherto I have written of tradesmen ruined by lawful and innocent diversions; and, indeed, these are some of the most dangerous pits for a tradesman to fall into, because men are so apt to be insensible of the danger: a ship may as well be lost in a calm smooth sea, and an easy fair gale of wind, as in a storm, if they have no pilot, or the pilot be ignorant or unwary; and disasters of that nature happen as frequently as any others, and are as fatal. When rocks are apparent, and the pilot, bold and wilful, runs directly upon them, without fear or wit, we know the fate of the ship – it must perish, and all that are in it will inevitably be lost; but in a smooth sea, a bold shore, an easy gale, the unseen rocks or shoals are the only dangers, and nothing can hazard them but the skilfulness of the pilot: and thus it is in trade. Open debaucheries and extravagances, and a profusion of expense, as well as a general contempt of business, these are open and current roads to a tradesman's destruction; but a silent going on, in pursuit of innocent pleasures, a smooth and calm, but sure neglect of his shop, and time, and business, will as effectually and as surely ruin the tradesman as the other; and though the means are not so scandalous, the effect is as certain. But I proceed to the other.

Next to immoderate pleasures, the tradesman ought to be warned against immoderate expense. This is a terrible article, and more particularly so to the tradesman, as custom has now, as it were on purpose for their undoing, introduced a general habit of, and as it were a general inclination among all sorts of people to, an expensive way of living; to which might be added a kind of necessity of it; for that even with the greatest prudence and frugality a man cannot now support a family with the ordinary expense, which the same family might have been maintained with some few years ago: there is now (1) a weight of taxes upon almost all the necessaries of life, bread and flesh excepted, as coals, salt, malt, candles, soap, leather, hops, wine, fruit, and all foreign consumptions; (2) a load of pride upon the temper of the nation, which, in spite of taxes and the unusual dearness of every thing, yet prompts people to a profusion in their expenses.

This is not so properly called a *tax* upon the tradesmen; I think rather, it may be called a *plague* upon them: for there is, first, the dearness of every necessary thing to make living expensive; and secondly, an unconquerable aversion to any restraint; so that the poor will be like the rich, and the rich like the great, and the great like the greatest – and thus the world runs on to a kind of distraction at this time: where it will end, time must discover.

Now, the tradesman I speak of, if he will thrive, he must resolve to begin as he can go on; and if he does so, in a word, he must resolve to live more under restraint than ever tradesmen of his class used to do; for every necessary thing being, as I have said, grown dearer than before, he must entirely omit all the enjoyment of the unnecessaries which he might have allowed himself before, or perhaps be obliged to an expense beyond the income of his trade: and in either of these cases he has a great hardship upon him.

When I talk of immoderate expenses, I must be understood not yet to mean the extravagances of wickedness and debaucheries; there are so many sober extravagances, and so many grave sedate ways for a tradesman's ruin, and they are so much more dangerous than those hair-brained desperate ways of gaming and debauchery, that I think it is the best service I can do the tradesmen to lay before them those sunk rocks (as the seamen call them), those secret dangers in the first place, that they may know how to avoid them; and as for the other common ways, common discretion will supply them with caution for those, and their senses will be their protection.

The dangers to the tradesmen whom I am directing myself to, are from lawful things, and such as before are called innocent; for I am speaking to the sober part of tradesmen, who yet are often ruined and overthrown in trade; and perhaps as many such miscarry, as of the mad and extravagant, particularly because their number far exceeds them. Expensive living is a kind of slow fever; it is not so open, so threatening and dangerous, as the ordinary distemper which goes by that name, but it preys upon the spirits, and, when its degrees are increased to a height, is as fatal and as sure to kill as the other: it is a secret enemy, that feeds upon the vitals; and when it has gone its full length, and the languishing tradesman is weakened in his solid part, I mean his stock, then it overwhelms him at once.

Expensive living feeds upon the life and blood of the tradesman, for it eats into the two most essential branches of his trade, namely, his credit and his cash; the first is its triumph, and the last is its food: nothing goes out to cherish the exorbitance, but the immediate money; expenses seldom go on trust, they are generally supplied and supported with ready money, whatever are not.

This expensive way of living consists in several things, which are all indeed in their degree ruinous to the tradesman; such as

1. Expensive house-keeping, or family extravagance.
2. Expensive dressing, or the extravagance of fine clothes.
3. Expensive company, or keeping company above himself.
4. Expensive equipages, making a show and ostentation of figure in the world.

I might take them all in bulk, and say, what has a young tradesman to do with these? and yet where is there a tradesman now to be found, who is not more or less guilty? It is, as I have said, the general vice of the times; the whole nation are more or less in the crime; what with necessity and inclination, where is the man or the family that lives as such families used to live?

In short, good husbandry and frugality is quite out of fashion, and he that goes about to set up for the practice of it, must mortify every thing about him that has the least tincture of frugality; it is the mode to live high, to spend more than we get, to neglect trade, contemn care and concern, and go on without forecast, or without consideration; and, in consequence, it is the mode to go on to extremity, to break, become bankrupt and beggars, and so going off the trading stage, leave it open for others to come after us, and do the same.[1]

To begin with house-keeping. I have already hinted, that every thing belonging to the family subsistence bears a higher price than usual, I may say, than ever; at the same time I can neither undertake to prove that there is more got by selling, or more ways to get it, I mean to a tradesman, than there was formerly; the consequence then must be, that the tradesmen do not grow rich faster than formerly; at least we may venture to say this of tradesmen and their families, comparing them with former times, namely, that there is not more got, and I am satisfied there is less laid up, than was then; or, if you will have it, that tradesmen get less and spend more than they ever did. How they should be richer than they were in those times, is very hard to say.

That all things are dearer than formerly to a house-keeper, needs little demonstration; the taxes necessarily infer it from the weight of them, and the many things charged; for, besides the things enumerated above, we find all articles of foreign importation are increased by the high duties laid on them; such as linen, especially fine linen; silk, especially foreign wrought silk: every thing eatable, drinkable,

1 [Now, as in Defoe's time, a common observer is apt to be impressed with the idea, that expenses, with a large part of the community, exceed gains. Certainly, this is true at all times with a certain portion of society, but probably at no time with a large portion. There is a tendency to great self-deception in all such speculations; and no one ever thinks of bringing them to the only true test – statistical facts. The reader ought, therefore, to pay little attention to the complaints in the text, as to an increased extravagance in the expenses of tradesmen, and only regard the general recommendation, and the reasons by which that recommendation is enforced, to live within income.]

and wearable, are made heavy to us by high and exorbitant customs and excises, as brandies, tobacco, sugar; deals and timber for building; oil, wine, spice, raw silks, calico, chocolate, coffee, tea; on some of these the duties are more than doubled: and yet that which is most observable is, that such is the expensive humour of the times, that not a family, no, hardly of the meanest tradesman, but treat their friends with wine, or punch, or fine ale; and have their parlours set off with the tea-table and the chocolate-pot – treats and liquors all exotic, foreign and new among tradesmen, and terrible articles in their modern expenses; which have nothing to be said for them, either as to the expense of them, or the helps to health which they boast of: on the contrary, they procure us rheumatic bodies and consumptive purses, and can no way pass with me for necessaries; but being needless, they add to the expense, by sending us to the doctors and apothecaries to cure the breaches which they make in our health, and are themselves the very worst sort of superfluities.

But I come back to necessaries; and even in them, family-expenses are extremely risen, provisions are higher rated – no provisions that I know of, except only bread, mutton, and fish, but are made dearer than ever – house-rent, in almost all the cities and towns of note in England, is excessively and extremely dearer, and that in spite of such innumerable buildings as we see almost everywhere raised up, as well in the country as in London, and the parts adjacent.

Add to the rents of houses, the wages of servants. A tradesman, be he ever so much inclined to good husbandry, cannot always do his kitchen-work himself, suppose him a bachelor, or can his wife, suppose him married, and suppose her to have brought him any portion, be his bedfellow and his cook too. These maid-servants, then, are to be considered, and are an exceeding tax upon house-keepers; those who were formerly hired at three pounds to four pounds a-year wages, now demand five, six and eight pounds a-year; nor do they double anything upon us but their wages and their pride; for, instead of doing more work for their advance of wages, they do less: and the ordinary work of families cannot now be performed by the same number of maids, which, in short, is a tax upon the upper sort of tradesmen, and contributes very often to their disasters, by the extravagant keeping three or four maid-servants in a house, nay, sometimes five, where two formerly were thought sufficient. This very extravagance is such, that talking lately with a man very well experienced in this matter, he told me he had been making his calculations on that very particular, and he found by computation, that the number of servants kept by all sorts of people, tradesmen as well as others, was so much increased, that there are in London, and the towns within ten miles of it, take it every way, above a hundred thousand more maid-servants and footmen, at this time in place, than used to be in the same compass of ground thirty years ago;[2] and that their wages amounted to above forty shillings a-head per annum, more than the wages of the like number of servants did amount to at the same length of time past; the advance to the whole body amounting to no less than two hundred thousand pounds a-year.

Indeed, it is not easy to guess what the expense of wages to servants amounts to in a year, in this nation; and consequently we cannot easily determine what the increase of that expense amounts to in England, but certainly it must rise to many hundred thousand pounds a-year in the whole.

The tradesmen bear their share of this expense, and indeed too great a share, very ordinary tradesmen in London keeping at least two maids, and some more, and some a footman or two besides; for it is an ordinary thing to see the tradesmen and shopkeepers of London keep footmen, as well as the gentlemen: witness the infinite number of blue liveries, which are so common now that they are called the tradesmen's liveries; and few gentlemen care to give blue to their servants for that very reason.

In proportion to their servants, the tradesmen now keep their tables, which are also advanced in their proportion of expense to other things: indeed, the citizen's and tradesmen's tables are now the emblems, not of plenty, but of luxury, not of good house-keeping, but of profusion, and that of the highest kind of extravagance; insomuch, that it was the opinion of a gentleman who had been not a traveller only, but a nice observer of such things abroad, that there is at this time more waste of provisions in England than in any other nation in the world, of equal extent of ground; and that England consumes for their whole subsistence more flesh than half Europe besides; that the beggars of London, and within ten miles round it, eat more white bread than the whole kingdom of Scotland,[3] and the like.

But this is an observation only, though I believe it is very just; I am bringing it in here only as an example of the dreadful profusion of this age, and how an extravagant way of expensive living, perfectly negligent of all degrees of frugality or good husbandry, is the reigning vice of the people. I could enlarge upon it, and very much to the purpose here, but I shall have occasion to speak of it again.

The tradesman, whom I am speaking to by way of direction, will not, I hope, think this the way for him to thrive, or find it for his convenience to

2 [There can be little doubt, that the calculation of this experienced gentleman is grossly inconsistent with the truth. Nevertheless, this part of Defoe's work contains some curious traits of manners, which are probably not exaggerated.]

3 [Defoe, from his having been employed for several years in Scotland at the time of the Union, must have well known how rare was then the use of white or wheaten bread in that country.]

fall in with this common height of living presently, in his beginning; if he comes gradually into it after he has gotten something considerable to lay by, I say, if he does it then, it is early enough, and he may be said to be insensibly drawn into it by the necessity of the times; because, forsooth, it is a received notion, 'We must be like other folks:' I say, if he does fall into it then, when he will pretend he cannot help it, it is better than worse, and if he can afford it, well and good; but to begin thus, to set up at this rate, when he first looks into the world, I can only say this, he that begins in such a manner, it will not be difficult to guess where he will end; for a tradesman's pride certainly precedes his destruction, and an expensive living goes before his fall.

We are speaking now to a tradesman, who, it is supposed, must live by his business, a young man who sets up a shop, or warehouse, and expects to get money; one that would be a rich tradesman, rather than a poor, fine, gay man; a grave citizen, not a peacock's feather; for he that sets up for a Sir Fopling Flutter, instead of a complete tradesman, is not to be thought capable of relishing this discourse; neither does this discourse relish him; for such men seem to be among the incurables, and are rather fit for an hospital of fools (so the French call our Bedlam) than to undertake trade, and enter upon business.

Trade is not a ball, where people appear in masque, and act a part to make sport; where they strive to seem what they really are not, and to think themselves best dressed when they are least known: but it is a plain visible scene of honest life, shown best in its native appearance, without disguise; supported by prudence and frugality; and like strong, stiff, clay land, grows fruitful only by good husbandry, culture, and manuring.

A tradesman dressed up fine, with his long wig and sword, may go to the ball when he pleases, for he is already dressed up in the habit; like a piece of counterfeit money, he is brass washed over with silver, and no tradesman will take him for current; with money in his hand, indeed, he may go to the merchant's warehouse and buy any thing, but no body will deal with him without it: he may write upon his edged hat, as a certain tradesman, after having been once broke and set up again, 'I neither give nor take credit:' and as others set up in their shops, 'No trust by retail,' so he may say, 'No trust by wholesale.' In short, thus equipped, he is truly a tradesman in masquerade, and must pass for such wherever he is known. How long it may be before his dress and he may suit, it not hard to guess.

Some will have it that this expensive way of living began among the tradesmen first, that is to say, among the citizens of London; and that their eager resolved pursuit of that empty and meanest kind of pride, called imitation, namely, to look like the gentry, and appear above themselves, drew them into it. It has indeed been a fatal custom, but it has been too long a city vanity. If men of quality lived like themselves, men of no quality would strive to live not like themselves: if those had plenty, these would have profusion; if those had enough, these would have excess; if those had what was good, these would have what was rare and exotic; I mean as to season, and consequently dear. And this is one of the ways that have worn out so many tradesmen before their time.

This extravagance, wherever it began, had its first rise among those sorts of tradesmen, who, scorning the society of their shops and customers, applied themselves to rambling to courts and plays; kept company above themselves, and spent their hours in such company as lives always above them; this could not but bring great expense along with it, and that expense would not be confined to the bare keeping such company abroad, but soon showed itself in a living like them at home, whether the tradesmen could support it or no.

Keeping high company abroad certainly brings on visitings and high treatings at home; and these are attended with costly furniture, rich clothes, and dainty tables. How these things agree with a tradesman's income, it is easy to suggest; and that, in short, these measures have sent so many tradesmen to the Mint and to the Fleet, where I am witness to it that they have still carried on their expensive living till they have come at last to starving and misery; but have been so used to it, they could not abate it, or at least not quite leave it off, though they wanted the money to pay for it.

Nor is the expensive dressing a little tax upon tradesmen, as it is now come up to an excess not formerly known to tradesmen; and though it is true that this particularly respects the ladies (for the tradesmen's wives now claim that title, as they do by their dress claim the appearance), yet to do justice to them, and not to load the women with the reproach, as if it were wholly theirs, it must be acknowledged the men have their share in dress, as the times go now, though, it is true, not so antic and gay as in former days; but do we not see fine wigs, fine Holland shirts of six to seven shillings an ell, and perhaps laced also, all lately brought down to the level of the apron, and become the common wear of tradesmen – nay, I may say, of tradesmen's apprentices – and that in such a manner as was never known in England before?

If the tradesman is thriving, and can support this and his credit too, that makes the case differ, though even then it cannot be said to be suitable; but for a tradesman to begin thus, is very imprudent, because the expense of this, as I said before, drains the very life-blood of his trade, taking away his ready money only, and making no return, but the worst of return, poverty and reproach; and, in case of miscarriage, infinite scandal and offence.

I am loth to make any part of my writing a satire upon the women; nor, indeed, does the extravagance either of dress or house-keeping, lie all, or always, at the door of the tradesmen's wives – the husband is often the prompter of it; at least he does not let his wife into the detail of his circumstances, he does not make her mistress of her own condition, but either flatters her with notions of his wealth, his profits, and his flourishing circumstances, and so the innocent woman spends high and lives great, believing that she is in a condition to afford it, and that her husband approves of it; at least, he does not offer to retrench or restrain her, but lets her go on, and indeed goes on with her, to the ruin of both.

I cannot but mention one thing here (though I purpose to give you one discourse on that subject by itself), namely, the great and indispensable obligation there is upon a tradesman always to acquaint his wife with the truth of his circumstances, and not to let her run on in ignorance, till she falls with him down the precipice of an unavoidable ruin – a thing no prudent woman would do, and therefore will never take amiss a husband's plainness in that particular case. But I reserve this to another place, because I am rather directing my discourse at this time to the tradesman at his beginning, and, as it may be supposed, unmarried.

Next to the expensive dressing, I place the expensive keeping company, as one thing fatal to a tradesman, and which, if he would be a complete tradesman, he should avoid with the utmost diligence. It is an agreeable thing to be seen in good company; for a man to see himself courted and valued, and his company desired by men of fashion and distinction, is very pleasing to any young tradesman, and it is really a snare which a young tradesman, if he be a man of sense, can very hardly resist. There is in itself indeed nothing that can be objected against, or is not very agreeable to the nature of man, and that not to his vicious part merely, but even to his best faculties; for who would not value himself upon being, as above, rendered acceptable to men both in station and figure above themselves? and it is really a piece of excellent advice which a learned man gave to his son, always to keep company with men above himself, not with men below himself.

But take me now to be talking, as I really am, not to the man merely, but to his circumstances, if he were a man of fortune, and had the view of great things before him, it would hold good; but if he is a young tradesman, such as I am now speaking of, who is newly entered into business, and must depend upon his said business for his subsistence and support, and hopes to raise himself by it – I say, if I am talking to such a one, I must say to him, that keeping company as above, with men superior to himself in knowledge, in figure, and estate, is not his business; for, first, as such conversation must necessarily take up a great deal of his time, so it ordinarily must occasion a great expense of money, and both destructive of his prosperity; nay, sometimes the first may be as fatal to him as the last, and it is often-times true in that sense of trade, that while by keeping company he is drawn out of his business, his absence from his shop or warehouse is the most fatal to him; and while he spends one crown in the tavern, he spends forty crowns' worth of his time; and with this difference, too, which renders it the worse to the tradesman, namely, that the money may be recovered, and gotten up again, but the time cannot. For example –

1. Perhaps in that very juncture a person comes to his warehouse. Suppose the tradesman to be a warehouse-keeper, who trades by commission, and this person, being a clothier in the country, comes to offer him his business, the commission of which might have been worth to him thirty to forty or fifty pounds per annum; but finding him abroad, or rather, not finding him at home and in his business, goes to another, and fixes with him at once. I once knew a dealer lose such an occasion as this, for an afternoon's pleasure, he being gone a-fishing into Hackney-marsh. This loss can never be restored, this expense of time was a fatal expense of money; and no tradesman will deny but they find many such things as this happen in the course of trade, either to themselves or others.

2. Another tradesman is invited to dinner by his great friend; for I am now speaking chiefly upon the subject of keeping high company, and what the tradesman sometimes suffers by it; it is true, that there he finds a most noble entertainment, the person of quality, and that professes a friendship for him, treats him with infinite respect, is fond of him, makes him welcome as a prince – for I am speaking of the acquaintance as really valuable and good in itself – but then, see it in its consequences. The tradesman on this occasion misses his 'Change, that is, omits going to the Exchange for that one day only, and not being found there, a merchant with whom he was in treaty for a large parcel of foreign goods, which would have been to his advantage to have bought, sells them to another more diligent man in the same way; and when he comes home, he finds, to his great mortification, that he has lost a bargain that would have been worth a hundred pounds buying; and now being in want of the goods, he is forced to entreat his neighbour who bought them to part with some of them at a considerable advance of price, and esteem it a favour too. Who now paid dearest for the visit to a person of figure? – the gentleman, who perhaps spent twenty shillings extraordinary to give him a handsome dinner, or the tradesman who lost a bargain worth a hundred pounds buying to go to eat it?

3. Another tradesman goes to 'Change in the ordinary course of his business, intending to speak with some of the merchants, his customers, as is usual, and get orders for goods, or perhaps an appointment to come to his warehouse to buy; but a snare of the like kind falls in his way, and a couple of friends, who perhaps have little or no business, at least with him, lay hold of him, and they agree to go off' Change to the tavern together. By complying with this invitation, he omits speaking to some of those merchants, as above, who, though he knew nothing of their minds, yet it had been his business to have shown himself to them, and have put himself in the way of their call; but omitting this, he goes and drinks a bottle of wine, as above, and though he stays but an hour, or, as we say, but a little while, yet unluckily, in that interim, the merchant, not seeing him on the Exchange, calls at his warehouse as he goes from the Exchange, but not finding him there either, he goes to another warehouse, and gives his orders to the value of £300 or £400, to a more diligent neighbour of the same business; by which he (the warehouse-keeper) not only loses the profit of selling that parcel, or serving that order, but the merchant is shown the way to his neighbour's warehouse, who, being more diligent than himself, fails not to cultivate his interest, obliges him with selling low, even to little or no gain, for the first parcel; and so the unhappy tradesman loses not his selling that parcel only, but loses the very customer, which was, as it were, his peculiar property before.

All these things, and many more such, are the consequences of a tradesman's absence from his business; and I therefore say, the expense of time on such light occasions as these, is one of the worst sorts of extravagance, and the most fatal to the tradesman, because really he knows not what he loses.

Above all things, the tradesman should take care not to be absent in the season of business, as I have mentioned above; for the warehouse-keeper to be absent from 'Change, which is his market, or from his warehouse, at the times when the merchants generally go about to buy, he had better be absent all the rest of the day.

I know nothing is more frequent, than for the tradesman, when company invites, or an excursion from business presses, to say, 'Well, come, I have nothing to do; there is no business to hinder, there is nothing neglected, I have no letters to write;' and the like; and away he goes to take the air for the afternoon, or to sit and enjoy himself with a friend – all of them things innocent and lawful in themselves; but here is the crisis of a tradesman's prosperity. In that very moment business presents, a valuable customer comes to buy, an unexpected bargain offers to be sold; another calls to pay money; and the like: nay, I would almost say, but that I am loth to concern the devil in more evils than he is guilty of – that the devil frequently draws a man out of his business when something extraordinary is just at hand for his advantage.

But not, as I have said, to charge the devil with what he is not guilty of, the tradesman is generally his own tempter; his head runs off from his business by a secret indolence; company, and the pleasure of being well received among gentlemen, is a cursed snare to a young tradesman, and carries him away from his business, for the mere vanity of being caressed and complimented by men who mean no ill, and perhaps know not the mischief they do to the man they show respect to; and this the young tradesman cannot resist, and that is in time his undoing.

The tradesman's pleasure should be in his business, his companions should be his books; and if he has a family, he makes his excursions up stairs, and no farther; when he is there, a bell or a call brings him down; and while he is in his parlour, his shop or his warehouse never misses him; his customers never go away unserved, his letters never come in and are unanswered. None of my cautions aim at restraining a tradesman from diverting himself, as we call it, with his fireside, or keeping company with his wife and children: there are so few tradesmen ruin themselves that way, and so few ill consequences happen upon an uxorious temper, that I will not so much as rank it with the rest; nor can it be justly called one of the occasions of a tradesman's disasters; on the contrary, it is too often that the want of a due complacency there, the want of taking delight there, estranges the man from not his parlour only, but his warehouse and shop, and every part of business that ought to engross both his mind and his time. That tradesman who does not delight in his family, will never long delight in his business; for, as one great end of an honest tradesman's diligence is the support of his family, and the providing for the comfortable subsistence of his wife and children, so the very sight of, and above all, his tender and affectionate care for his wife and children, is the spur of his diligence; that is, it puts an edge upon his mind, and makes him hunt the world for business, as hounds hunt the woods for their game. When he is dispirited, or discouraged by crosses and disappointments, and ready to lie down and despair, the very sight of his family rouses him again, and he flies to his business with a new vigour; 'I must follow my business,' says he, 'or we must all starve, my poor children must perish;' in a word, he that is not animated to diligence by the very sight and thought of his wife and children being brought to misery and distress, is a kind of a deaf adder that no music will charm, or a Turkish mute that no pity can move: in a word, he is a creature not to be called human, a wretch hardened against all the passions and affections that nature has furnished to other animals; and as there is no rhetoric of use to such a kind of man as that, so I am not talking to such a one, he must go among the incurables; for, where nature cannot work, what can argument assist?

CHAPTER XI

OF THE TRADESMAN'S MARRYING TOO SOON

It was a prudent provision which our ancestors made in the indenture of tradesmen's apprentices, that they should not contract matrimony during their apprenticeship; and they bound it with a penalty that was then thought sufficient. However, custom has taken off the edge of it since; namely, that they who did thus contract matrimony should forfeit their indentures, that is to say, should lose the benefit of their whole service, and not be made free.

Doubtless our forefathers were better acquainted with the advantages of frugality than we are, and saw farther into the desperate consequences of expensive living in the beginning of a tradesman's setting out into the world than we do; at least, it is evident they studied more and practised more of the prudential part in those cases, than we do.

Hence we find them very careful to bind their youth under the strongest obligations they could, to temperance, modesty, and good husbandry, as the grand foundations of their prosperity in trade, and to prescribe to them such rules and methods of frugality and good husbandry, as they thought would best conduce to their prosperity.

Among these rules this was one of the chief – namely, 'that they should not wed before they had sped?' It is an old homely rule, and coarsely expressed, but the meaning is evident, that a young beginner should never marry too soon. While he was a servant, he was bound from it as above; and when he had his liberty, he was persuaded against it by all the arguments which indeed ought to prevail with a considering man – namely, the expenses that a family necessarily would bring with it, and the care he ought to take to be able to support the expense before he brought it upon himself.

On this account it is, I say, our ancestors took more of their youth than we now do; at least, I think, they studied well the best methods of thriving, and were better acquainted with the steps by which a young tradesman ought to be introduced into the world than we are, and of the difficulties which those people would necessarily involve themselves in, who, despising those rules and methods of frugality, involved themselves in the expense of a family before they were in a way of gaining sufficient to support it.

A married apprentice will always make a repenting tradesman; and those stolen matches, a very few excepted, are generally attended with infinite broils and troubles, difficulties, and cross events, to carry them on at first by way of intrigue, to conceal them afterwards under fear of superiors, to manage after that to keep off scandal, and preserve the character as well of the wife as of the husband; and all this necessarily attended with a heavy expense, even before the young man is out of his time; before he has set a foot forward, or gotten a shilling in the world; so that all this expense is out of his original stock, even before he gets it, and is a sad drawback upon him when it comes.

Nay, this unhappy and dirty part is often attended with worse consequences still; for this expense coming upon him while he is but a servant, and while his portion, or whatever it is to be called, is not yet come into his hand, he is driven to terrible exigencies to supply this expense. If his circumstances are mean, and his trade mean, he is frequently driven to wrong his master, and rob his shop or his till for money, if he can come at it: and this, as it begins in madness, generally ends in destruction; for often he is discovered, exposed, and perhaps punished, and so the man is undone before he begins. If his circumstances are good, and he has friends that are able, and expectations that are considerable, then his expense is still the greater, and ways and means are found out, or at least looked for, to supply the expense, and conceal the fact, that his friends may not know it, till he has gotten the blessing he expects into his hands, and is put in a way to stand upon his own legs; and then it comes out, with a great many grieving aggravations to a parent to find himself tricked and defeated in the expectations of his son's marrying handsomely, and to his advantage; instead of which, he is obliged to receive a dish-clout for a daughter-in-law, and see his family propagated by a race of beggars, and yet perhaps as haughty, as insolent, and as expensive, as if she had blessed the family with a lady of fortune, and brought a fund with her to have supported the charge of her posterity.

When this happens, the poor young man's case is really deplorable. Before he is out of his time, he is obliged to borrow of friends, if he has any, on pretence his father does not make him a sufficient allowance, or he trenches upon his master's cash, which perhaps, he being the eldest apprentice, is in his hands; and this he does, depending, that when he is out of his time, and his father gives him wherewith to set up, he will make good the deficiency; and all this happens accordingly so that his reputation as to his master is preserved, and he comes off clear as to dishonesty in his trust.

But what a sad chasm does it make in his fortune! I knew a certain young tradesman, whose father, knowing nothing of his son's measures, gave him £2000 to set up with, straining himself to the utmost for the well introducing his son into the world; but who, when he came to set up, having near a year before married the servant-maid of the house where he lodged, and kept her privately at a great expense, had above £600 of his stock already wasted and sunk, before he began for himself; the consequence of which was, that going in partner with another young man, who had likewise £2000 to begin with, he was, instead of half of the profits, obliged to make a private article to accept of a third of the trade; and the beggar-wife proving more expensive, by far, than the partner's wife (who married afterwards, and doubled his fortune), the first young man was obliged to quit the trade, and with his remaining stock set up by himself; in which case his expenses continuing, and his stock being insufficient, he sank gradually, and then broke, and died poor. In a word, he broke the heart of his father, wasted what he had, and could never recover it, and at last it broke his own heart too.

But I shall bring it a little farther. Suppose the youth not to act so grossly neither; not to marry in his apprenticeship, not to be forced to keep a wife privately, and eat the bread he never got; but suppose him to be entered upon the world, that he has set up, opened shop, or fitted up his warehouse, and is ready to trade, the next thing, in the ordinary course of the world, at this time is *a wife*; nay, I have met with some parents, who have been indiscreet enough themselves to prompt their sons to marry as soon as they are set up; and the reason they give for it is, the wickedness of the age, that youth are drawn in a hundred ways to ruinous matches or debaucheries, and are so easily ruined by the mere looseness of their circumstances, that it is needful to marry them to keep them at home, and to preserve them diligent, and bind them close to their business.

This, be it just or not, is a bad cure of an ill disease; it is ruining the young man to make him sober, and making him a slave for life to make him diligent. Be it that the wife he shall marry is a sober, frugal, housewifely woman, and that nothing is to be laid to her charge but the mere necessary addition of a family expense, and that with the utmost moderation, yet, at the best, he cripples his fortune, stock-starves his business, and brings a great expense upon himself at first, before, by his success in trade, he had laid up stock enough to support the charge.

First, it is reasonable to suppose, that at his beginning in the world he cannot expect to get so good a portion with a wife, as he might after he had been set up a few years, and by his diligence and frugality, joined to a small expense in house-keeping, had increased both his stock in trade and the trade itself; then he would be able to look forward boldly, and would have some pretence for insisting on a fortune, when he could make out his improvements in trade, and show that he was both able to maintain a wife, and able to live without her. When a young tradesman in Holland or Germany goes a-courting, I am told the first question the young woman asks of him, or perhaps her friends for her, is, 'Are you able to pay the charges?' that is to say, in English, 'Are you able to keep a wife when you have got her?' The question is a little Gothic indeed, and would be but a kind of gross way of receiving a lover here, according to our English good breeding; but there is a great deal of reason in the inquiry, that must be confessed; and he that is not able to *pay the charges*, should never begin the journey; for, be the wife what she will, the very state of life that naturally attends the marrying a woman, brings with it an expense so very considerable, that a tradesman ought to consider very well of it before he engages.

But it is to be observed, too, that abundance of young tradesmen, especially in England, not only marry early, but by the so marrying they are obliged to take up with much less fortunes in their haste, than when they allow themselves longer time of consideration. As it stands now, generally speaking, the wife and the shop make their first show together; but how few of these early marriages succeed – how hard such a tradesman finds it to stand, and support the weight that attends it – I appeal to the experience of those, who having taken this wrong step, and being with difficulty got over it, are yet good judges of that particular circumstance in others that come after them.[1]

I know it is a common cry that is raised against the woman, when her husband fails in business, namely, that it is the wife has ruined him; it is true, in some particular cases it may be so, but in general it is wrong placed – they may say marrying has ruined the man, when they cannot say his wife has done it, for the woman was not in fault, but her husband.

When a tradesman marries, there are necessary consequences, I mean of expenses, which the wife ought not be charged with, and cannot be made accountable for – such as, first, furnishing the house;

1 [Defoe's views on the subject of the too early marrying of young tradesmen, are in every particular sound. Though there are instances of premature marriages followed by no evil result, but rather the contrary, there can be no doubt, that the only prudent course is to wait till a settlement in life, and a regular income, have been secured. A young man, anxious for other reasons to marry, is sometimes heard to express his conviction that he might live more cheaply married than single. There could be no assertion more inconsistent with all common experience. Even if no positively ruinous consequences arise from an over-early marriage, it almost always occasions much hardship. It saddens a period of life which nature has designed to be peculiarly cheerful. The whole life of such a man becomes like a year in which there has been no May or June. The grave cares of matrimony do not appear to be naturally suitable to the human character, till the man has approached his thirtieth, and the woman her twenty-fourth year.]

and let this be done with the utmost plainness, so as to be decent; yet it must be done, and this calls for ready money, and that ready money by so much diminishes his stock in trade; nor is the wife at all to be charged in this case, unless she either put him to more charge than was needful, or showed herself dissatisfied with things needful, and required extravagant gaiety and expense. Secondly, servants, if the man was frugal before, it may be he shifted with a shop, and a servant in it, an apprentice, or journeyman, or perhaps without one at first, and a lodging for himself, where he kept no other servant, and so his expenses went on small and easy; or if he was obliged to take a house because of his business and the situation of his shop, he then either let part of the house out to lodgers, keeping himself a chamber in it, or at the worst left it unfurnished, and without any one but a maid-servant to dress his victuals, and keep the house clean; and thus he goes on when a bachelor, with a middling expense at most.

But when he brings home a wife, besides the furnishing his house, he must have a formal house-keeping, even at the very first; and as children come on, more servants, that is, maids, or nurses, that are as necessary as the bread he eats – especially if he multiplies apace, as he ought to suppose he may – in this case let the wife be frugal and managing, let her be unexceptionable in her expense, yet the man finds his charge mount high, and perhaps too high for his gettings, notwithstanding the additional stock obtained by her portion. And what is the end of this but inevitable decay, and at last poverty and ruin?

Nay, the more the woman is blameless, the more certain is his overthrow, for if it was an expense that was extravagant and unnecessary, and that his wife ran him out by her high living and gaiety, he might find ways to retrench, to take up in time, and prevent the mischief that is in view. A woman may, with kindness and just reasoning, be easily convinced, that her husband cannot maintain such an expense as she now lives at; and let tradesmen say what they will, and endeavour to excuse themselves as much as they will, by loading their wives with the blame of their miscarriage, as I have known some do, and as old father Adam, though in another case, did before them, I must say so much in the woman's behalf at a venture. It will be very hard to make me believe that any woman, that was not fit for Bedlam, if her husband truly and timely represented his case to her, and how far he was or was not able to maintain the expense of their way of living, would not comply with her husband's circumstances, and retrench her expenses, rather than go on for a while, and come to poverty and misery. Let, then, the tradesman lay it early and seriously before his wife, and with kindness and plainness tell her his circumstances, or never let him pretend to charge her with being the cause of his ruin. Let him tell her how great his annual expense is; for a woman who receives what she wants as she wants it, that only takes it with one hand, and lays it out with another, does not, and perhaps cannot, always keep an account, or cast up how much it comes to by the year. Let her husband, therefore, I say, tell her honestly how much his expense for her and himself amounts to yearly; and tell her as honestly, that it is too much for him, that his income in trade will not answer it; that he goes backward, and the last year his family expenses amounted to so much, say £400 – for that is but an ordinary sum now for a tradesman to spend, whatever it has been esteemed formerly – and that his whole trade, though he made no bad debts, and had no losses, brought him in but £320 the whole year, so that he was £80 that year a worse man than he was before, that this coming year he had met with a heavy loss already, having had a shopkeeper in the country broke in his debt £200, and that he offered but eight shillings in the pound, so that he should lose £120 by him, and that this, added to the £80 run out last year, came to £200, and that if they went on thus, they should be soon reduced.

What could the woman say to so reasonable a discourse, if she was a woman of any sense, but to reply, she would do any thing that lay in her to assist him, and if her way of living was too great for him to support, she would lessen it as he should direct, or as much as he thought was reasonable? – and thus, going hand in hand, she and he together abating what reason required, they might bring their expenses within the compass of their gettings, and be able to go on again comfortably.

But now, when the man, finding his expenses greater than his income, and yet, when he looks into those expenses, finds that his wife is frugal too, and industrious, and applies diligently to the managing her family, and bringing up her children, spends nothing idly, saves every thing that can be saved; that instead of keeping too many servants, is a servant to every body herself; and that, in short, when he makes the strictest examination, finds she lays out nothing but what is absolutely necessary, what now must this man do? He is ruined inevitably – for all his expense is necessary; there is no retrenching, no abating any thing.

This, I say, is the worst case of the two indeed; and this man, though he may say he is undone by marrying, yet cannot blame the woman, and say he is undone by his wife. This is the very case I am speaking of; the man should not have married so soon; he should have staid till he had, by pushing on his trade, and living close in his expense, increased his stock, and been what we call beforehand in the world; and had he done thus, he had not been undone by marrying.

It is a little hard to say it, but in this respect it is very true, there is many a young tradesman ruined by marrying a good wife – in which, pray take notice that I observe my own just distinction: I do not say they are ruined or undone by a good wife, or by their wives being good, but by their marrying – their unseasonable, early, and hasty marrying – before they had cast up the cost of one, or the income of the other – before they had inquired into the necessary charge of a wife and a family, or seen the profits of their business, whether it would maintain them or no; and whether, as above, they could pay the charges, the increasing necessary charge, of a large and growing family. How to persuade young men to consider this in time, and beware and avoid the mischief of it, that is a question by itself.

Let no man, then, when he is brought to distress by this early rashness, turn short upon his wife, and reproach her with being the cause of his ruin, unless, at the same time, he can charge her with extravagant living, needless expense, squandering away his money, spending it in trifles and toys, and running him out till the shop could not maintain the kitchen, much less the parlour; nor even then, unless he had given her timely notice of it, and warned her that he was not able to maintain so large a family, or so great an expense, and that, therefore, she would do well to consider of it, and manage with a straiter hand, and the like. If, indeed, he had done so, and she had not complied with him, then she had been guilty, and without excuse too; but as the woman cannot judge of his affairs, and he sees and bears a share in the riotous way of their living, and does not either show his dislike of it, or let her know, by some means or other, that he cannot support it, the woman cannot be charged with being his ruin – no, though her way of extravagant expensive living were really the cause of it. I met with a short dialogue, the other day, between a tradesman and his wife, upon such a subject as this, some part of which may be instructing in the case before us.

The tradesman was very melancholy for two or three days, and had appeared all that time to be pensive and sad, and his wife, with all her arts, entreaties, anger, and tears, could not get it out of him; only now and then she heard him fetch a deep sigh, and at another time say, he wished he was dead, and the like expressions. At last, she began the discourse with him in a respectful, obliging manner, but with the utmost importunity to get it out of him, thus:–

Wife. – My dear, what is the matter with you?

Husb. – Nothing.

Wife. – Nay, don't put me off with an answer that signifies nothing; tell me what is the matter, for I am sure something extraordinary is the case – tell me, I say, do tell me. [*Then she kisses him.*

Husb. – Prithee, don't trouble me.

Wife. – I will know what is the matter

Husb. – I tell you nothing is the matter – what should be the matter?

Wife. – Come, my dear, I must not be put off so; I am sure, if it be any thing ill, I must have my share of it; and why should I not be worthy to know it, whatever it is, before it comes upon me.

Husb. – Poor woman! [*He kisses her.*

Wife. – Well, but let me know what it is; come, don't distract yourself alone; let me bear a share of your grief, as well as I have shared in your joy.

Husb. – My dear, let me alone, you trouble me now, indeed. [*Still he keeps her off.*

Wife. – Then you will not trust your wife with knowing what touches you so sensibly?

Husb. – I tell you, it is nothing, it is a trifle, it is not worth talking of.

Wife. – Don't put me off with such stuff as that; I tell you, it is not for nothing that you have been so concerned, and that so long too; I have seen it plain enough; why, you have drooped upon it for this fortnight past, and above.

Husb. – Ay, this twelvemonth, and more.

Wife. – Very well, and yet it is nothing.

Husb. – It is nothing that you can help me in.

Wife. – Well, but how do you know that? Let me see, and judge whether I can, or no.

Husb. – I tell you, you cannot.

Wife. – Sure it is some terrible thing then. Why must not I know it? What! are you going to break? Come, tell me the worst of it.

Husb. – Break! no, no, I hope not – Break! no, I'll never break.

Wife. – As good as you have broke; don't presume; no man in trade can say he won't break.

Husb. – Yes, yes; I can say I won't break.

Wife. – I am glad to hear it; I hope you have a knack, then, beyond other tradesmen.

Husb. – No, I have not neither; any man may say so as well as I; and no man need break, if he will act the part of an honest man.

Wife. – How is that, pray?

Husb. – Why, give up all faithfully to his creditors, as soon as he finds there is a deficiency in his stock, and yet that there is enough left to pay them.

Wife. – Well, I don't understand those things, but I desire you would tell me what it is troubles you now; and if it be any thing of that kind, yet I think you should let me know it.

Husb. – Why should I trouble you with it?

Wife. – It would be very unkind to let me know nothing till it comes and swallows you up and me too, all on a sudden; I must know it, then; pray tell it me now.

Husb. – Why, then, I will tell you; indeed, I am not going to break, and I hope I am in no danger of it, at least not yet.

Wife. – I thank you, my dear, for that; but still, though it is some satisfaction to me to be assured of so much, yet I find there is something in it; and your way of speaking is ambiguous and doubtful. I entreat you, be plain and free with me. What is at the bottom of it? – why won't you tell me? – what have I done, that I am not to be trusted with a thing that so nearly concerns me?

Husb. – I have told you, my dear; pray be easy; I am not going to break, I tell you.

Wife. – Well, but let us talk a little more seriously of it; you are not going to break, that is, not just now, not yet, you said; but, my dear, if it is then not just at hand, but may happen, or is in view at some distance, may not some steps be taken to prevent it for the present, and to save us from it at last too.

Husb. – What steps could you think of, if that were the case?

Wife. – Indeed it is not much that is in a wife's power, but I am ready to do what lies in me, and what becomes me; and first, pray let us live lower. Do you think I would live as I do, if I thought your income would not bear it? No, indeed.

Husb. – You have touched me in the most sensible part, my dear; you have found out what has been my grief; you need make no further inquiries.

Wife. – Was that your grief? – and would you never be so kind to your wife as to let her know it?

Husb. – How could I mention so unkind a thing to you?

Wife. – Would it not have been more unkind to have let things run on to destruction, and left your wife to the reproach of the world, as having ruined you by her expensive living?

Husb. – That's true, my dear; and it may be I might have spoke to you at last, but I could not do it now; it looks so cruel and so hard to lower your figure, and make you look little in the eyes of the world, for you know they judge all by outsides, that I could not bear it.

Wife. – It would be a great deal more cruel to let me run on, and be really an instrument to ruin my husband, when, God knows, I thought I was within the compass of your gettings, and that a great way; and you know you always prompted me to go fine, to treat handsomely, to keep more servants, and every thing of that kind. Could I doubt but that you could afford it very well?

Husb. – That's true, but I see it is otherwise now; and though I cannot help it, I could not mention it to you, nor, for ought I know, should I ever have done it.

Wife. – Why! you said just now you should have done it.

Husb. – Ay, at last, perhaps, I might, when things had been past recovery.

Wife. – That is to say, when you were ruined and undone, and could not show your head, I should know it; or when a statute of bankrupt had come out, and the creditors had come and turned us out of doors, then I should have known it – that would have been a barbarous sort of kindness.

Husb. – What could I do? I could not help it.

Wife. – Just so our old acquaintance G — W — did; his poor wife knew not one word of it, nor so much as suspected it, but thought him in as flourishing circumstances as ever; till on a sudden he was arrested in an action for a great sum, so great that he could not find bail, and the next day an execution on another action was served in the house, and swept away the very bed from under her; and the poor lady, that brought him £3000 portion, was turned into the street with five small children to take care of.

Husb. – Her case was very sad, indeed.

Wife. – But was not he a barbarous wretch to her, to let her know nothing of her circumstances? She was at the ball but the day before, in her velvet suit, and with her jewels on, and they reproach her with it every day.

Husb. – She did go too fine, indeed.

Wife. – Do you think she would have done so, if she had known any thing of his circumstances?

Husb. – It may be not.

Wife. – No, no; she is a lady of too much sense, to allow us to suggest it.

Husb. – And why did he not let her have some notice of it?

Wife. – Why, he makes the same dull excuse you speak of; he could not bear to speak to her of it, and it looked so unkind to do any thing to straiten her, he could not do it, it would break his heart, and the like; and now he has broke her heart.

Husb. – I know it is hard to break in upon one's wife in such a manner, where there is any true kindness and affection; but —

Wife. – But! but what? Were there really a true kindness and affection, as is the pretence, it would be quite otherwise; he would not break his own heart, forsooth, but chose rather to break his wife's heart! he could not be so cruel to tell her of it, and therefore left her to be cruelly and villanously insulted, as she was, by the bailiffs and creditors. Was that his kindness to her?

Husb. – Well, my dear, I have not brought you to that, I hope.

Wife. – No, my dear, and I hope you will not; however, you shall not say I will not do every thing I can to prevent it; and, if it lies on my side, you are safe.

Husb. – What will you do to prevent it? Come, let's see, what can you do?

Wife. – Why, first, I keep five maids, you see, and a footman; I shall immediately give three of my maids warning, and the fellow also, and save you that part of the expense.

Husb. – How can you do that? – you can't do your business.

Wife. – Yes, yes, there's nobody knows what they can do till they are tried; two maids may do all my house-business, and I'll look after my children myself; and if I live to see them grown a little bigger, I'll make them help one another, and keep but one maid; I hope that will be one step towards helping it.

Husb. – And what will all your friends and acquaintance, and the world, say to it?

Wife. – Not half so much as they would to see you break, and the world believe it be by my high living, keeping a house full of servants, and do nothing myself.

Husb. – They will say I am going to break upon your doing thus, and that's the way to make it so.

Wife. – I had rather a hundred should say you were going to break, than one could say you were really broke already.

Husb. – But it is dangerous to have it talked of, I say.

Wife. – No, no; they will say we are taking effectual ways to prevent breaking.

Husb. – But it will put a slur upon yourself too. I cannot bear any mortifications upon you, any more than I can upon myself.

Wife. – Don't tell me of mortifications; it would be a worse mortification, a thousand times over, to have you ruined, and have your creditors insult me with being the occasion of it.

Husb. – It is very kind in you, my dear, and I must always acknowledge it; but, however, I would not have you straiten yourself too much neither.

Wife. – Nay, this will not be so much a mortification as the natural consequence of other things; for, in order to abate the expense of our living, I resolve to keep less company. I assure you I will lay down all the state of living, as well as the expense of it; and, first, I will keep no visiting days; secondly, I'll drop the greatest part of the acquaintance I have; thirdly, I will lay down our treats and entertainments, and the like needless occasions of expense, and then I shall have no occasion for so many maids.

Husb. – But this, my dear, I say, will make as much noise almost, as if I were actually broke.

Wife. – No, no; leave that part to me.

Husb. – But you may tell me how you will manage it then.

Wife. – Why, I'll go into the country.

Husb. – That will but bring them after you, as it used to do.

Wife. – But I'll put off our usual lodgings at Hampstead, and give out that I am gone to spend the summer in Bedfordshire, at my aunt's, where every body knows I used to go sometimes; they can't come after me thither.

Husb. – But when you return, they will all visit you.

Wife. – Yes, and I will make no return to all those I have a mind to drop, and there's an end of all their acquaintance at once.

Husb. – And what must I do?

Wife. – Nay, my dear, it is not for me to direct that part; you know how to cure the evil which you sensibly feel the mischief of. If I do my part, I don't doubt you know how to do yours.

Husb. – Yes, I know, but it is hard, very hard.

Wife. – Nay, I hope it is no harder for you than it is for your wife.

Husb. – That is true, indeed, but I'll see.

Wife. – The question to me is not whether it is hard, but whether it is necessary.

Husb. – Nay, it is necessary, that is certain.

Wife. – Then I hope it is as necessary to you as to your wife.

Husb. – I know not where to begin.

Wife. – Why, you keep two horses and a groom, you keep rich high company, and you sit long at the Fleece every evening. I need say no more; you know where to begin well enough.

Husb. – It is very hard; I have not your spirit, my dear.

Wife. – I hope you are not more ashamed to retrench, than you would be to have your name in the Gazette.

Husb. – It is sad work to come down hill thus.

Wife. – It would be worse to fall down at one blow from the top; better slide gently and voluntarily down the smooth part, than to be pushed down the precipice, and be dashed all in pieces.

There was more of this dialogue, but I give the part which I think most to the present purpose; and as I strive to shorten the doctrine, so I will abridge the application also; the substance of the case lies in a few particulars, thus:–

I. The man was melancholy, and oppressed with the thoughts of his declining circumstances, and yet had not any thought of letting his wife know it, whose way of living was high and expensive, and more than he could support; but though it must have ended in ruin, he would rather let it have gone on till she was surprised in it, than to tell her the danger that was before her.

His wife very well argues the injustice and unkindness of such usage, and how hard it was to a wife, who, being of necessity to suffer in the fall, ought certainly to have the most early notice of it – that, if possible, she might prevent it, or, at least, that she might not be overwhelmed with the suddenness and the terror of it.

II. Upon discovering it to his wife, or rather her drawing the discovery from him by her importunity, she immediately, and most readily and cheerfully, enters into measures to retrench her expenses, and, as far as she was able, to prevent the blow, which was otherwise apparent and unavoidable.

Hence it is apparent, that the expensive living of most tradesmen in their families, is for want of a serious acquainting their wives with their circumstances, and acquainting them also in time; for there are very few ladies so unreasonable, who, if their husbands seriously informed them how things stood with them, and that they could not support their way of living, would not willingly come into measures to prevent their own destruction.

III. That it is in vain, as well as unequal, for a tradesman to preach frugality to his wife, and to bring his wife to a retrenching of her expenses, and not at the same time to retrench his own; seeing that keeping horses and high company is every way as great and expensive, and as necessary to be abated, as any of the family extravagances, let them be which they will.

All this relates to the duty of a tradesman in preventing his family expenses being ruinous to his business; but the true method to prevent all this, and never to let it come so far, is still, as I said before, not to marry too soon; not to marry, till by a frugal industrious management of his trade in the beginning, he has laid a foundation for maintaining a wife, and bringing up a family, and has made an essay by which he knows what he can and cannot do, and also before he has laid up and increased his stock, that he may not cripple his fortune at first, and be ruined before he has begun to thrive.

CHAPTER XII

OF THE TRADESMAN'S LEAVING HIS BUSINESS TO SERVANTS

It is the ordinary excuse of the gentlemen tradesmen of our times, that they have good servants, and that therefore they take more liberty to be out of their business, than they would otherwise do. 'Oh!' says the shopkeeper, 'I have an apprentice – it is an estate to have such a servant. I am as safe in him as if I had my eye upon the business from morning till night; let me be where I will, I am always satisfied he is at home; if I am at the tavern, I am sure he is in the counting-house, or behind the counter; he is never out of his post.

'And then for my other servants, the younger apprentices,' says he, 'it is all one as if I were there myself – they would be idle it may be, but he won't let them, I assure you; they must stick close to it, or he will make them do it; he tells them, boys do not come apprentices to play, but to work; not to sit idle, and be doing nothing, but to mind their master's business, that they may learn how to do their own.'

'Very well; and you think, Sir, this young man being so much in the shop, and so diligent and faithful, is an estate to you, and so indeed it is; but are your customers as well pleased with this man, too, as you are? or are they as well pleased with him, as they would be, if you were there yourself?'

'Yes, they are,' says the shopkeeper; 'nay, abundance of the customers take him for the master of the shop, and don't know any other; and he is so very obliging, and pleases so well, giving content to every body, that, if I am at any other part of the shop, and see him serving a customer, I never interrupt them, unless sometimes (he is so modest) he will call me, and turning to the ladies say, "There's my master, Madam; if you think he will abate you any thing, I'll call him;" and sometimes they will look a little surprised, and say, "Is that your master? indeed, we thought you had been the master of the shop yourself."'

'Well,' said I, 'and you think yourself very happy in all this, don't you? Pray, how long has this young gentleman to serve? how long is it before his time will be out?' 'Oh, he has almost a year and a half to serve,' says the shopkeeper. 'I hope, then,' said I, 'you will take care to have him knocked on the head, as soon as his time is out.' 'God forbid,' says the honest man; 'what do you mean by that?' 'Mean!' said I, 'why, if you don't, he will certainly knock your trade on the head, as soon as the year and a half comes to be up. Either you must dispose of him, as I say, or take care that he does not set up near you, no, not in the same street; if you do, your customers will all run thither. When they miss him in the shop, they will presently inquire for him; and as, you say, they generally take him for the master, they will ask whether the gentleman is removed that kept the shop before.'

All my shopkeeper could say, was, that he had got a salve for that sore, and that was, that when Timothy was out of his time, he resolved to take him in partner.

'A very good thing, indeed! so you must take Timothy into half the trade when he is out of his time, for fear he should run away with three-quarters of it, when he sets up for himself. But had not the master much better have been Timothy himself? – then he had been sure never to have the customers take Timothy for the master; and when he went away, and set up perhaps at next door, leave the shop, and run after him.'

It is certain, a good servant, a faithful, industrious, obliging servant, is a blessing to a tradesman, and, as he said, is an estate to his master; but the master, by laying the stress of his business upon him, divests himself of all the advantages of such a servant, and turns the blessing into a blast; for by giving up the shop as it were to him, and indulging himself in being abroad, and absent from his business, the apprentice gets the mastery of the business, the fame of the shop depends upon him, and when he sets up, certainly follows him. Such a servant would, with the master's attendance too, be very helpful, and yet not be dangerous; such a servant is well, when he is visibly an assistant to the master, but is ruinous when he is taken for the master. There is a great deal of difference between a servant's being the stay of his master, and his being the stay of his trade: when he is the first, the master is served by him; and when he is gone, he breeds up another to follow his steps; but when he is the last, he carries the trade with him, and does his master infinitely more hurt than good.

A good tradesman has a great deal of trouble with a bad servant, but must take heed that he is not wounded by a good one – the extravagant idle vagrant servant hurts himself, but the diligent servant endangers his master. The greater reputation the servant gets in his business, the more care the master has upon him, lest he gets within him, and worms him out of his business.

The only way to prevent this, and yet not injure a diligent servant, is that the master be as diligent as the servant; that the master be as much at the shop as the man. He that will keep in his business, need never fear keeping his business, let his servant be as diligent as he will.

It is a hard thing that a tradesman should have the blessing of a good servant, and make it a curse to him, by his appearing less capable than his man.

Let your apprentice be in the business, but let the master be at the head of the business at all times. There is a great deal of difference between being diligent in the business *in* the shop, and leading the whole business *of* the shop. An apprentice who is diligent may be master of his business, but should never be master of the shop; the one is to be useful to his master, the other is to be master of his master; and, indeed, this shows the absolute necessity of diligence and application in a tradesman, and how, for want of it, that very thing which is the blessing of another tradesman's business is the ruin of his.

Servants, especially apprentices, ought to be considered, as they really are, in their moveable station, that they are here with you but seven years, and that then they act or move in a sphere or station of their own: their diligence is now for you, but ever after it is for themselves; that the better servants they have been while they were with you, the more dangerous they will be to you when you part; that, therefore, though you are bound in justice to them to let them into your business in every branch of it, yet you are not bound to give your business away to them; the diligence, therefore, of a good servant in the master's business, should be a spur to the master's diligence to take care of himself.

There is a great deal of difference also between trusting a servant in your business, and trusting him with your business: the first is leaving your business with him, the other is leaving your business to him. He that trusts a servant in his business, leaves his shop only to him; but he that leaves his business to his servant, leaves his wife and children at his disposal – in a word, such a trusting, or leaving the business to the servant, is no less than a giving up all to him, abandoning the care of his shop and all his affairs to him; and when such a servant is out of his time, the master runs a terrible risk, such as, indeed, it is not fit any tradesman should run – namely, of losing the best of his business.

What I have been now saying, is of the tradesman leaving his business to his apprentices and servants, when they prove good, when they are honest and diligent, faithful, and industrious; and if there are dangers even in trusting good servants, and such as do their duty perfectly well, what, then, must it be when the business is left to idle, negligent, and extravagant servants, who both neglect their masters' business and their own, who neither learn their trade for themselves, nor regard it for the interest of their masters? If the first are a blessing to their masters, and may only be made dangerous by their carrying away the trade with them when they go, these are made curses to their masters early, for they lose the trade for themselves and their masters too. The first carry the customers away with them, the last drive the customers away before they go. 'What signifies going to such a shop?' say the ladies, either speaking of a mercer or a draper, or any other trade; 'there is nothing to be met with there but a crew of saucy boys, that are always at play when you come in, and can hardly refrain it when you are there: one hardly ever sees a master in the shop, and the young rude boys hardly mind you when you are looking on their goods; they talk to you as if they cared not whether you laid out your money or no, and as if they had rather you were gone, that they might go to play again. I will go there no more, not I.'

If this be not the case, then you are in danger of worse still, and that is, that they are often thieves – idle ones are seldom honest ones – nay, they cannot indeed be honest, in a strict sense, if they are idle: but by dishonest, I mean downright thieves; and what is more dangerous than for an apprentice, to whom the whole business, the cash, the books, and all is committed, to be a thief?

For a tradesman, therefore, to commit his business thus into the hand of a false, a negligent, and a thievish servant, is like a man that travels a journey, and takes a highwayman into the coach with him: such a man is sure to be robbed, and to be fully and effectually plundered, because he discovers where he hides his treasure. Thus the tradesman places his confidence in the thief, and how should he avoid being robbed?

It is answered, that, generally tradesmen, who have any considerable trust to put into the hands of an apprentice, take security of them for their honesty by their friends, when their indentures are signed; and it is their fault then, if they are not secure. True, it is often so; but in a retail business, if the servant be unfaithful, there are so many ways to defraud a master, besides that of merely not balancing the cash, that it is impossible to detect them; till the tradesman, declining insensibly by the weight of the loss, is ruined and undone.

What need, then, has the tradesman to give a close attendance, and preserve himself from plunder, by acquainting himself in and with his business and servants, by which he makes it very difficult for them to deceive him, and much easier to him to discover it if he suspects them. But if the tradesman lives abroad, keeps at his country-house or lodgings, and leaves his business thus in the hands of his servants, committing his affairs to them, as is often the case; if they prove thieves, negligent, careless, and idle, what is the consequence? – he is insensibly wronged, his substance wasted, his business neglected; and how shall a tradesman thrive under such circumstances? Nay, how is it possible he should avoid ruin and destruction? – I mean, as to his business; for, in short, every such servant has his hand in his master's pocket, and may use him as he pleases.

Again, if they are not thieves, yet if they are idle and negligent, it is, in some cases, the same thing; and I wish it were well recommended to all such servants as call themselves honest, that it is as criminal to neglect their master's business as to rob him; and he is as really a thief who robs him of his time, as he that robs him of his money.

I know, as servants are now, this is a principle they will not allow, neither does one servant in fifty act by it; but if the master be absent, the servant is at his heels – that is to say, is as soon out of doors as his master, and having none but his conscience to answer to, he makes shift to compound with himself, like a bankrupt with his creditor, to pay half the debt – that is to say, half the time to his master, and half to himself, and think it good pay too.

The point of conscience, indeed, seems to be out of the question now, between master and servant; and as few masters concern themselves with the souls, nay, scarce with the morals of their servants, either to instruct them, or inform them of their duty either to God or man, much less to restrain them by force, or correct them, as was anciently practised, so, few servants concern themselves in a conscientious discharge of their duty to their masters – so that the great law of subordination is destroyed, and the relative duties on both sides are neglected; all which, as I take it, is owing to the exorbitant sums of money which are now given with servants to the masters, as the present or condition of their apprenticeship, which, as it is extravagant in itself, so it gives the servant a kind of a different figure in the family, places him above the ordinary class of servants hired for wages, and exempts him from all the laws of family government, so that a master seems now to have nothing to do with his apprentice, any other than in what relates to his business.

And as the servant knows this, so he fails not to take the advantage of it, and to pay no more service than he thinks is due; and the hours of his shop business being run out, he claims all the rest for himself, without the above restraint. Nor will the servants, in these times, bear any examinations with respect to the disposing of their waste time, or with respect to the company they keep, or the houses or places they go to.

The use I make of it is this, and herein it is justly applicable to the case in hand; by how much the apprentices and servants in this age are loose, wild, and ungovernable, by so much the more should a master think himself obliged not to depend upon them, much less to leave his business to them, and dispense with his own attendance in it. If he does, he must have much better luck then his neighbours, if he does not find himself very much wronged and abused, seeing, as I said above, the servants and apprentices of this age do very rarely act from a principle of conscience in serving their master's interest, which, however, I do not see they can be good Christians without.

I knew one very considerable tradesman in this city, and who had always five or six servants in his business, apprentices and journeymen, who lodged in his house; and having a little more the spirit of government in him than most masters I now meet with, he took this method with them. When he took apprentices, he told them beforehand the orders of his family, and which he should oblige them to; particularly, that they should none be absent from his business without leave, nor out of the house after nine o'clock at night; and that he would not have it thought hard, if he exacted three things of them:–

1. That, if they had been out, he should ask them where they had been, and in what company? and that they should give him a true and direct answer.

2. That, if he found reason to forbid them keeping company with any particular person, or in any particular house or family, they should be obliged to refrain from such company.

3. That, in breach of any of those two, after being positively charged with it, he would, on their promising to amend it, forgive them, only acquainting their friends of it; but the second time, he would dismiss them his service, and not be obliged to return any of the money he had with them. And to these he made their parents consent when they were bound; and yet he had large sums of money with them too, not less than £200 each, and sometimes more.

As to his journeymen, he conditioned with them as follows:–

1. They should never dine from home without leave asked and obtained, and telling where, if required.

2. After the shutting in of the shop, they were at liberty to go where they pleased, only not to be out of the house after nine o'clock at night.

3. Never to be in drink, or to swear, on pain of being immediately dismissed without the courtesy usual with such servants, namely, of a month's warning.

These were excellent household laws; but the question is, how shall a master see them punctually obeyed, for the life of all laws depends upon their being well executed; and we are famous in England for being remiss in that very point; and that we have the best laws the worst executed of any nation in the world.

But my friend was a man who knew as well how to make his laws be well executed, as he did how to make the laws themselves. His case was thus: he kept a country-house about two miles from London, in the summer-time, for the air of his wife and children, and there he maintained them very comfortably: but it was a rule with him, that he who expects his servants to obey his orders, must be always upon the spot with them to see it done: to this purpose he confined himself to lie always at home, though his family was in the country; and every afternoon he walked out to see them, and to give himself the air too; but always so ordered his diversions, that he was sure to be at home before nine at night, that he might call over his family, and see that they observed orders, that is, that they were all at home at their time, and all sober.

As this was, indeed, the only way to have good servants, and an orderly family, so he had both; but it was owing much, if not all, to the exactness of his government; and would all masters take the same method, I doubt not they would have the like success; but what servants can a man expect when he leaves them to their own government, not regarding whether they serve God or the devil?

Now, though this man had a very regular family, and very good servants, yet he had this particular qualification, too, for a good tradesman, namely, that he never left his business entirely to them, nor could any of them boast that they were trusted to more than another.

This is certainly the way to have regular servants and to have business thrive; but this is not practised by one master to a thousand at this time – if it were, we should soon see a change in the families of tradesmen, and that very much for the better: nor, indeed, would this family government be good for the tradesman only, but it would be the servant's advantage too; and such a practice, we may say, would in time reform all the next age, and make them ashamed of us that went before them.

If, then, the morals of servants are thus loose and debauched, and that it is a general and epidemic evil, how much less ought tradesmen of this age to trust them, and still less to venture their all upon them, leave their great design, the event of all their business with them, and go into the country in pursuit of their pleasure.

The case of tradesmen differs extremely in this age from those in the last, with respect to their apprentices and servants; and the difference is all to the disadvantage of the present age, namely, in the last age, that is to say, fifty or sixty years ago, for it is not less, servants were infinitely more under subjection than they are now, and the subordination of mankind extended effectually to them; they were content to submit to family government; and the just regulations which masters made in their houses were not scorned and contemned, as they are now; family religion also had some sway upon them; and if their masters did keep good orders, and preserve the worship of God in their houses, the apprentices thought themselves obliged to attend at the usual hours for such services; nay, it has been known, where such orders have been observed, that if the master of the family has been sick, or indisposed, or out of town, the eldest apprentice has read prayers to the family in his place.

How ridiculous, to speak in the language of the present times, would it be for any master to expect this of a servant in our days! and where is the servant that would comply with it? Nay, it is but very rarely now that masters themselves do it; it is rather thought now to be a low step, and beneath the character of a man in business, as if worshipping God were a disgrace, and not an honour, to a family, or to the master of a family; and I doubt not but in a little while more, either the worship of God will be quite banished out of families, or the better sort of tradesmen, and such as have any regard to it, will keep chaplains, as other persons of quality do. It is confessed, the first is most probable, though the last, as I am informed, is already begun in the city, in some houses, where the reader of the parish is allowed a small additional salary to come once a-day, namely, every evening, to read prayers in the house.

But I am not talking on this subject; I am not directing myself to citizens or townsmen, as masters of families, but as heads of trade, and masters in their business; the other part would indeed require a whole book by itself, and would insensibly run me into a long satirical discourse upon the loss of all family government among us; in which, indeed, the practice of house-keepers and heads of families is grown not remiss only in all serious things, but even scandalous in their own morals, and in the personal examples they show to their servants, and all about them.

But to come back to my subject, namely, that the case of tradesmen differs extremely from what it was formerly: the second head of difference is this; that whereas, in former times, the servants were better and humbler than they are now, submitted more to family government, and to the regulations made by their masters, and masters were more moral, set better examples, and kept better order in their houses, and, by consequence of it, all servants were soberer, and fitter to be trusted, than they are now; yet, on the other hand, notwithstanding all their sobriety, masters did not then so much depend upon them, leave business to them, and commit the management of their affairs so entirely to their servants, as they do now.

All that I meet with, which masters have to say to this, is contained in two heads, and these, in my opinion, amount to very little.

I. That they have security for their servants' honesty, which in former times they had not.

II. That they receive greater premiums, or present-money, now with their apprentices, than they did formerly.

The first of these is of no moment; for, first, it does not appear that apprentices in those former days gave no security to their masters for their integrity, which, though perhaps not so generally as now, yet I have good reason to know was then practised among tradesmen of note, and is not now among inferior tradesmen: but, secondly, this security extends to nothing, but to make the master satisfaction for any misapplications or embezzlements which are discovered, and can be proved, but extend to no secret concealed mischiefs: neither, thirdly, do those securities reach to the negligence, idleness, or debaucheries of servants; but, which is still more than all the rest, they do not reach to the worst of robbery between the servant and his master, I mean the loss of his time; so that still there is as much reason for the master's inspection, both into his servants and their business, as ever.

But least of all does this security reach to make the master any satisfaction for the loss of his business, the ill management of his shop, the disreputation brought upon it by being committed to servants, and those servants behaving ill, slighting, neglecting, or disobliging customers; this does not relate to securities given or taken, nor can the master make himself any amends upon his servant, or upon his securities, for this irrecoverable damage. He, therefore, that will keep up the reputation of his shop, or of his business, and preserve his trade to his own advantage, must resolve to attend it himself, and not leave it to servants, whether good or bad; if he leaves it to good servants, they improve it for themselves, and carry the trade away with them when they go; if to bad servants, they drive his customers away, bring a scandal upon his shop, and destroy both their master and themselves.

Secondly, As to the receiving great premiums with their apprentices, which, indeed, is grown up to a strange height in this age, beyond whatever it was before, it is an unaccountable excess, which is the ruin of more servants at this time than all the other excesses they are subject to, nay, in some respect it is the cause of it all; and, on the contrary, is far from being an equivalent to their masters for the defect of their service, but is an unanswerable reason why the master should not leave his business to their management.

This premium was originally not a condition of indenture, but was a kind of usual or customary present to the tradesman's wife to engage her to be kind to the youth, and take a motherly care of him, being supposed to be young when first put out.

By length of time this compliment or present became so customary as to be made a debt, and to be conditioned for as a demand, but still was kept within bounds, and thirty or forty pounds was sufficient to a very good merchant, which now is run up to five hundred, nay, to a thousand pounds with an apprentice; a thing which formerly would have been thought monstrous, and not to be named.

The ill consequences of giving these large premiums are such and so many, that it is not to be entered upon in such a small tract as this; nor is it the design of this work: but it is thus far to the purpose here – namely, as it shows that this sets up servants into a class of gentlemen above their masters, and above their business; and they neither have a sufficient regard to one or other, and consequently are the less fit to be trusted by the master in the essential parts of his business; and this brings it down to the case in hand.

Upon the whole, the present state of things between masters and servants is such, that now more than ever the caution is needful and just, that he that leaves his business to the management of his servants, it is ten to one but he ruins his business and his servants too.

Ruining his business is, indeed, my present subject; but ruining his servants also is a consideration that an honest, conscientious master ought to think is of weight with him, and will concern himself about. Servants out of government are like soldiers without an officer, fit for nothing but to rob and plunder; without order, and without orders, they neither know what to do, or are directed how to do it.

Besides, it is letting loose his apprentices to levity and liberty in that particular critical time of life, when they have the most need of government and restraint. When should laws and limits be useful to mankind but in their youth, when unlimited liberty is most fatal to them, and when they are least capable of governing themselves? To have youth left without government, is leaving fire in a magazine of powder, which will certainly blow it all up at last, and ruin all the houses that are near it.

If there is any duty on the side of a master to his servant, any obligation on him as a Christian, and as a trustee for his parents, it lies here – to limit and restrain them, if possible, in the liberty of doing evil; and this is certainly a debt due to the trust reposed in masters by the parents of the youth committed to them. If he is let loose here, he is undone, of course, and it may be said, indeed, he was ruined by his master; and if the master is afterwards ruined by such a servant, what can be said for it but this? He could expect no other.

To leave a youth without government is indeed unworthy of any honest master; he cannot discharge himself as a master; for instead of taking care of him he indeed casts him off, abandons him, and, to put it into Scripture words, he leads him into temptation: nay, he goes farther, to use another Scripture expression: he delivers him over to Satan.

It is confessed – and it is fatal both to masters and servants at this time – that not only servants are made haughty, and above the government of their masters, and think it below them to submit to any family government, or any restraints of their masters, as to their morals and religion; but masters also seem to have given up all family government, and all care or concern for the morals and manners, as well as for the religion of their servants, thinking themselves under no obligation to meddle with those things, or to think any thing about them, so that their business be but done, and their shop or warehouse duly looked after.

But to bring it all home to the point in hand, if it is so with the master and servant, there is the less room still for the master of such servants to leave any considerable trust in the hands of such apprentices, or to expect much from them, to leave the weight of their affairs with them, and, living at their country lodgings, and taking their own diversions, depend upon such servants for the success of their business. This is indeed abandoning their business, throwing it away, and committing themselves, families, and fortunes, to the conduct of those, who, they have all the reason in the world to believe, have no concern upon them for their good, or care one farthing what becomes of them.

CHAPTER XIII

OF TRADESMEN MAKING COMPOSITION WITH DEBTORS, OR WITH CREDITORS

There is an alternative in the subject of this chapter, which places the discourse in the two extremes of a tradesman's fortunes.

I. The *fortunate tradesman*, called upon by his poor unfortunate neighbour, who is his debtor, and is become insolvent, to have compassion on him, and to compound with him for part of his debt, and accept his offer in discharge of the whole.

II. The *unfortunate tradesman* become insolvent and bankrupt himself, and applying himself to his creditor to accept of a composition, in discharge of his debt.

I must confess, a tradesman, let his circumstances be what they will, has the most reason to consider the disasters of the unfortunate, and be compassionate to them under their pressures and disasters, of any other men; because they know not – no, not the most prosperous of them – what may be their own fate in the world. There is a Scripture proverb, if I may call it so, very necessary to a tradesman in this case, 'Let him that thinketh he standeth, take heed lest he fall.'

N.B. It is not said, let him that standeth take heed, but him *that thinketh* he standeth. Men in trade can but think they stand; and there are so many incidents in a tradesman's circumstances, that sometimes when he thinks himself most secure of standing, he is in most danger of falling.

If, then, the contingent nature of trade renders every man liable to disaster that is engaged in it, it seems strange that tradesmen should be outrageous and unmerciful to one another when they fall; and yet so it is, that no creditor is so furious upon an unhappy insolvent tradesman, as a brother-tradesman of his own class, and who is at least liable to the same disaster, in the common event of his business.

Nay, I have lived to see – such is the uncertainty of human affairs, and especially in trade – the furious and outrageous creditor become bankrupt himself in a few years, or perhaps months after, and begging the same mercy of others, which he but just before denied to his not more unfortunate fellow-tradesman, and making the same exclamations at the cruelty and hard-heartedness of his creditors in refusing to comply with him, when, at the same time, his own heart must reproach him with his former conduct; how inexorable he was to all the entreaties and tears of his miserable neighbour and his distressed family, who begged his compassion with the lowest submission, who employed friends to solicit and entreat for them, laying forth their misery in the most lively expressions, and using all the arguments which the most moving distress could dictate, but in vain.

The tradesman is certainly wrong in this, as compassion to the miserable is a debt of charity due from all mankind to their fellow-creatures; and though the purse-proud tradesman may be able to say he is above the fear of being in the like circumstances, as some may be, yet, even then, he might reflect that perhaps there was a time when he was not so, and he ought to pay that debt of charity, in acknowledgement of the mercy that has set him above the danger.

And yet, speaking in the ordinary language of men who are subject to vicissitudes of fortune, where is the man that is sure he shall meet with no shock? And how have we seen men, who have to-day been immensely rich, be to-morrow, as it were, reduced to nothing! What examples were made in this city of such precipitations within the memory of some living, when the Exchequer shutting up ruined the great bankers of Lombard Street.[1] To what fell Sir Robert Viner – the great Alderman Backwell – the three brothers of the name of Forth, of whom King Charles II. made that severe pun, that '*Three-fourths* of the city were broke?'

To what have we seen men of prodigious bulk in trade reduced – as Sir Thomas Cook, Sir Basil Firebrass, Sheppard, Coggs, and innumerable bankers, money-scriveners, and merchants, who thought themselves as secure against the shocks of trade, as any men in the world could be? Not to instance our late South Sea directors, and others, reduced by the terrible fate of bubbles, whose names I omit because they yet live, though sinking still under the oppression of their fortunes, and whose weight I would be far from endeavouring to make heavier.

Why, then, should any tradesman, presuming on his own security, and of his being out of the reach of disaster, harden his heart against the miseries and distresses of a fellow-tradesman, who sinks, as it were, by his side, and refuse to accept his offer of composition; at least, if he cannot object against the integrity of his representations, and cannot charge him with fraud and deceit, breaking with a wicked design to cheat and delude his creditors, and to get money by a pretended breach? I say, why should any tradesman harden his heart in such a case, and not, with a generous pity, comply with a reasonable and fair proposal, while it is to be had?

1 [This event took place in 1671, Charles II. finding it necessary to suspend the national payments for a year.]

I do acknowledge, if there is an evident fraud, if he can detect the bankrupt in any wicked design, if he can prove he has effects sufficient to pay his debts, and that he only breaks with a purpose to cheat his creditors, and he conceals a part of his estate, when he seems to offer a sincere surrender; if this be the case, and it can be made appear to be so – for in such a case, too, we ought to be very sure of the fact – then, indeed, no favour is due, and really none ought to be shown.

And, therefore, it was a very righteous clause which was inflicted on the fraudulent bankrupt, in a late act of Parliament, namely, that in case he concealed his effects, and that it appeared he had, though upon his oath, not given in a full account of his estate, but willingly and knowingly concealed it, or any part of it, with design to defraud his creditors, he should be put to death as a felon: the reason and justice of which clause was this, and it was given as the reason of it when the act was passed in the House of Commons, namely, that the act was made for the relief of the debtor, as well as of the creditor, and to procure for him a deliverance on a surrender of his effects; but then it was made also for the relief of the creditor, too, that he might have as much of his debt secured to him as possible, and that he should not discharge the debtor with his estate in his pocket, suffering him to run away with his (the creditor's) money before his face.

Also it was objected, that the act, without a penalty, would be only an act to encourage perjury, and would deliver the hard-mouthed knave that could swear what he pleased, and ruin and reject the modest conscientious tradesman, that was willing and ready to give up the utmost farthing to his creditors. On this account the clause was accepted, and the act passed, which otherwise had been thrown out.

Now, when the poor insolvent has thus surrendered his all, stript himself entirely upon oath, and that oath taken on the penalty of death if it be false, there seems to be a kind of justice due to the bankrupt. He has satisfied the law, and ought to have his liberty given him *as a prey*, as the text calls it, Jer. xxxix. 18., that he may try the world once again, and see, if possible, to recover his disasters, and get his bread; and it is to be spoken in honour of the justice as well as humanity of that law for delivering bankrupts, that there are more tradesmen recover themselves in this age upon their second endeavours, and by setting up again after they have thus failed and been delivered, than ever were known to do so in ten times the number of years before.

To break, or turn bankrupt, before this, was like a man being taken by the Turks; he seldom recovered liberty to try his fortune again, but frequently languished under the tyranny of the commissioners of bankrupt, or in the Mint, or Friars, or rules of the Fleet, till he wasted the whole estate, and at length his life, and so his debts were all paid at once.

Nor was the case of the creditor much better – I mean as far as respected his debt, for it was very seldom that any considerable dividend was made; on the other hand, large contributions were called for before people knew whether it was likely any thing would be made of the debtor's effects or no, and oftentimes the creditor lost his whole debt, contribution-money and all; so that while the debtor was kept on the rack, as above, being held in suspense by the creditors, or by the commissioners, or both, he spent the creditor's effects, and subsisted at their expense, till, the estate being wasted, the loss fell heavy on every side, and generally most on those who were least able to bear it.

By the present state of things, this evil is indeed altered, and the ruin of the creditor's effects is better prevented; the bankrupt can no more skulk behind the door of the Mint and Rules, and prevent the commissioners' inspection; he must come forth, be examined, give in an account, and surrender himself and effects too, or fly his country, and be seen here no more; and if he does come in, he must give a full account upon oath, on the penalty of his neck.

When the effects are thus surrendered, the commissioners' proceedings are short and summary. The assignees are obliged to make dividends, and not detain the estate in their own hands, as was the case in former days, till sometimes they became bankrupts themselves, so that the creditors are sure now what is put into the hands of the assignees, shall in due time, and without the usual delay, be fairly divided. On the other hand, the poor debtor having honestly discharged his part, and no objection lying against the sincerity of the discovery, has a certificate granted him, which being allowed by the Lord Chancellor, he is a clear man, and may begin the world again, as I have said above.

The creditor, being thus satisfied that the debtor has been faithful, does not answer the end of the act of Parliament, if he declines to assent to the debtor's certificate; nor can any creditor decline it, but on principles which no man cares to own – namely, that of malice, and the highest resentment, which are things a Christian tradesman will not easily act upon.

But I come now to the other part of the case; and this is supposing a debtor fails, and the creditors do not think fit to take out a commission of bankrupt against him, as sometimes is the case, at least, where they see the offers of the debtor are any thing reasonable: my advice in such case is (and I speak it from long experience in such things), that they should always accept the first reasonable proposal of the debtor; and I am not in this talking on the foot of charity and mercy to the debtor, but of the real and undoubted interest of the creditor; nor could I urge it, by such arguments as I shall bring, upon any other foundation; for, if I speak in behalf of the debtor, I must argue commiseration to the miserable, compassion and pity of his family, and a reflection upon the sad changes which human life exposes us all to, and so persuade the creditor to have pity upon not him only, but upon all families in distress.

But, I say, I argue now upon a different foundation, and insist that it is the creditor's true interest, as I hinted before, that if he finds the debtor inclined to be honest, and he sees reason to believe he makes the best offer he can, he should accept the first offer, as being generally the best the debtor can make;[2] and, indeed, if the debtor be wise as well as honest, he will make it so, and generally it is found to be so. And there are, indeed, many reasons why the first offers of the debtor are generally the best, and why no commission of bankrupt ordinarily raises so much, notwithstanding all its severities, as the bankrupt offers before it is sued out – not reckoning the time and expense which, notwithstanding all the new methods, attend such things, and are inevitable. For example –

When the debtor, first looking into his affairs, sees the necessity coming upon him of making a stop in trade, and calling his creditors together, the first thought which by the consequence of the thing comes to be considered, is, what offers he can make to them to avoid the having a commission sued out against him, and to which end common prudence, as well as honest principles, move him to make the best offers he can. If he be a man of sense, and, according to what I mentioned in another chapter, has prudently come to a stop in time, before things are run to extremities, and while he has something left to make an offer of that may be considerable, he will seldom meet with creditors so weak or so blind to their own interest not to be willing to end it amicably, rather than to proceed to a commission. And as this is certainly best both for the debtor and the creditor, so, as I argued with the debtor, that he should be wise enough, as well as honest enough, to break betimes, and that it was infinitely best for his own interest, so I must add, on the other hand, to the creditor, that it is always his interest to accept the first offer; and I never knew a commission make more of an estate, where the debtor has been honest, than he (the debtor) proposed to give them without it.

It is true, there are cases where the issuing out a commission may be absolutely necessary. For example –

1. Where the debtor is evidently knavish, and discovers himself to be so, by endeavours to carry off his effects, or alter the property of the estate, confessing judgments, or any the usual ways of fraud, which in such cases are ordinarily practised. Or –

2 [The truth of this continues to be matter of daily observation in our own times.]

2. Where some creditors, by such judgments, or by attachments of debts, goods delivered, effects made over, or any other way, have gotten some of the estate into their hands, or securities belonging to it, whereby they are in a better state, as to payment, than the rest. Or–

3. Where some people are brought in as creditors, whose debts there is reason to believe are not real, but who place themselves in the room of creditors, in order to receive a dividend for the use of the bankrupt, or some of his family.

In these, and such like cases, a commission is inevitable, and must be taken out; nor does the man merit to be regarded upon the foot of what I call compassion and commiseration at all, but ought to be treated like a *rapparee*,[3] or plunderer, who breaks with a design to make himself whole by the composition; and as many did formerly, who were beggars when they broke, be made rich by the breach. It was to provide against such harpies as these that the act of Parliament was made; and the only remedy against them is a commission, in which the best thing they can do for their creditors is to come in and be examined, give in a false account upon oath, be discovered, convicted of it, and sent to the gallows, as they deserve.

But I am speaking of honest men, the reverse of such thieves as these, who being brought into distress by the ordinary calamities of trade, are willing to do the utmost to satisfy their creditors. When such as these break in the tradesman's debt, let him consider seriously my advice, and he shall find – I might say, he shall *always* find, but I do affirm, he shall *generally* find – the first offer the best, and that he will never lose by accepting it. To refuse it is but pushing the debtor to extremities, and running out some of the effects to secure the rest.

First, as to collecting in the debts. Supposing the man is honest, and they can trust him, it is evident no man can make so much of them as the bankrupt. (1.) He knows the circumstances of the debtors, and how best to manage them; he knows who he may best push at, and who best forbear. (2.) He can do it with the least charge; the commissioners or assignees must employ other people, such as attorneys, solicitors, &c., and they are paid dear. The bankrupt sits at home, and by letters into the country, or by visiting them, if in town, can make up every account, answer every objection, judge of every scruple, and, in a word, with ease, compared to what others must do, brings them to comply.

Next, as to selling off a stock of goods. The bankrupt keeps open the shop, disperses or disposes of the goods with advantage; whereas the commission brings all to a sale, or an outcry, or an appraisement, and all sinks the value of the stock; so that the bankrupt can certainly

3 [A name applied, in the seventeenth century, to a certain class of robbers in Ireland.]

make more of the stock than any other person (always provided he is honest, as I said before), and much more than the creditors can do.

For these reasons, and many others, the bankrupt is able to make a better offer upon his estate than the creditors can expect to raise any other way; and therefore it is their interest always to take the first offer, if they are satisfied there is no fraud in it, and that the man has offered any thing near the extent of what he has left in the world to offer from.

If, then, it be the tradesman's interest to accept of the offer made, there needs no stronger argument to be used with him for the doing it; and nothing is more surprising to me than to see tradesmen, the hardest to come into such compositions, and to push on severities against other tradesmen, as if they were out of the reach of the shocks of fortune themselves, or that it was impossible for them ever to stand in need of the same mercy – the contrary to which I have often seen.

To what purpose should tradesmen push things to extremities against tradesmen, if nothing is to be gotten by it, and if the insolvent tradesman will take proper measures to convince the creditor that his intentions are honest? The law was made for offenders; there needs no law for innocent men: commissions are granted to manage knaves, and hamper and entangle cunning and designing rogues, who seek to raise fortunes out of their creditors' estates, and exalt themselves by their own downfall; they are not designed against honest men, neither, indeed, is there any need of them for such.

Let no man mistake this part, therefore, and think that I am moving tradesmen to be easy and compassionate to rogues and cheats: I am far from it, and have given sufficient testimony of the contrary; having, I assure you, been the only person who actually formed, drew up, and first proposed that very cause to the House of Commons, which made it felony to the bankrupt to give in a false account. It cannot, therefore, be suggested, without manifest injustice, that I would with one breath prompt creditors to be easy to rogues, and to cheating fraudulent bankrupts, and with another make a proposal to have them hanged.

But I move the creditor, on account of his own interest, always to take the first offer, if he sees no palpable fraud in it, or sees no reason to suspect such fraud; and my reason is good, namely, because I believe, as I said before, it is generally the best.

I know there is a new method of putting an end to a tradesman's troubles, by that which was formerly thought the greatest of all troubles; I mean a fraudulent method, or what they call taking out friendly statutes; that is, when tradesmen get statutes taken out against themselves, moved first by some person in kindness to them, and done at the request of the bankrupt himself. This is generally done when the circumstances of the debtor are very low, and he has little or nothing to surrender; and the end is, that the creditors may be obliged to take what there is, and the man may get a full discharge.

This is, indeed, a vile corruption of a good law, and turning the edge of the act against the creditor, not against the debtor; and as he has nothing to surrender, they get little or nothing, and the man is as effectually discharged as if he had paid twenty shillings in the pound; and so he is in a condition to set up again, take fresh credit, break again, and have another commission against him; and so round, as often as he thinks fit. This, indeed, is a fraud upon the act, and shows that all human wisdom is imperfect, that the law wants some repairs, and that it will in time come into consideration again, to be made capable of disappointing the people that intend to make such use of it.

I think there is also wanting a law against twice breaking, and that all second commissions should have some penalty upon the bankrupt, and a third a farther penalty, and if the fourth brought the man to the gallows, it could not be thought hard; for he that has set up and broke, and set up again, and broke again, and the like, a third time, I think merits to be hanged, if he pretends to venture any more.

Most of those crimes against which any laws are published in particular, and which are not capital, have generally an addition of punishment upon a repetition of the crime, and so on – a further punishment to a further repetition. I do not see why it should not be so here; and I doubt not but it would have a good effect upon tradesmen, to make them cautious, and to warn them to avoid such scandalous doings as we see daily practised, breaking three or four, or five times over; and we see instances of some such while I am writing this very chapter.

To such, therefore, I am so far from moving for any favour, either from the law, or from their creditors, that I think the only deficiency of the law at this time is, that it does not reach to inflict a corporal punishment in such a case, but leaves such insolvents to fare well, in common with those whose disasters are greater, and who, being honest and conscientious, merit more favour, but do not often find it.

CHAPTER XIV

OF THE UNFORTUNATE TRADESMAN COMPOUNDING WITH HIS CREDITORS

This is what in the last chapter I called an alternative to that of the fortunate tradesman yielding to accept the composition of his insolvent debtor.

The poor unhappy tradesman, having long laboured in the fire, and finding it is in vain to struggle, but that whether he strives or not strives, he must break; that he does but go backward more and more, and that the longer he holds out, he shall have the less to offer, and be the harder thought of, as well as the harder dealt with – resolves to call his creditors together in time, while there is something considerable to offer them, and while he may have some just account to give of himself, and of his conduct, and that he may not be reproached with having lived on the spoil, and consumed their estates; and thus, being satisfied that the longer he puts the evil day from him, the heavier it will fall when it comes; I say, he resolves to go no farther, and so gets a friend to discourse with and prepare them, and then draws up a state of his case to lay before them.

First, He assures them that he has not wasted his estate, either by vice and immorality, or by expensive and riotous living, luxury, extravagance, and the like.

Secondly, He makes it appear that he has met with great losses, such as he could not avoid; and yet such and so many, that he has not been able to support the weight of them.

Thirdly, That he could have stood it out longer, but that he was sensible if he did, he should but diminish the stock, which, considering his debts, was properly not his own; and that he was resolved not to spend one part of their debts, as he had lost the other.

Fourthly, That he is willing to show them his books, and give up every farthing into their hands, that they might see he acted the part of an honest man to them.

And,

Fifthly, That upon his doing so, they will find, that there is in goods and good debts sufficient to pay them fifteen shillings in the pound; after which, and when he has made appear that they have a faithful and just account of every thing laid before them, he hopes they will give him his liberty, that he may try to get his bread, and to maintain his family in the best manner he can; and, if possible, to pay the remainder of the debt.

You see I go all the way upon the suggestion of the poor unfortunate tradesman being critically honest, and showing himself so to the full satisfaction of his creditors; that he shows them distinctly a true state of his case, and offers his books and vouchers to confirm every part of his account.

Upon the suggestion of his being thus sincerely honest, and allowing that the state of his account comes out so well as to pay fifteen shillings in the pound, what and who but a parcel of outrageous hot-headed men would reject such a man? What would they be called, nay, what would they say of themselves, if they should reject such a composition, and should go and take out a commission of bankrupt against such a man? I never knew but one of the like circumstances, that was refused by his creditors; and that one held them out, till they were all glad to accept of half what they said should be first paid them: so may all those be served, who reject such wholesome advice, and the season for accepting a good offer, when it was made them. But I return to the debtor.

When he looks into his books, he finds himself declined, his own fortune lost, and his creditors' stock in his hands wasted in part, and still wasting, his trade being for want of stock much fallen off, and his family expense and house-rent great; so he draws up the general articles thus:–

STOCK DEBTOR

To cash of my father (being my stock) to begin with in trade	£800	0	0
To cash of my father-in-law, being my wife's portion	600	0	0
To household-goods, plate, &c. of both	100	0	0
To profits in trade for ten years, as by the yearly balance in the journal appears	2469	10	0
To debts abroad esteemed good, as by the ledger appears	1357	8	0
To goods in the warehouse at the prime cost	672	12	0
Plate and some small jewels of my wife's left, and old household-goods altogether	103	0	0
	£6102	10	0
Estate deficient to balance	1006	2	0
	£7108	12	0

STOCK CREDITOR

	£	s.	d.
By losses by bad debts in trade, in the year 1715	£ 50	0	0
By do. 1716	66	10	0
By do. 1717	234	15	0
By do. 1718	43	0	0
By do. 1719	25	0	0
By do. by the South Sea stock, 1720	1280	0	0
By do. in trade, 1721	42	0	0
By do. 1722	106	0	0
By do. 1723	302	0	0
By do. 1724	86	15	0
By house-keeping and expenses, taxes included, as by the cash-book appears, for ten years	1836	12	0
By house-rents at £50 per annum	500	0	0
By credits now owing to sundry persons, as by the ledger appears	2536	0	0
	£7108	12	0

This account is drawn out to satisfy himself how his condition stands, and what it is he ought to do: upon the stating which account he sees to his affliction that he has sunk all his own fortune and his wife's, and is a thousand pounds worse than nothing in the world; and that, being obliged to live in the same house for the sake of his business and warehouse, though the rent is too great for him, his trade being declined, his credit sunk, and his family being large, he sees evidently he cannot go on, and that it will only be bringing things from bad to worse; and, above all the rest, being greatly perplexed in his mind that he is spending other people's estates, and that the bread he eats is not his own, he resolves to call his creditors all together, lay before them the true state of his case, and lie at their mercy for the rest.

The account of his present and past fortune standing as it did, and as appears above, the result is as follows, namely, that he has not sufficient to pay all his creditors, though his debts should prove to be all good, and the goods in his warehouse should be fully worth the price they cost, which, being liable to daily contingencies, add to the reasons which pressed him before to make an offer of surrender to his creditors both of his goods and debts, and to give up all into their hands.

The state of his case, as to his debts and credits, stands as follows:–

	£	s.	d.
His debts esteemed good, as by the ledger, are	£1357	8	0
His goods in the warehouse	672	12	0
	£2030	0	0
His creditors demands, as by the same ledger appears, are	£3036	0	0

This amounts to fifteen shillings in the pound upon all his debts, which, if the creditors please to appoint an assignee or trustee to sell the goods, and collect the debts, he is willing to surrender wholly into their hands, hoping they will, as a favour, give him his household goods, as in the account, for his family use, and his liberty, that he may seek out for some employment to get his bread.

The account being thus clear, the books exactly agreeing, and the man appearing to have acted openly and fairly, the creditors meet, and, after a few consultations, agree to accept his proposals, and the man is a free man immediately, gets fresh credit, opens his shop again, and, doubling his vigilance and application in business, he recovers in a few years, grows rich; then, like an honest man still, he calls all his creditors together again, tells them he does not call them now to a second composition, but to tell them, that having, with God's blessing and his own industry, gotten enough to enable him, he was resolved to pay them the remainder of his old debt; and accordingly does so, to the great joy of his creditors, to his own very great honour, and to the encouragement of all honest men to take the same measures. It is true, this does not often happen, but there have been instances of it, and I could name several within my own knowledge.

But here comes an objection in the way, as follows: It is true this man did very honestly, and his creditors had a great deal of reason to be satisfied with his just dealing with them; but is every man bound thus to strip himself naked? Perhaps this man at the same time had a family to maintain, and had he no debt of justice to them, but to beg his household goods back of them for his poor family, and that as an alms? – and would he not have fared as well, if he had offered his creditors ten shillings in the pound, and took all the rest upon himself, and then he had reserved to himself sufficient to have supported himself in any new undertaking?

The answer to this is short and plain, and no debtor can be at a loss to know his way in it, for otherwise people may make difficulties where there are none; the observing the strict rules of justice and honesty will chalk out his way for him.

The man being deficient in stock, and his estate run out to a thousand pounds worse than nothing by his losses, &c., it is evident all he has left is the proper estate of his creditors, and he has no right to one shilling of it; he owes it them, it is a just debt to them, and he ought to discharge it fairly, by giving up all into their hands, or at least to offer to do so.

But to put the case upon a new foot; as he is obliged to make an offer, as above, to put all his effects, books, and goods into their power, so he may add an alternative to them thus, namely – that if, on the other hand, they do not think proper to take the trouble, or run the risk, of collecting the debts, and selling the goods, which may be difficult, if they will leave it to him to do it, he will undertake to pay them — shillings in the pound, and stand to the hazard both of debts and goods.

Having thus offered the creditors their choice, if they accept the proposal of a certain sum, as sometimes I know they have chosen to do, rather than to have the trouble of making assignees, and run the hazard of the debts, when put into lawyers' hands to collect, and of the goods, to sell them by appraisement; if, I say, they choose this, and offer to discharge the debtor upon payment, suppose it be of ten or twelve shillings in the pound in money, within a certain time, or on giving security for the payment; then, indeed, the debtor is discharged in conscience, and may lawfully and honestly take the remainder as a gift given him by his creditors for undertaking their business, or securing the remainder of their debt to them – I say, the debtor may do this with the utmost satisfaction to his conscience.

But without thus putting it into the creditors' choice, it is a force upon them to offer them any thing less than the utmost farthing that he is able to pay; and particularly to pretend to make an offer as if it were his utmost, and, as is usual, make protestations that it is the most he is able to pay (indeed, every offer of a composition is a kind of protestation that the debtor is not able to pay any more) – I say, to offer thus, and declare he offers as much as possible, and as much as the effects he has left will produce, if his effects are able to produce more, he is then a cheat; for he acts then like one that stands at bay with his creditors, make an offer, and if the creditors do not think fit to accept of it, they must take what methods they think they can take to get more; that is to say, he bids open defiance to their statutes and commissions of bankrupt, and any other proceedings: like a town besieged, which offers to capitulate and to yield upon such and such articles; which implies, that if those articles are not accepted, the garrison will defend themselves to the last extremity, and do all the mischief to the assailants that they can.

Now, this in a garrison-town, I say, may be lawful and fair, but in a debtor to his creditor it is quite another thing: for, as I have said above, the debtor has no property in the effects which he has in his hands; they are the goods and the estate of the creditor; and to hold out against the creditor, keep his estate by violence, and make him accept of a small part of it, when the debtor has a larger part in his power, and is able to give it – this is not fair, much less is it honest and conscientious; but it is still worse to do this, and at the same time to declare that it is the utmost the debtor can do; this, I say, is still more dishonest, because it is not true, and is adding falsehood to the other injustice.

Thus, I think, I have stated the case clearly, for the conduct of the debtor; and, indeed, this way of laying all before the creditors, and putting it into their choice, seems a very happy method for the comfort of the debtor, cast down and dejected with the weight of his circumstances; and, it may be, with the reproaches of his own conscience too, that he has not done honestly in running out the effects of his creditors, and making other families suffer by him, and perhaps poor families too – I say, this way of giving up all with an honest and single desire to make all the satisfaction he is able to his creditors, greatly heals the breach in his peace, which his circumstances had made before; for, by now doing all that is in his power, he makes all possible amends for what is past, I mean as to men; and they are induced, by this open, frank usage, to give him the reward of his honesty, and freely forgive him the rest of the debt.

There is a manifest difference to the debtor, in point of conscience, between surrendering his whole effects, or estate, to his creditors for satisfaction of their debts, and offering them a composition, unless, as I have said, the composition is offered, as above, to the choice of the creditor. By surrendering the whole estate, the debtor acknowledges the creditors' right to all he has in his possession, and gives it up to them as their own, putting it in their full power to dispose of it as they please.

But, by a composition, the debtor, as I have said above, stands at bay with the creditors, and, keeping their estates in his hands, capitulates with them, as it were, sword in hand, telling them he can give them no more, when perhaps, and too often it is the case, it is apparent that he is in condition to offer more. Now, let the creditors consent to these proposals, be what it will; and, however voluntary it may be pretended to be, it is evident that a force is the occasion of it, and the creditor complies, and accepts the proposal, upon the supposition that no better conditions can be had. It is the plain language of the thing, for no man accepts of less than he thinks he can get: if he believed he could have more, he would certainly get it if he could.

And if the debtor is able to pay one shilling more than he offers, it is a cheat, a palpable fraud, and of so much he actually robs his creditor. But in a surrender the case is altered in all its parts; the debtor says to his creditors, 'Gentlemen, there is a full and faithful account of all I have left; it is your own, and there it is; I am ready to put it into your hands, or into the hands of whomsoever you shall appoint to receive it, and to lie at your mercy.' This is all the man is able to do, and therefore is so far honest; whether the methods that reduced him were honest or no, that is a question by itself. If on this surrender he finds the creditors desirous rather to have it digested into a composition, and that they will voluntarily come into such a proposal, then, as above, they being judges of the equity of the composition, and of what ability the debtor is to perform it, and, above all, of what he may or may not gain by it, if they accept of such a composition, instead of the surrender of his effects, then the case alters entirely, and the debtor is acquitted in conscience, because the creditor had a fair choice, and the composition is rather their proposal to the debtor, than the debtor's proposal to them.

Thus, I think, I have stated the case of justice and conscience on the debtor's behalf, and cleared up his way, in case of a necessity, to stop trading, that he may break without wounding his conscience, as well as his fortunes; and he that thinks fit to act thus, will come off with the reputation of an honest man, and will have the favour of his creditors to begin again, with whatever he may have as to stock; and sometimes that favour is better to him than a stock, and has been the raising of many a broken tradesman, so that his latter end has been better than his beginning.

CHAPTER XV

OF TRADESMEN RUINING ONE ANOTHER BY RUMOUR AND CLAMOUR, BY SCANDAL AND REPROACH

I have dwelt long upon the tradesman's management of himself, in order to his due preserving both his business and his reputation: let me bestow one chapter upon the tradesman for his conduct among his neighbours and fellow-tradesmen.

Credit is so much a tradesman's blessing that it is the choicest ware he deals in, and he cannot be too chary of it when he has it, or buy it too dear when he wants it; it is a stock to his warehouse, it is current money in his cash-chest, it accepts all his bills, for it is on the fund of his credit that he has any bills to accept; demands would else be made upon the spot, and he must pay for his goods before he has them – therefore, I say, it accepts all his bills, and oftentimes pays them too; in a word, it is the life and soul of his trade, and it requires his utmost vigilance to preserve it.

If, then, his own credit should be of so much value to him, and he should be so nice in his concern about it, he ought in some degree to have the same care of his neighbour's. Religion teaches us not to slander and defame our neighbour, that is to say, not to raise or promote any slander or scandal upon his good name. As a good name is to another man, and which the wise man says, 'is better than life,' the same is credit to a tradesman – it is the life of his trade; and he that wounds a tradesman's credit without cause, is as much a murderer in trade, as he that kills a man in the dark is a murderer in matters of blood.

Besides, there is a particular nicety in the credit of a tradesman, which does not reach in other cases: a man is slandered in his character, or reputation, and it is injurious; and if it comes in the way of a marriage, or of a preferment, or post, it may disappoint and ruin him; but if this happens to a tradesman, he is immediately and unavoidably blasted and undone; a tradesman has but two sorts of enemies to encounter with, namely, thieves breaking open his shop, and ill neighbours blackening and blasting his reputation; and the latter are the worst thieves of the two, by a great deal; and, therefore, people should indeed be more chary of their discourse of tradesmen, than of other men, and that as they would not be guilty of murder.

I knew an author of a book, who was drawn in unwarily, and without design, to publish a scandalous story of a tradesman in London. He (the author) was imposed upon by a set of men, who did it maliciously, and he was utterly ignorant of the wicked design; nor did he know the person, but rashly published the thing, being himself too fond of a piece of news, which he thought would be grateful to his readers; nor yet did he publish the person's name, so cautious he was, though that was not enough, as it proved, for the person was presently published by those who had maliciously done it.

The scandal spread; the tradesman, a flourishing man, and a considerable dealer, was run upon by it with a torrent of malice; a match which he was about with a considerable fortune was blasted and prevented, and that indeed was the malicious end of the people that did it; nor did it stop there – it brought his creditors upon him, it ruined him, it brought out a commission of bankrupt against him, it broke his heart, and killed him; and after his death, his debts and effects coming in, there appeared to be seven shillings in the pound estate, clear and good over and above all demands, all his debts discharged, and all the expenses of the statute paid.

It was to no purpose that the man purged himself of the crime laid to his charge – that the author, who had ignorantly and rashly published the scandal, declared himself ignorant; the man was run down by a torrent of reproach; scandal oppressed him; he was buried alive in the noise and dust raised both against his morals and his credit, and yet his character was proved good, and his bottom in trade was so too, as I have said above.

It is not the least reason of my publishing this to add, that even the person who was ignorantly made the instrument of publishing the scandal, was not able to retrieve it, or to prevent the man's ruin by all the public reparation he could make in print, and by all the acknowledgement he could make of his having been ignorantly drawn in to do it. And this I mention for the honest tradesman's caution, and to put him in mind, that when he has unwarily let slip anything to the wounding the reputation of his neighbour tradesman, whether in his trading credit, or the credit of his morals, it may not be in his power to unsay it again, that is, so as to prevent the ruin of the person; and though it may grieve him as long as he lives, as the like did the author I mention, yet it is not in his power to recall it, or to heal the wound he has given; and that he should consider very well of beforehand.

A tradesman's credit and a virgin's virtue ought to be equally sacred from the tongues of men; and it is a very unhappy truth, that as times now go, they are neither of them regarded among us as they ought to be.

The tea-table among the ladies, and the coffee-house among the men, seem to be places of new invention for a depravation of our manners and morals, places devoted to scandal, and where the characters of all kinds of persons and professions are handled in the most merciless manner, where reproach triumphs, and we seem to give ourselves a loose to fall upon one another in the most unchristian and unfriendly manner in the world.

It seems a little hard that the reputation of a young lady, or of a new-married couple, or of people in the most critical season of establishing the characters of their persons and families, should lie at the mercy of the tea-table; nor is it less hard, that the credit of a tradesman, which is the same thing in its nature as the virtue of a lady, should be tossed about, shuttle-cock-like, from one table to another, in the coffee-house, till they shall talk all his creditors about his ears, and bring him to the very misfortune which they reported him to be near, when at the same time he owed them nothing who raised the clamour, and owed nothing to all the world, but what he was able to pay.

And yet how many tradesmen have been thus undone, and how many more have been put to the full trial of their strength in trade, and have stood by the mere force of their good circumstances; whereas, had they been unfurnished with cash to have answered their whole debts, they must have fallen with the rest.

We need go no farther than Lombard Street for an exemplification of this truth. There was a time when Lombard Street was the only bank, and the goldsmiths there were all called bankers. The credit of their business was such, that the like has not been seen in England since, in private hands: some of those bankers, as I have had from their own mouths, have had near two millions of paper credit upon them at a time; that is to say, have had bills under their hands running abroad for so much at a time.

On a sudden, like a clap of thunder, King Charles II. shut up the Exchequer, which was the common centre of the overplus cash these great bankers had in their hands. What was the consequence? Not only the bankers who had the bulk of their cash there, but all Lombard Street, stood still. The very report of having money in the Exchequer brought a run upon the goldsmiths that had no money there, as well as upon those that had, and not only Sir Robert Viner, Alderman Backwell, Farringdon, Forth, and others, broke and failed, but several were ruined who had not a penny of money in the Exchequer, and only sunk by the rumour of it; that rumour bringing a run upon the whole street, and giving a check to the paper credit that was run up to such an exorbitant height.

I remember a shopkeeper who one time took the liberty (foolish liberty!) with himself, in public company in a coffee-house, to say that he was broke. 'I assure you,' says he, 'that I am broke, and to-morrow

I resolve to shut up my shop, and call my creditors together.' His meaning was, that he had a brother just dead in his house, and the next day was to be buried, when, in civility to the deceased, he kept his shop shut; and several people whom he dealt with, and owed money to, were the next day invited to the funeral, so that he did actually shut up his shop, and call some of his creditors together.

But he sorely repented the jest which he put upon himself. 'Are you broke?' says one of his friends to him, that was in the coffee-house; 'then I wish I had the little money you owe me' (which however, it seems, was not much). Says the other, still carrying on his jest, 'I shall pay nobody, till, as I told you, I have called my people together.' The other did not reach his jest, which at best was but a dull one, but he reached that part of it that concerned himself, and seeing him continue carelessly sitting in the shop, slipped out, and, fetching a couple of sergeants, arrested him. The other was a little surprised; but however, the debt being no great sum, he paid it, and when he found his mistake, told his friends what he meant by his being broke.

But it did not end there; for other people of his neighbours, who were then in the coffee-house, and heard his discourse, and had thought nothing more of it, yet in the morning seeing his shop shut, concluded the thing was so indeed, and immediately it went over the whole street that such a one was broke; from thence it went to the Exchange, and from thence into the country, among all his dealers, who came up in a throng and a fright to look after him. In a word, he had as much to do to prevent his breaking as any man need to desire, and if he had not had very good friends as well as a very good bottom, he had inevitably been ruined and undone.

So small a rumour will overset a tradesman, if he is not very careful of himself; and if a word in jest from himself, which though indeed no man that had considered things, or thought before he spoke, would have said (and, on the other hand, no man who had been wise and thinking would have taken as it was taken) – I say, if a word taken from the tradesman's own mouth could be so fatal, and run such a dangerous length, what may not words spoken slyly, and secretly, and maliciously, be made to do?

A tradesman's reputation is of the nicest nature imaginable; like a blight upon a fine flower, if it is but touched, the beauty of it, or the flavour of it, or the seed of it, is lost, though the noxious breath which touched it might not reach to blast the leaf, or hurt the root; the credit of a tradesman, at least in his beginning, is too much at the mercy of every enemy he has, till it has taken root, and is established on a solid foundation of good conduct and success. It is a sad truth, that every idle tongue can blast a young shopkeeper; and therefore, though I would not discourage any young beginner, yet it is highly beneficial to alarm them, and to let them know that they must expect a storm of scandal and reproach upon the least slip they make: if they but stumble, fame will throw them down; it is true, if they recover, she will set them up as fast; but malice generally runs before, and bears down all with it; and there are ten tradesmen who fall under the weight of slander and an ill tongue, to one that is lifted up again by the common hurry of report.

To say I am broke, or in danger of breaking, is to break me: and though sometimes the malicious occasion is discovered, and the author detected and exposed, yet how seldom is it so; and how much oftener are ill reports raised to ruin and run down a tradesman, and the credit of a shop; and like an arrow that flies in the dark, it wounds unseen. The authors, no nor the occasion of these reports, are never discovered perhaps, or so much as rightly guessed at; and the poor tradesman feels the wound, receives the deadly blow, and is perhaps mortally stabbed in the vitals of his trade, I mean his trading credit, and never knows who hurt him.

I must say, in the tradesman's behalf, that he is in such a case to be esteemed a sacrifice to the worst and most hellish of all secret crimes, I mean envy; which is made up of every hateful vice, a complication of crimes which nothing but the worst of God's reasonable world can be guilty of; and he will indeed merit and call for every honest man's pity and concern. But what relief is this to him? for, in the meantime, though the devil himself were the raiser of the scandal, yet it shall go about; the blow shall take, and every man, though at the same time expressing their horror and aversion at the thing, shall yet not be able, no not themselves, to say they receive no impression from it.

Though I know the clamour or rumour was raised maliciously, and from a secret envy at the prosperity of the man, yet if I deal with him, it will in spite of all my abhorrence of the thing, in spite of all my willingness to do justice, I say it will have some little impression upon me, it will be some shock to my confidence in the man; and though I know the devil is a liar, a slanderer, a calumniator, and that his name *devil* is derived from it; and that I knew, if that, as I said, were possible, that the devil in his proper person raised and began, and carried on, this scandal upon the tradesman, yet there is a secret lurking doubt (about him), which hangs about me concerning him; the devil is a liar, but he may happen to speak truth just then, he may chance to be right, and I know not what there may be in it, and whether there may be any thing or no, but I will have a little care, &c.

Thus, insensibly and involuntarily, nay, in spite of friendship, good wishes, and even resolution to the contrary, it is almost impossible to prevent our being shocked by rumour, and we receive an impression whether we will or not, and that from the worst enemy; there is such a powerful sympathy between our thoughts and our interest, that the first being but touched, and that in the lightest manner imaginable, we cannot help it, caution steps on in behalf of the last, and the man is jealous and afraid, in spite of all the kindest and best intentions in the world.

Nor is it only dangerous in case of false accusations and false charges, for those indeed are to be expected fatal; but even just and true things may be as fatal as false, for the truth is not always necessary to be said of a tradesman: many things a tradesman may perhaps allow himself to do, and may be lawfully done, but if they should be known to be part of his character, it would sink deep into his trading fame, his credit would suffer by it, and in the end it might be his ruin; so that he that would not set his hand to his neighbour's ruin, should as carefully avoid speaking some truths, as raising some forgeries upon him.

Of what fatal consequence, then, is the raising rumours and suspicions upon the credit and characters of young tradesmen! and how little do those who are forward to raise such suspicions, and spread such rumours, consult conscience, or principle, or honour, in what they do! How little do they consider that they are committing a trading murder, and that, in respect to the justice of it, they may with much more equity break open the tradesman's house, and rob his cash-chest, or his shop; and what they can carry away thence will not do him half the injury that robbing his character of what is due to it from an upright and diligent conduct, would do. The loss of his money or goods is easily made up, and may be sometimes repaired with advantage, but the loss of credit is never repaired; the one is breaking open his house, but the other is burning it down; the one carries away some goods, but the other shuts goods out from coming in; one is hurting the tradesman, but the other is undoing him.

Credit is the tradesman's life; it is, as the wise man says, 'marrow to his bones;' it is by this that all his affairs go on prosperously and pleasantly; if this be hurt, wounded, or weakened, the tradesman is sick, hangs his head, is dejected and discouraged; and if he does go on, it is heavily and with difficulty, as well as with disadvantage; he is beholding to his fund of cash, not his friends; and he may be truly said to stand upon his own legs, for nothing else can do it.

And therefore, on the other hand, if such a man is any way beholding to his credit, if he stood before upon the foundation of his credit, if he owes any thing considerable, it is a thousand to one but he sinks under the oppression of it; that is to say, it brings every body upon him – I mean, every one that has any demand upon him – for in pushing for their own, especially in such cases, men have so little mercy, and are so universally persuaded that he that comes first is first served, that I did not at all wonder, that in the story of the tradesman who so foolishly exposed himself in the coffee-house, as above, his friend whom he said the words to, began with him that very night, and before he went out of the coffee-house; it was rather a wonder to me he did not go out and bring in half-a-dozen more upon him the same evening.

It is very rarely that men are wanting to their own interest; and the jealousy of its being but in danger, is enough to make men forget, not friendship only, and generosity, but good manners, civility, and even justice itself, and fall upon the best friends they have in the world, if they think they are in the least danger of suffering by them.

On these accounts it is, and many more, that a tradesman walks in continual jeopardy, from the looseness and inadvertency of men's tongues, ay, and women's too; for though I am all along very tender of the ladies, and would do justice to the sex, by telling you, they were not the dangerous people whom I had in view in my first writing upon this subject, yet I must be allowed to say, that they are sometimes fully even with the men, for ill usage, when they please to fall upon them in this nice article, in revenge for any slight, or but pretended slight, put upon them.

It was a terrible revenge a certain lady, who was affronted by a tradesman in London, in a matter of love, took upon him in this very article. It seems a tradesman had courted her some time, and it was become public, as a thing in a manner concluded, when the tradesman left the lady a little abruptly, without giving a good reason for it, and, indeed, she afterwards discovered, that he had left her for the offer of another with a little more money, and that, when he had done so, he reported that it was for another reason, which reflected a little on the person of the lady; and in this the tradesman did very unworthily indeed, and deserved her resentment: but, as I said, it was a terrible revenge she took, and what she ought not to have done.

First, she found out who it was that her former pretended lover had been recommended to, and she found means to have it insinuated to her by a woman-friend, that he was not only rakish and wicked, but, in short, that he had a particular illness, and went so far as to produce letters from him to a quack-doctor, for directions to him how to take his medicines, and afterwards a receipt for money for the cure; though both the letters and receipt also, as afterwards appeared, were forged, in which she went a dismal length in her revenge, as you may see.

Then she set two or three female instruments to discourse her case in all their gossips' companies, and at the tea-tables wherever they came, and to magnify the lady's prudence in refusing such a man, and what an escape she had had in being clear of him.

'Why,' says a lady to one of these emissaries, 'what was the matter? I thought she was like to be very well married.'

'Oh no, Madam! by no means,' says the emissary.

'Why, Madam,' says another lady, 'we all know Mr H——; he is a very pretty sort of a man.'

'Ay, Madam,' says the emissary again, 'but you know a pretty man is not all that is required.'

'Nay,' says the lady again, 'I don't mean so; he is no beauty, no rarity that way; but I mean a clever good sort of a man in his business, such as we call a pretty tradesman.'

'Ay,' says the lady employed, 'but that is not all neither.'

'Why,' says the other lady, 'he has a very good trade too, and lives in good credit.'

'Yes,' says malice, 'he has some of the first, but not too much of the last, I suppose.'

'No!' says the lady; 'I thought his credit had been very good.'

'If it had, I suppose,' says the first, 'the match had not been broke off.'

'Why,' says the lady, 'I understood it was broken off on his side.'

'And so did I,' says another.

'And so did I, indeed,' says a third.

'Oh, Madam!' says the tool, 'nothing like it, I assure you.'

'Indeed,' says another, 'I understood he had quitted Mrs ——, because she had not fortune enough for him, and that he courted another certain lady, whom we all know.'

Then the ladies fell to talking of the circumstances of his leaving her, and how he had broken from her abruptly and unmannerly, and had been too free with her character; at which the first lady, that is to say, the emissary, or tool, as I call her, took it up a little warmly, thus:–

1. *Lady*. – Well, you see, ladies, how easily a lady's reputation may be injured; I hope you will not go away with it so.

2. *Lady*. – Nay, we have all of us a respect for Mrs ——, and some of us visit there sometimes; I believe none of us would be willing to injure her.

1. *Lady*. – But indeed, ladies, she is very much injured in that story.

2. *Lady*. – Indeed, it is generally understood so, and every body believes it.

1. *Lady*. – I can assure you it is quite otherwise in fact.

2. *Lady*. – I believe he reports it so himself, and that with some very odd things about the lady too.

1. *Lady*. – The more base unworthy fellow he.

2. *Lady*. – Especially if he knows it to be otherwise.

1. *Lady*. – Especially if he knows the contrary to be true, Madam.

2. *Lady*. – Is that possible? Did he not refuse her, then?

1. *Lady*. – Nothing like it, Madam; but just the contrary.

2. *Lady*. – You surprise me!

3. *Lady*. – I am very glad to hear it, for her sake.

1. *Lady*. – I can assure you, Madam, she had refused him, and that he knows well enough, which has been one of the reasons that has made him abuse her as he has done.

2. *Lady*. – Indeed, she has been used very ill by him, or somebody for him.

1. *Lady*. – Yes, he has reported strange things, but they are all lies.

2. *Lady*. – Well; but pray, Madam, what was the reason, if we may be so free, that she turned him off after she had entertained him so long?

1. *Lady*. – Oh, Madam! reason enough; I wonder he should pretend, when he knew his own circumstances too, to court a lady of her fortune.

2. *Lady*. – Why, are not his circumstances good, then?

1. *Lady*. – No, Madam. Good! alas, he has no bottom.

2. *Lady*. – No bottom! Why, you surprise me; we always looked upon him to be a man of substance, and that he was very well in the world.

1. *Lady*. – It is all a cheat, Madam; there's nothing in it; when it came to be made out, nothing at all in it.

2. *Lady*. – That cannot be, Madam; Mr—— has lived always in good reputation and good credit in his business.

1. *Lady*. – It is all sunk again then, if it was so; I don't know.

2. *Lady*. – Why did she entertain him so long, then?

1. *Lady*. – Alas! Madam, how could she know, poor lady, till her friends inquired into things? But when they came to look a little narrowly into it, they soon found reason to give her a caution, that he was not the man she took him for.

2. *Lady*. – Well, it is very strange; I am sure he passed for another man among us.

1. *Lady*. – It must be formerly, then, for they tell me his credit has been sunk these three or four years; he had need enough indeed to try for a greater fortune, he wants it enough.

2. *Lady*. – It is a sad thing when men look out for fortunes to heal their trade-breaches with, and make the poor wife patch up their old bankrupt credit.

1. *Lady*. – Especially, Madam, when they know themselves to be gone so far, that even with the addition they can stand but a little while, and must inevitably bring the lady to destruction with them.

2. *Lady*. – Well, I could never have thought Mr—— was in such circumstances.

3. *Lady*. – Nor I; we always took him for a ten thousand pound man.

1. *Lady*. – They say he was deep in the bubbles, Madam.

2. *Lady*. – Nay, if he was gotten into the South Sea, that might hurt him indeed, as it has done many a gentleman of better estates than he.

1. *Lady*. – I don't know whether it was the South Sea, or some other bubbles, but he was very near making a bubble of her, and £3000 into the bargain.

2. *Lady*. – I am glad she has escaped him, if it be so; it is a sign her friends took a great deal of care of her.

1. *Lady*. – He won't hold it long; he will have his desert, I hope; I don't doubt but we shall see him in the Gazette quickly for a bankrupt.

2. *Lady*. – If he does not draw in some innocent young thing that has her fortune in her own hands to patch him up.

1. *Lady*. – I hope not, Madam; I hear he is blown where he went since, and there, they say, they have made another discovery of him, in a worse circumstance than the other.

2. *Lady*. – How, pray?

1. *Lady*. – Nothing, Madam, but a particular kind of illness, &c. I need say no more.

2. *Lady*. – You astonish me! Why, I always thought him a very civil, honest, sober man.

1. *Lady*. – This is a sad world, Madam; men are seldom known now, till it is too late; but sometimes murder comes out seasonably, and so I understand it is here; for the lady had not gone so far with him, but that she could go off again.

2. *Lady*. – Nay, it was time to go off again, if it were so.

1. *Lady*. – Nay, Madam, I do not tell this part of my own knowledge; I only heard so, but I am afraid there is too much in it.

Thus ended this piece of hellish wildfire, upon the character and credit of a tradesman, the truth of all which was no more than this – that the tradesman, disliking his first lady, left her, and soon after, though not presently, courted another of a superior fortune indeed, though not for that reason; and the first lady, provoked at being cast off, and, as she called it, slighted, raised all this clamour upon him, and persecuted him with it, wherever she was able.

Such a discourse as this at a tea-table, it could not be expected would be long a secret; it ran from one tittle-tattle society to another; and in every company, snow-ball like, it was far from lessening, and it went on, till at length it began to meet with some contradiction, and the tradesman found himself obliged to trace it as far and as well as he could.

But it was to no purpose to confront it; when one was asked, and another was asked, they only answered they heard so, and they heard it in company in such a place, and in such a place, and some could remember where they had it, and some could not; and the poor tradesman, though he was really a man of substance, sank under it prodigiously: his new mistress, whom he courted, refused him, and would never hear any thing in his favour, or trouble herself to examine whether it were true or no – it was enough, she said, to her, that he was laden with such a report; and, if it was unjust, she was sorry for it, but the misfortune must be his, and he must place it to the account of his having made some enemies, which she could not help.

As to his credit, the slander of the first lady's raising was spread industriously, and with the utmost malice and bitterness, and did him an inexpressible prejudice; every man he dealt with was shy of him; every man he owed any thing to came for it, and, as he said, he was sure he should see the last penny demanded; it was his happiness that he had wherewith to pay, for had his circumstances been in the least perplexed, the man had been undone; nay, as I have observed in another case, as his affairs might have lain, he might have been able to have paid forty shillings in the pound, and yet have been undone, and been obliged to break, and shut up his shop.

It is true, he worked through it, and he carried it so far as to fix the malice of all the reports pretty much upon the first lady, and particularly so far as to discover that she was the great reason of his being so positively rejected by the other; but he could never fix it so upon her as to recover any damages of her, only to expose her a little, and that she did not value, having, as she said wickedly, had her full revenge of him, and so indeed she had.

The sum of the matter is, and it is for this reason I tell you the story, that the reputation of a tradesman is too much at the mercy of men's tongues or women's either; and a story raised upon a tradesman, however malicious, however false, and however frivolous the occasion, is not easily suppressed, but, if it touches his credit, as a flash of fire it spreads over the whole air like a sheet; there is no stopping it.

My inference from all this shall be very brief; if the tongues of every ill-disposed envious gossip, whether man-gossip or woman-gossip, for there are of both sorts, may be thus mischievous to the tradesman, and he is so much at the mercy of the tattling slandering part of the world, how much more should tradesmen be cautious and wary how they touch or wound the credit and character of one another. There are but a very few tradesmen who can say they are out of the reach of slander, and that the malice of enemies cannot hurt them with the tongue. Here and there one, and those ancient and well established, may be able to defy the world; but there are so many others, that I think I may warn all tradesmen against making havoc of one another's reputation, as they would be tenderly used in the same case.

And yet I cannot but say it is too much a tradesman's crime, I mean to speak slightly and contemptibly of other tradesman, their neighbours, or perhaps rivals in trade, and to run them down in the characters they give of them, when inquiry may be made of them, as often is the case. The reputation of tradesmen is too often put into the hands of their fellow-tradesmen, when ignorant people think to inform themselves of their circumstances, by going to those whose interest it is to defame and run them down.

I know no case in the world in which there is more occasion for the golden rule, Do as you would be done unto; and though you may be established, as you may think, and be above the reach of the tongues of others, yet the obligation of the rule is the same, for you are to do as you would be done unto, supposing that you were in the same condition, or on a level with the person.

It is confessed that tradesmen do not study this rule in the particular case I am now speaking of. No men are apter to speak slightly and coldly of a fellow-tradesman than his fellow-tradesmen, and to speak unjustly so too; the reasons for which cannot be good, unless it can be pleaded for upon the foundation of a just and impartial concern in the interest of the inquirer; and even then nothing must be said but what is consistent with strict justice and truth: all that is more than that, is mere slander and envy, and has nothing of the Christian in it, much less of the neighbour or friend. It is true that friendship may be due to the inquirer, but still so much justice is due to the person inquired of, that it is very hard to speak in such cases, and not be guilty of raising dust, as they call it, upon your neighbour, and at least hurting, if not injuring him.

It is, indeed, so difficult a thing, that I scarce know what stated rule to lay down for the conduct of a tradesman in this case: – A tradesman at a distance is going to deal with another tradesman, my neighbour; and before he comes to bargain, or before he cares to trust him, he goes, weakly enough perhaps, to inquire of him, and of his circumstances, among his neighbours and fellow-tradesmen, perhaps of the same profession or employment, and who, among other things, it may be, are concerned by their interest, that this tradesman's credit should not rise too fast. What must be done in this case?

If I am the person inquired of, what must I do? If I would have this man sink in his reputation, or be discredited, and if it is for my interest to have him cried down in the world, it is a sore temptation to me to put in a few words to his disadvantage; and yet, if I do it in gratification of my private views or interest, or upon the foot of resentment of any kind whatever, and let it be from what occasion it will, nay, however just and reasonable the resentment is, or may be, it is utterly unjust and unlawful, and is not only unfair as a man, but unchristian, and is neither less nor more than a secret revenge, which is forbidden by the laws of God and man.

If, on the other hand, I give a good character of the man, or of his reputation, I mean, of his credit in business, in order to have the inquirer trust him, and at the same time know or believe that he is not a sound and good man (that is, as to trade, for it is his character in trade that I am speaking of), what am I doing then? It is plain I lay a snare for the inquirer, and am at least instrumental to his loss, without having really any design to hurt him; for it is to be supposed, before he came to me to inquire, I had no view of acting any thing to his prejudice.

Again, there is no medium, for to refuse or decline giving a character of the man, is downright giving him the worst character I can – it is, in short, shooting him through the head in his trade. A man comes to me for a character of my neighbouring tradesman; I answer him with a repulse to his inquiry thus—

A. – Good sir, do not ask me the character of my neighbours – I resolve to meddle with nobody's character; pray, do not inquire of me.

B. – Well, but, sir, you know the gentleman; you live next door to him; you can tell me, if you please, all that I desire to know, whether he is a man in credit, and fit to be trusted, or no, in the way of his business.

A. – I tell you, sir, I meddle with no man's business; I will not give characters of my neighbours – it is an ill office – a man gets no thanks for it, and perhaps deserves none.

B. – But, sir, you would be willing to be informed and advised, if it were your own case.

A. – It may be so, but I cannot oblige people to inform me.

B. – But you would entreat it as a favour, and so I come to you.

A. – But you may go to any body else.

B. – But you are a man of integrity; I can depend upon what you say; I know you will not deceive me; and, therefore, I beg of you to satisfy me.

A. – But I desire you to excuse me, for it is what I never do – I cannot do it.

B. – But, sir, I am in a great strait; I am just selling him a great parcel of goods, and I am willing to sell them too, and yet I am willing to be safe, as you would yourself, if you were in my case.

A. – I tell you, sir, I have always resolved to forbear meddling with the characters of my neighbours – it is an ill office. Besides, I mind my own business; I do not enter into the inquiries after other people's affairs.

B. – Well, sir, I understand you, then; I know what I have to do.

A. – What do you mean by that?

B. – Nothing, sir, but what I suppose you would have me understand by it.

A. – I would have you understand what I say – namely, that I will meddle with nobody's business but my own.

B. – And I say I understand you; I know you are a good man, and a man of charity, and loth to do your neighbours any prejudice, and that you will speak the best of every man as near as you can.

A. – I tell you, I speak neither the best nor the worst – I speak nothing.

B. – Well, sir, that is to say, that as charity directs you to speak well of every man, so, when you cannot speak well, you refrain, and will say nothing; and you do very well, to be sure; you are a very kind neighbour.

A. – But that is a base construction of my words; for I tell you, I do the like by every body.

B. – Yes, sir, I believe you do, and I think you are in the right of it – I am fully satisfied.

A. – You act more unjustly by me than by my neighbour; for you take my silence, or declining to give a character, to be giving an ill character.

B. – No, sir, not for an ill character.

A. – But I find you take it for a ground of suspicion.

B. – I take it, indeed, for a due caution to me, sir; but the man may be a good man for all that, only –

A. – Only what? I understand you – only you won't trust him with your goods.

B. – But another man may, sir, for all that, so that you have been kind to your neighbours and to me too, sir – and you are very just. I wish all men would act so one by another; I should feel the benefit of it myself among others, for I have suffered deeply by ill tongues, I am sure.

A. – Well, however unjust you are to me, and to my neighbour too, I will not undeceive you at present; I think you do not deserve it.

He used a great many more words with him to convince him that he did not mean any discredit to his neighbour tradesman; but it was all one; he would have it be, that his declining to give his said neighbour a good character was giving him an ill character, which the other told him was a wrong inference. However, he found that the man stood by his own notion of it, and declined trusting the tradesman with the goods, though he was satisfied he (the tradesman) was a sufficient man.

Upon this, he was a little uneasy, imagining that he had been the cause of it, as indeed he had, next to the positive humour of the inquirer, though it was not really his fault; neither was the construction the other made of it just to his intention, for he aimed at freeing himself from all inquiries of that nature, but found there was no prevailing with him to understand it any other way than he did; so, to requite the man a little in his own way, he contrived the following method: he met with him two or three days after, and asked him if he had sold his goods to the person his neighbour?

'No,' says he; 'you know I would not.'

'Nay,' says the other, 'I only knew you said so; I did not think you would have acted so from what I said, nor do I think I gave you any reason.'

'Why,' says he, 'I knew you would have given him a good character if you could, and I knew you were too honest to do it, if you were not sure it was just.'

'The last part I hope is true, but you might have believed me honest too, in what I did say, that I had resolved to give no characters of any body.'

'As to that, I took it, as any body would, to be the best and modestest way of covering what you would not have be disclosed, namely, that you could not speak as you would; and I also judged that you therefore chose to say nothing.'

'Well, I can say no more but this; you are not just to me in it, and I think you are not just to yourself neither.'

They parted again upon this, and the next day the first tradesman, who had been so pressed to give a character of his neighbour, sent a man to buy the parcel of goods of the other tradesman, and offering him ready money, bought them considerably cheaper than the neighbour-tradesman was to have given for them, besides reckoning a reasonable discount for the time, which was four months, that the first tradesman was to have given to his neighbour.

As soon as he had done, he went and told the neighbour-tradesman what he had done, and the reason of it, and sold the whole parcel to him again, giving the same four months' credit for them as the first man was to have given, and taking the discount for time only to himself, gave him all the advantage of the buying, and gave the first man the mortification of knowing it all, and that the goods were not only for the same man, but that the very tradesman, whom he would not believe when he declined giving a character of any man in general, had trusted him with them.

He pretended to be very angry, and to take it very ill; but the other told him, that when he came to him for a character of the man, and he told him honestly, that he would give no characters at all, that it was not for any ill to his neighbour that he declined it, he ought to have believed him; and that he hoped, when he wanted a character of any of his neighbours again, he would not come to him for it.

This story is to my purpose in this particular, which is indeed very significant; that it is the most difficult thing of its kind in the world to avoid giving characters of our neighbouring tradesmen; and that, let your reasons for it be what they will, to refuse giving a character is giving a bad character, and is generally so taken, whatever caution or arguments you use to the contrary.

In the next place, it is hard indeed, if an honest neighbour be in danger of selling a large parcel of goods to a fellow, who I may know it is not likely should be able to pay for them, though his credit may in the common appearance be pretty good at that time; and what must I do? If I discover the man's circumstances, which perhaps I am let into by some accident, I say, if I discover them, the man is undone; and if I do not, the tradesman, who is in danger of trusting him, is undone.

I confess the way is clear, if I am obliged to speak at all in the case: the man unsound is already a bankrupt at bottom, and must fail, but the other man is sound and firm, if this disaster does not befall him: the first has no wound given him, but negatively; he stands where he stood before; whereas the other is drawn in perhaps to his own ruin. In the next place, the first is a knave, or rather thief, for he offers to buy, and knows he cannot pay; in a word, he offers to cheat his neighbour; and if I know it, I am so far confederate with him in the cheat.

In this case I think I am obliged to give the honest man a due caution for his safety, if he desires my advice; I cannot say I am obliged officiously to go out of my way to do it, unless I am any way interested in the person – for that would be to dip into other men's affairs, which is not my proper work; and if I should any way be misinformed of the circumstances of the tradesman I am to speak of, and wrong him, I may be instrumental to bring ruin causelessly upon him.

In a word, it is a very nice and critical case, and a tradesman ought to be very sure of what he says or does in such a case, the good or evil fate of his neighbour lying much at stake, and depending too much on the breath of his mouth. Every part of this discourse shows how much a tradesman's welfare depends upon the justice and courtesy of his neighbours, and how nice and critical a thing his reputation is.

This, well considered, would always keep a tradesman humble, and show him what need he has to behave courteously and obligingly among his neighbours; for one malicious word from a man much meaner than himself, may overthrow him in such a manner, as all the friends he has may not be able to recover him; a tradesman, if possible, should never make himself any enemies.

But if it is so fatal a thing to tradesmen to give characters of one another, and that a tradesman should be so backward in it for fear of hurting his neighbour, and that, notwithstanding the character given should be just, and the particular reported of him should be true, with how much greater caution should we act in like cases where what is suggested is really false in fact, and the tradesman is innocent, as was the case in the tradesman mentioned before about courting the lady. If a tradesman may be ruined and undone by a true report, much more may he be so by a false report, by a malicious, slandering, defaming tongue. There is an artful way of talking of other people's reputation, which really, however some people salve the matter, is equal, if not superior, in malice to the worst thing they can say; this is, by rendering them suspected, talking doubtfully of their characters, and of their conduct, and rendering them first doubtful, and then strongly suspected. I don't know what to say to such a man. A gentleman came to me the other day, but I knew not what to say; I dare not say he is a good man, or that I would trust him with five hundred pounds myself; if I should say so, I should belie my own opinion. I do not know, indeed, he may be a good man at bottom, but I cannot say he minds his business; if I should, I must lie; I think he keeps a great deal of company, and the like.

Another, he is asked of the currency of his payments, and he answers suspiciously on that side too; I know not what to say, he may pay them at last, but he does not pay them the most currently of any man in the street, and I have heard saucy boys huff him at his door for bills, on his endeavouring to put them off; indeed, I must needs say I had a bill on him a few weeks ago for a hundred pounds, and he paid me very currently, and without any dunning, or often calling upon, but it was I believe because I offered him a bargain at that time, and I supposed he was resolved to put a good face upon his credit.

A tradesman, that would do as he would be done by, should carefully avoid these people who come always about, inquiring after other tradesman's characters. There are men who make it their business to do thus; and as they are thereby as ready to ruin and blow up good fair-dealing tradesmen as others, so they do actually surprise many, and come at their characters earlier and nearer than they expect they would.

Tradesmen, I say, that will thus behave to one another, cannot be supposed to be men of much principle, but will be apt to lay hold of any other advantage, how unjust soever, and, indeed, will wait for an occasion of such advantages; and where is there a tradesman, but who, if he be never so circumspect, may some time or other give his neighbour, who watches for his halting, advantage enough against him. When such a malicious tradesman appears in any place, all the honest tradesmen about him ought to join to expose him, whether they are afraid of him or no: they should blow him among the neighbourhood, as a public nuisance, as a common *barrettor*, or raiser of scandal; by such a general aversion to him they would depreciate him, and bring him into so just a contempt, that no body would keep him company, much less credit any thing he said; and then his tongue would be no slander, and his breath would be no blast, and nobody would either tell him any thing, or hear any thing from him: and this kind of usage, I think, is the only way to put a stop to a defamer; for when he has no credit of his own left, he would be unable to hurt any of his neighbour's.

CHAPTER XVI

OF THE TRADESMAN'S ENTERING INTO PARTNERSHIP IN TRADE, AND THE MANY DANGERS ATTENDING IT

There are some businesses which are more particularly accustomed to partnerships than others, and some that are very seldom managed without two, three, or four partners, and others that cannot be at all carried on without partnership; and there are those again, in which they seldom join partners together.

Mercers, linen-drapers, banking goldsmiths, and such considerable trades, are often, and indeed generally, carried on in partnership; but other meaner trades, and of less business, are carried on, generally speaking, single-handed.

Some merchants, who carry on great business in foreign ports, have what they call houses in those ports, where they plant and breed up their sons and apprentices; and these are such as I hinted could not carry on their business without partnership.

The trading in partnership is not only liable to more hazards and difficulties, but it exposes the tradesman to more snares and disadvantages by a great deal, than the trading with a single hand does; and some of those snares are these:–

1. If the partner is a stirring, diligent, capable man, there is danger of his slipping into the whole trade, and, getting in between you and home, by his application, thrusting you at last quite out; so that you bring in a snake into your chimney corner, which, when it is warmed and grown vigorous, turns about at you, and hisses you out of the house. It is with the tradesman, in the case of a diligent and active partner, as I have already observed it was in the case of a trusty and diligent apprentice, namely, that if the master does not appear constantly at the head of the business, and make himself be known by his own application and diligence to be what he is, he shall soon look to be what he is not, that is to say, one not concerned in the business.

He will never fail to be esteemed the principal person concerned in the shop, and in the trade, who is principally and most constantly found there, acting at the head of every business; and be it a servant or a partner, the master or chief loses himself extremely by the advances the other makes of that kind; for, whenever they part again, either the apprentice by being out of his time, or the partner by the expiration of the articles of partnership, or by any other determination of their agreement, the customers most certainly desire to deal with the man whom they have so often been obliged by; and if they miss him, inquire after and follow him.

It is true, the apprentice is the more dangerous of the two, because his separation is supposed to be more certain, and generally sooner than the partner; the apprentice is not known, and cannot have made his interest among the buyers, but for perhaps a year, or a year and a half, before his time expired: sooner than that he could not put himself in the way of being known and observed; and then, when his time is out, he certainly removes, unless he is taken into the shop as a partner, and that, indeed, prolongs the time, and places the injury at a greater distance, but still it makes it the more influencing when it comes; and unless he is brought some how or other into the family, and becomes one of the house, perhaps by marriage, or some other settled union with the master, he never goes off without making a great chasm in the master's affairs, and the more, by how much he has been more diligent and useful in the trade, the wounds of which the master seldom if ever recovers.

If the partner were not an apprentice, but that they either came out of their times together, or near it, or had a shop and business before, but quitted it to come in, it may then be said that he brought part of the trade with him, and so increased the trade when he joined with the other in proportion to what he may be said to carry away when he went off; this is the best thing that can be said of a partnership; and then I have this to add, first, that the tradesman who took the partner in has a fair field, indeed, to act in with his partner, and must take care, by his constant attendance, due acquaintance with the customers, and appearing in every part of the business, to maintain not his interest only, but the appearance of his interest, in the shop or warehouse, that he may, on every occasion, and to every customer, not only be, but be known to be, the master and head of the business; and that the other is at best but a partner, and not a chief partner, as, in case of his absence and negligence, will presently be suggested; for he that chiefly appears will be always chief partner in the eye of the customers, whatever he is in the substance of the thing.

This, indeed, is much the same case with what is said before of a diligent servant, and a negligent master, and therefore I forbear to enlarge upon it; but it is so important in both cases, that indeed it cannot well be mentioned too often: the master's full application, in his own person, is the only answer to both. He that takes a partner only to ease him of the toil of his business, that he may take his pleasure, and leave the drudgery, as they call it, to the partner, should take care not to do it till about seven years before he resolves to leave off trade, that, at the end of the partnership, he may be satisfied to give up the trade to his partner, or see him run away with it, and not trouble himself about it.

But if he takes a partner at his beginning, with an intent, by their joint enlarged stock, to enlarge their business, and so carry on a capital trade, which perhaps neither of them were able to do by themselves, and which is the only justifiable reason for taking a partner at all, he must resolve then to join with his partner, not only in stock, but in mutual diligence and application, that the trade may flourish by their joint assistance and constant labour, as two oxen yoked together in the same draught, by their joint assistance, draw much more than double what they could either of them draw by their single strength; and this, indeed, is the only safe circumstance of a partnership: then, indeed, they are properly partners when they are assistants to one another, whereas otherwise they are like two gamesters striving to worm one another out, and to get the mastery in the play they are engaged in.

The very word *partner* imports the substance of the thing, and they are, as such, engaged to a mutual application, or they are no more partners, but rather one is the trading gentleman, and the other is the trading drudge; but even then, let them depend, the drudge will carry away the trade, and the profit too, at last. And this is the way how one partner may honestly ruin another, and for ought I know it is the only one: for it cannot be said but that the diligent partner acts honestly in acting diligently, and if the other did the same, they would both thrive alike; but if one is negligent and the other diligent, one extravagant and expensive, the other frugal and prudent, it cannot be said to be his fault that one is rich and the other poor – that one increases in the stock, and the other is lessened, and at last worked quite out of it.

As a partner, then, is taken in only for ease, to abate the first tradesman's diligence, and take off the edge of his application, so far a partner, let him be as honest and diligent as he will, is dangerous to the tradesman – nay, the more honest and the more diligent he is, the more dangerous he is, and the more a snare to the tradesman that takes him in; and a tradesman ought to be very cautious in the adventure, for, indeed, it is an adventure – that he be not brought in time to relax his diligence, by having a partner, even contrary to his first intention; for laziness is a subtle insinuating thing, and it is a sore temptation to a man of ease and indolence to see his work done for him, and less need of him in the business than used to be, and yet the business to go on well too; and this danger is dormant, and lies unseen, till after several years it rises, as it were, out of its ambuscade, and surprises the tradesman, letting him see by his loss what his neglect has cost him.

2. But there are other dangers in partnership, and those not a few; for you may not only be remiss and negligent, remitting the weight of

the business upon him, and depending upon him for its being carried on, by which he makes himself master, and brings you to be forgot in the business; but he may be crafty too, and designing in all this, and when he has thus brought you to be as it were *nobody*, he shall make himself be all *somebody* in the trade, and in that particular he by degrees gets the capital interest, as well as stock in the trade, while the true original of the shop, who laid the foundation of the whole business, brought a trade to the shop, or brought commissions to the house, and whose the business more particularly is, is secretly supplanted, and with the concurrence of his own negligence – for without that it cannot be – is, as it were, laid aside, and at last quite thrust out.

Thus, whether honest or dishonest, the tradesman is circumvented, and the partnership is made fatal to him; for it was all owing to the partnership the tradesman was diligent before, understood his business, and kept close to it, gave up his time to it, and by employing himself, prevented the indolence which he finds breaking insensibly upon him afterwards, by being made easy, as they call it, in the assistance of a partner.

3. But there are abundance of other cases which make a partnership dangerous; for if it be so where the partner is honest and diligent, and where he works into the heart of the business by his industry and application, or by his craft and insinuation, what may it not be if he proves idle and extravagant; and if, instead of working him out, he may be said to play him out of the business, that is to say, prove wild, expensive, and run himself and his partner out by his extravagance?

There are but too many examples of this kind; and here the honest tradesman has the labouring oar indeed; for instead of being assisted by a diligent industrious partner, whom on that account he took into the trade, he proves a loose, extravagant, wild fellow, runs abroad into company, and leaves him (for whose relief he was taken in) to bear the burden of the whole trade, which, perhaps, was too heavy for him before, and if it had not been so, he had not been prevailed with to have taken in a partner at all.

This is, indeed, a terrible disappointment, and is very discouraging, and the more so, because it cannot be recalled; for a partnership is like matrimony, it is almost engaged in for better or for worse, till the years expire; there is no breaking it off, at least, not easily nor fairly, but all the inconveniences which are to be feared will follow and stare in your face: as, first, the partner in the first place draws out all his stock; and this sometimes is a blow fatal enough, for perhaps the partner cannot take the whole trade upon himself, and cannot carry on the trade upon his own stock: if he could, he would not have taken in a partner at all. This withdrawing the stock has sometimes been very dangerous to a partner; nay, has many times been the overthrow and undoing of him and of the family that is left.

He that takes a partner into his trade on this account – namely, for the support of his stock, to enjoy the assistance of so much cash to carry on the trade, ought seriously to consider what he shall be able to do when the partner, breaking off the partnership, shall carry all his stock, and the improvement of it too, with him: perhaps the tradesman's stock is not much increased, perhaps not at all; nay, perhaps the stock is lessened, instead of being increased, and they have rather gone backward than forward. What shall the tradesman do in such a case? And how shall he bear the breach in his stock which that separation would make?

Thus he is either tied down to the partner, or the partner is pinned down to him, for he cannot separate without a breach. It is a sad truth to many a partner, that when the partnership comes to be finished and expired, the man would let his partner go, but the other cannot go without tearing him all to pieces whom he leaves behind him; and yet the partner being loose, idle, and extravagant, in a word, will ruin both if he stays.

This is the danger of partnership in some of the best circumstances of it; but how hazardous and how fatal is it in other cases! And how many an honest and industrious tradesman has been prevailed with to take in a partner to ease himself in the weight of the business, or on several other accounts, some perhaps reasonable and prudent enough, but has found himself immediately involved in a sea of trouble, is brought into innumerable difficulties, concealed debts, and unknown incumbrances, such as he could no ways extricate himself out of, and so both have been unavoidably ruined together!

These cases are so various and so uncertain, that it is not easy to enumerate them: but we may include the particulars in a general or two.

1. One partner may contract debts, even in the partnership itself, so far unknown to the other, as that the other may be involved in the danger of them, though he was not at all concerned in, or acquainted with, them at the same time they were contracted.

2. One partner may discharge debts for both partners; and so, having a design to be knavish, may go and receive money, and give receipts for it, and not bringing it to account, or not bringing the money into cash, may wrong the stock to so considerable a sum as may be to the ruin of the other partner.

3. One partner may confess judgment, or give bonds, or current notes in the name, and as for the account of the company, and yet

convert the effects to his own private use, leaving the stock to be answerable for the value.

4. One partner may sell and give credit, and deliver parcels of goods to what sum, or what quantity, he thinks fit, and to whom, and so, by his indiscretion, or perhaps by connivance and knavery, lose to the stock what parcel of goods he pleases, to the ruin of the other partner, and bring themselves to be both bankrupt together.

5. Nay, to sum up all, one partner may commit acts of bankruptcy without the knowledge of the other, and thereby subject the united stock, and both or all the partners, to the danger of a commission, when they may themselves know nothing of it till the blow is given, and given so as to be too late to be retrieved.

All these, and many more, being the ill consequences and dangers of partnership in trade, I cannot but seriously warn the honest industrious tradesman, if possible, to stand upon his own legs, and go on upon his own bottom; to pursue his business diligently, but cautiously, and what we call fair and softly; not eagerly pushing to drive a vast trade, and enjoy but half of it, rather carry on a middling business, and let it be his own.

There may be cases, indeed, which may have their exceptions to this general head of advice; partnerships may sometimes prove successful, and in some particular business they are more necessary than in others, and in some they tell us that they are absolutely necessary, though the last I can by no means grant; but be that as it will, there are so many cases more in number, and of great consequence too, which miscarry by the several perplexed circumstances, differing tempers, and open knavery of partners, that I cannot but give it as a friendly advice to all tradesmen – if possible, to avoid partnerships of all kinds.

But if the circumstances of trade require partnerships, and the risk must be run, I would recommend to the tradesman not to enter into partnerships, but under the following circumstances:–

1. Not to take in any partner who should be allowed to carry on any separate business, in which the partnership is not concerned. Depend upon it, whatever other business your partner carries on, you run the risk of it as much as you do of your own; and you run the risk with this particular circumstance too, that you have the hazard without the profit or success: that is, without a share in the profit or success, which is very unequal and unfair. I know cunning men will tell you, that there may be provision made so effectually in the articles of partnership, that the stock in partnership should be concerned in no other interest or engagements but its own; but let such cunning gentlemen tell me, if the partner meets with a disappointment in his other undertakings, which wounds him so deep as to break him, will it not

affect the partnership thus far? 1. That it may cause his stock to be drawn hastily out, and perhaps violently too. 2. That it touches and taints the credit of the partner to be concerned with such a man; and though a man's bottom may support him, if it be very good, yet it is a blow to him, touches his credit, and makes the world stand a little at a stay about him, if it be no more, for a while, till they see that he shows himself upon the Exchange, or at his shop-door again, in spite of all the apprehensions and doubts that have been handed about concerning him. Either of these are so essential to the tradesman, whose partner thus sinks by his own private breaches, in which the parnership is not concerned, that it is worth while to caution the tradesman against venturing. And I must add, too, that many a tradesman has fallen under the disaster by the partner's affairs thus affecting him, though the immediate losses which the partner had suffered have not been charged upon him; and yet I believe it is not so easy to avoid being fallen upon for those debts also.

It is certain, as I formerly noted, rumour will break a tradesman almost at any time. It matters not, at first, whether the rumour be true or false. What rumour can sit closer to a man in business – his own personal misfortunes excepted – than such as this – *that his partner is broke*? That his partner has met with a loss, suppose an insurance, suppose a fall of stocks, suppose a bubble or a cheat, or we know not what, the partner is sunk, no man knows whether the partnership be concerned in it or no; and while it is not known, every man will suppose it, for mankind always think the worst of every thing.

What can be a closer stroke at the poor tradesman? He knows not what his partner has done; he has reason to fear the worst; he even knows not himself, for a while, whether he can steer clear of the rocks or no; but soon recovers, knows his own circumstances, and struggles hard with the world, pays out his partner's stock, and gets happily over it. And it is well he does so, for that he is at the brink of ruin must be granted; and where one stands and keeps up his reputation and his business, there are twenty would be undone in the same circumstance.

Who, then, would run the venture of a partner, if it were possible to avoid it? And who, if they must have a partner, would have one that was concerned in separate business, in which the partnership was not engaged?

2. If you must have a partner, always choose to have the partner rather under than over you; by this I mean, take him in for a fifth, a fourth, or at most a third, never for a half. There are many reasons to be given for this, besides that of having the greater share of profits, for that I do not give as a reason here at all; but the principal reasons are these: – First, in case of any disaster in any of the particular supposed accidents which I have mentioned, and that you should be obliged to

pay out your partner's stock, it will not be so heavy, or be so much a blow to you: and, secondly, you preserve to yourself the governing influence in your own business; you cannot be overruled, overawed, or dogmatically told, it shall, or shall not, be thus, or thus. He that takes in a partner for a third, has a partner servant; he that takes him in for a half, has a partner master – that is to say, a director, or preceptor: let your partner have always a lesser interest in the business than yourself, and be rather less acquainted with the business than yourself, at least not better. You should rather have a partner to be instructed, than a partner to instruct you; for he that teaches you, will always taunt you.

3. If you must have a partner, let him always be your junior, rather than your senior; by this I mean, your junior in business, whether he is so in years or not. There are many reasons why the tradesman should choose this, and particularly the same as the other of taking him in for a junior or inferior part of the trade – that is to say, to maintain the superiority of the business in his own hands; and this I mention, not at all upon account of the pride or vanity of the superiority, for that is a trifle compared to the rest; but that he may have the more authority to inspect the conduct of his partner, in which he is so much and so essentially concerned; and to inquire whether he is doing any thing, or taking any measures, dangerous or prejudicial to the stock, or to the credit of the partnership, that so if he finds any thing, he may restrain him, and prevent in time the mischief which would otherwise be inevitable to them both.

There are many other advantages to a tradesman who is obliged to take a partner, by keeping in his own hands the major part of the trade, which are too long to repeat here; such as his being always able to put a check to any rash adventure, any launching out into bubbles and projects, and things dangerous to the business: and this is a very needful thing in a partnership, that one partner should be able to correct the rash resolves of another in hazardous cases.

By this correcting of rash measures, I mean over-ruling them with moderation and temper, for the good of the whole, and for their mutual advantage. The Romans frequently had two generals, or consuls, to command their armies in the field: one of which was to be a young man, that by his vigour and sprightly forwardness he might keep up the spirits and courage of the soldiers, encourage them to fight, and lead them on by his example; the other an old soldier, that by his experience in the military affairs, age, and counsels, he might a little abate the fire of his colleague, and might not only know how to fight, but know when to fight, that is to say, when to avoid fighting; and the want of this lost them many a victory, and the great battle of Cannae in particular, in which 80,000 Romans were killed in one day.

To compare small things with great, I may say it is just so in the affair of trade. You should always join a sober grave head, weighed to business, and acquainted with trade, to the young trader, who having been young in the work will the easier give up his judgment to the other, and who is governed with the solid experience of the other; and so you join their ways together, the rash and the sedate, the grave and the giddy.

Again, if you must go into partnership, be sure, if possible, you take nobody into partnership but such as whose circumstances in trade you are fully acquainted with. Such there are frequently to be had among relations and neighbours, and such, if possible, should be the man that is taken into partnership, that the hazard of unsound circumstances may be avoided. A man may else be taken into partnership who may be really bankrupt even before you take him; and such things have been done, to the ruin of many an honest tradesman.

If possible, let your partner be a beginner, that his stock may be reasonably supposed to be free and unentangled; and let him be one that you know personally, and his circumstances, and did know even before you had any thoughts of engaging together.

All these cautions are with a supposition that the partner must be had; but I must still give it as my opinion, in the case of such tradesmen as I have all along directed myself to, that if possible they should go on single-handed in trade; and I close it with this brief note, respecting the qualifications of a partner, as above, that, next to no partner, such a partner is best.

CHAPTER XVII

OF HONESTY IN DEALING, AND LYING

There is some difference between an honest man and an honest tradesman; and though the distinction is very nice, yet, I must say, it is to be supported. Trade cannot make a knave of an honest man, for there is a specific difference between honesty and knavery which can never be altered by trade or any other thing; nor can that integrity of mind which describes and is peculiar to a man of honesty be ever abated to a tradesman; the rectitude of his soul must be the same, and he must not only intend or mean honestly and justly, but he must do so; he must act honestly and justly, and that in all his dealings; he must neither cheat nor defraud, over-reach nor circumvent his neighbour, nor indeed anybody he deals with; nor must he design to do so, or lay any plots or snares to that purpose in his dealing, as is frequent in the general conduct of too many, who yet call themselves honest tradesmen, and would take it very ill to have any one tax their integrity.

But after all this is premised, there are some latitudes, like poetical licences in other cases, which a tradesman is and must be allowed, and which by the custom and usage of trade he may give himself a liberty in, which cannot be allowed in other cases to any man, no, nor to the tradesman himself out of his business – I say, he may take some liberties, but within bounds; and whatever some pretenders to strict living may say, yet that tradesman shall pass with me for a very honest man, notwithstanding the liberty which he gives himself of this kind, if he does not take those liberties in an exorbitant manner; and those liberties are such as these.

1. The liberty of asking more than he will take. I know some people have condemned this practice as dishonest, and the Quakers for a time stood to their point in the contrary practice, resolving to ask no more than they would take, upon any occasion whatsoever, and choosing rather to lose the selling of their goods, though they could afford sometimes to take what was offered, rather than abate a farthing of the price they had asked; but time and the necessities of trade made them wiser, and brought them off of that severity, and they by degrees came to ask, and abate, and abate again, just as other business tradesmen do, though not perhaps as some do, who give themselves a fuller liberty that way.

Indeed, it is the buyers that make this custom necessary; for they, especially those who buy for immediate use, will first pretend positively to tie themselves up to a limited price, and bid them a little and a little more, till they come so near the sellers' price, that they, the sellers, cannot find in their hearts to refuse it, and then they are tempted to take it, notwithstanding their first words to the contrary. It is common, indeed, for the tradesman to say, 'I cannot abate anything,' when yet they do and can afford it; but the tradesman should indeed not be understood strictly and literally to his words, but as he means it, namely, that he cannot reasonably abate, and that he cannot afford to abate: and there he may be in earnest, namely, that he cannot make a reasonable profit of his goods, if he is obliged to abate, and so the meaning is honest, that he cannot abate; and yet rather than not take your money, he may at last resolve to do it, in hopes of getting a better price for the remainder, or being willing to abate his ordinary gain, rather than disoblige the customer; or being perhaps afraid he should not sell off the quantity; and many such reasons may be given why he submits to sell at a lower price than he really intended, or can afford to do; and yet he cannot be said to be dishonest, or to lie, in saying at first he cannot, or could not, abate.

A man in trade is properly to be said not to be able to do what he cannot do to his profit and advantage. The English cannot trade to Hungary, and into Slavonia – that is to say, they cannot do it to advantage; but it is better for them to trade to Venice with their goods, and let the Venetians carry on a trade into Hungary through Dalmatia, Croatia, &c., and the like in other places.

To bring it down to particular cases: one certain merchant cannot deal in one sort of goods which another merchant is eminent for; the other merchant is as free to the trade as he, but he cannot do it to profit; for he is unacquainted with the trade, and it is out of his way, and therefore he cannot do it.

Thus, to the case in hand. The tradesman says he cannot sell his goods under such a price, which in the sense of his business is true; that is to say, he cannot do it to carry on his trade with the usual and reasonable advantage which he ought to expect, and which others make in the same way of business.

Or, he cannot, without underselling the market, and undervaluing the goods, and seeming to undersell his neighbour-shopkeepers, to whom there is a justice due in trade, which respects the price of sale; and to undersell is looked upon as an unfair kind of trading.

All these, and many more, are the reasons why a tradesman may be said not to lie, though he should say he *cannot* abate, or *cannot* sell his goods under such a price, and yet may after think fit to sell you his goods something lower than he so intended, or can afford to do, rather than lose your custom, or rather than lose the selling of his goods, and taking your ready money, which at that time he may have occasion for.

In these cases, I cannot say a shopkeeper should be tied down to the literal meaning of his words in the price he asks, or that he is guilty of lying in not adhering stiffly to the letter of his first demand; though, at the same time, I would have every tradesman take as little liberty that way as may be: and if the buyer would expect the tradesman should keep strictly to his demand, he should not stand and haggle, and screw the shop-keeper down, bidding from one penny to another, to a trifle within his price, so, as it were, to push him to the extremity, either to turn away his customer for a sixpence, or some such trifle, or to break his word: as if he would say, I will force you to speak falsely, or turn me away for a trifle.

In such cases, if, indeed, there is a breach, the sin is the buyer's: at least, he puts himself in the devil's stead, and makes himself both tempter and accuser; nor can I say that the seller is in that case so much to blame as the buyer. However, it were to be wished that on both sides buying and selling might be carried on without it; for the buyer as often says, 'I won't give a farthing more,' and yet advances, as the seller says, 'I can't abate a farthing,' and yet complies. These are, as I call them, *trading lies*; and it were to be wished they could be avoided on both sides; and the honest tradesman does avoid them as much as possible, but yet must not, I say, in all cases, be tied up to the strict, literal sense of that expression, *I cannot abate*, as above.[1]

2. Another trading licence is that of appointing, and promising payments of money, which men in business are oftentimes forced to make, and forced to break, without any scrupple; nay, and without any reproach upon their integrity. Let us state this case as clearly as we can, and see how it stands as to the morality of it, for that is the point in debate.

The credit usually given by one tradesman to another, as particularly by the merchant to the wholesale-man, and by the wholesale-man to the retailer, is such, that, without tying the buyer up to a particular day of payment, they go on buying and selling, and the buyer pays money upon account, as his convenience admits, and as the seller is content to take it. This occasions the merchant, or the wholesale-man, to go about, as they call it, *a-dunning* among their dealers, and which is generally the work of every Saturday. When the merchant comes to his customer the wholesale-man, or warehouse-keeper, for money, he tells him, 'I have no money, Sir; I cannot pay

1 [The practice of haggling about prices is now very properly abandoned by all respectable dealers in goods, greatly to the comfort of both sellers and buyers.]

you now; if you call next week, I will pay you.' Next week comes, and the merchant calls again; but it is the same thing, only the warehouseman adds, 'Well, I will pay you next week, *without fail.*' When the week comes, he tells him he has met with great disappointments, and he knows not what to do, but desires his patience another week: and when the other week comes, perhaps he pays him, and so they go on.

Now, what is to be said for this? In the first place, let us look back to the occasion. This warehouse-keeper, or wholesale-man, sells the goods which he buys of the merchant – I say, he sells them to the retailers, and it is for that reason I place it first there. Now, as they buy in smaller quantities than he did of the merchant, so he deals with more of them in number, and he goes about among them the same Saturday, to get in money that he may pay his merchant, and he receives his bag full of promises, too, every where instead of money, and is put off from week to week, perhaps by fifty shopkeepers in a day; and their serving him thus obliges him to do the same to the merchant.

Again, come to the merchant. Except some, whose circumstances are above it, they are by this very usage obliged to put off the Blackwell-hall factor, or the packer, or the clothier, or whoever they deal with, in proportion; and thus promises go round for payment, and those promises are kept or broken as money comes in, or as disappointments happen; and all this while there is no breach of honesty, or parole; no lying, or supposition of it, among the tradesmen, either on one side or other.

But let us come, I say, to the morality of it. To break a solemn promise is a kind of prevarication; that is certain, there is no coming off of it; and I might enlarge here upon the first fault, namely, of making the promise, which, say the strict objectors, they should not do. But the tradesman's answer is this: all those promises ought to be taken as they are made – namely, with a contingent dependence upon the circumstances of trade, such as promises made them by others who owe them money, or the supposition of a week's trade bringing in money by retail, as usual, both of which are liable to fail, or at least to fall short; and this the person who calls for the money knows, and takes the promise with those attending casualties; which if they fail, he knows the shopkeeper, or whoever he is, must fail him too.

The case is plain, if the man had the money in cash, he need not make a promise or appointment for a farther day; for that promise is no more or less than a capitulation for a favour, a desire or condition of a week's forbearance, on his assurance, that if possible he will not fail to pay him at the time. It is objected, that the words *if possible* should then be mentioned, which would solve the morality of the case: to this I must answer, that I own I think it needless, unless the man to whom the promise was made could be supposed to believe the promise was to be performed, whether it were possible or no; which no reasonable man can be supposed to do.

There is a parallel case to this in the ordinary appointment of people to meet either at place or time, upon occasions of business. Two friends make an appointment to meet the next day at such a house, suppose a tavern at or near the Exchange: one says to the other, 'Do not fail me at that time, for I will certainly be there;' the other answers, 'I will not fail.' Some people, who think themselves more religious than others, or at least would be thought so, object against these positive appointments, and tell us we ought to say, 'I will, if it pleases God.' or 'I will, life and health permitting;'[2] and they quote the text for it, where our Saviour expressly commands to use such a caution, and which I shall say nothing to lessen the force of.

But to say a word to our present custom. Since Christianity is the public profession of the country, and we are to suppose we not only are Christians ourselves, but that all those we are talking to, or of, are also Christians, we must add that Christianity supposes we acknowledge that life, and all the contingencies of life, are subjected to the dominion of Providence, and liable to all those accidents which God permits to befall us in the ordinary course of our living in the world, therefore we expect to be taken in that sense in all such appointments; and it is but justice to us as Christians, in the common acceptation of our words, that when I say, *I will certainly* meet my friend at such a place, and at such a time, he should understand me to mean, if it pleases God to give me life and health, or that his Providence permits me to come, or, as the text says, 'If the Lord will;' for we all know that unless the Lord will, I cannot meet, or so much as live.

Not to understand me thus, is as much as to say, you do not understand me to be a Christian, or to act like a Christian in any thing; and on the other hand, they that understand it otherwise, I ought not to understand them to be Christians. Nor should I be supposed to put any neglect or dishonour upon the government of Providence in the world, or to suggest that I did not think myself subjected to it, because I omitted the words in my appointment.

2 [It was a fashion of trade in Defoe's time, and down to a somewhat later period, to thrust the phrase 'God willing' into almost every promise or announcement, the purport of which might possibly be thwarted by death or any other accident. The phrase, in particular, appeared at the beginning of all letters in which a merchant announced his design of visiting retail dealers in the provinces; as, 'God willing, I shall have the honour of waiting on you on the 15th proximo:' hence English *riders*, or commercial travellers, came to be known in Scotland by the nickname of 'God-willings.' This pious phraseology seems now to be banished from all mercantile affairs, except the shipping of goods.]

In like manner, when a man comes to me for money, I put him off: that, in the first place, supposes I have not the money by me, or cannot spare it to pay him at that time; if it were otherwise, it may be supposed I would pay him just then. He is then perhaps impatient, and asks me when I will pay him, and I tell him at such a time. This naturally supposes, that by that time I expect to be supplied, so as to be able to pay; I have current bills, or promises of money, to be paid me, or I expect the ordinary takings in my shop or warehouse will supply me to make good my promise: thus my promise is honest in its foundation, because I have reason to expect money to come in to make me in a condition to perform it; but so it falls out, contrary to my expectation, and contrary to the reason of things, I am disappointed, and cannot do it; I am then, indeed, a trespasser upon my creditor, whom I ought to have paid, and I am under affliction enough on that account, and I suffer in my reputation for it also; but I cannot be said to be a liar, an immoral man, a man that has no regard to my promise, and the like; for at the same time I have perhaps used my utmost endeavour to do it, but am prevented by many several men breaking promise with me, and I am no way able to help myself.

It is objected to this, that then I should not make my promises absolute, but conditional. To this I say, that the promises, as is above observed, are really not absolute, but conditional in the very nature of them, and are understood so when they are made, or else they that hear them do not understand them, as all human appointments ought to be understood; I do confess, it would be better not to make an absolute promise at all, but to express the condition or reserve with the promise, and say, 'I will if I can,' or, 'I will if people are just to me, and perform their promises to me.'

But to this I answer, the importunity of the person who demands the payment will not permit it – nothing short of a positive promise will satisfy – they never believe the person intends to perform if he makes the least reserve or condition in his promise, though, at the same time, they know that even the nature of the promise and the reason of the promise strongly implies the condition – I say, the importunity of the creditor occasions the breach, which he reproaches the debtor with the immorality of.[3]

3 [Notwithstanding all this ingenious reasoning, we cannot help thinking that it would be better if conditional promises were made in conditional language. It is not necessarily to be understood in all cases that a direct unreserved promise means something conditional, so that there is a liability to being much deceived and grievously disappointed by all such promises. A sound morality certainly demands that the tradesman should use the practices described in the text as rarely, and with as much reluctance, as possible, and that, like other men, he should make his words, as nearly as may be, the echo of his thoughts.]

Custom, indeed, has driven us beyond the limits of our morals in many things, which trade makes necessary, and which we cannot now avoid; so that if we must pretend to go back to the literal sense of the command; if our yea must be yea, and our nay nay; if no man must go beyond, or defraud his neighbour; if our conversation must be without covetousness, and the like – why, then, it is impossible for tradesmen to be Christians, and we must unhinge all business, act upon new principles in trade, and go on by new rules – in short, we must shut up shop, and leave off trade, and so in many things we must leave off living; for as conversation is called life, we must leave off to converse: all the ordinary communication of life is now full of lying; and what with table-lies, salutation-lies, and trading-lies, there is no such thing as every man speaking truth with his neighbour.

But this is a subject would launch me out beyond the bounds of a chapter, and make a book by itself. I return to the case particularly in hand – promises of payment of money. Men in trade, I say, are under this unhappy necessity, they are forced to make them, and they are forced to break them; the violent pressing and dunning, and perhaps threatening too, of the creditor, when the poor shopkeeper cannot comply with his demand, forces him to promise; in short, the importunate creditor will not be otherwise put off, and the poor shopkeeper, almost worried, and perhaps a little terrified too, and afraid of him, is glad to do and say any thing to pacify him, and this extorts a promise, which, when the time comes, he is no more able to perform than he was before, and this multiplies promises, and consequently breaches, so much of which are to be placed to the accounts of force, that I must acknowledge, though the debtor is to blame, the creditor is too far concerned in the crime of it to be excused, and it were to be wished some other method could be found out to prevent the evil, and that tradesmen would resolve with more courage to resist the importunities of the creditor, be the consequence what it would, rather than break in upon their morals, and load their consciences with the reproaches of it for all their lives after.

I remember I knew a tradesman, who, labouring long under the ordinary difficulties of men embarrassed in trade, and past the possibility of getting out, and being at last obliged to stop and call his people together, told me, that after he was broke, though it was a terrible thing to him at first too, as it is to most tradesmen, yet he thought himself in a new world, when he was at a full stop, and had no more the terror upon him of bills coming for payment, and creditors knocking at his door to dun him, and he without money to pay. He was no more obliged to stand in his shop, and be bullied and ruffled by his creditors, nay, by their apprentices and boys, and sometimes by porters and footmen, to whom he was forced to give good words, and sometimes strain his patience to the utmost limits: he was now no more obliged to make promises, which he knew he could not perform, and break promises as fast as he made them, and so lie continually both to God and man; and, he added, the ease of his mind which he felt upon that occasion was so great, that it balanced all the grief he was in at the general disaster of his affairs; and, farther, that even in the lowest of his circumstances which followed, he would not go back to live as he had done, in the exquisite torture of want of money to pay his bills and his duns.

Nor was it any satisfaction to him to say, that it was owing to the like breach of promise in the shopkeepers, and gentlemen, and people whom he dealt with, who owed him money, and who made no conscience of promising and disappointing him, and thereby drove him to the necessity of breaking his own promises; for this did not satisfy his mind in the breaches of his word, though they really drove him to the necessity of it: but that which lay heaviest upon him was the violence and clamour of creditors, who would not be satisfied without such promises, even when he knew, or at least believed, he should not be able to perform.

Nay, such was the importunity of one of his merchants, that when he came for money, and he was obliged to put him off, and to set him another day, the merchant would not be satisfied, unless he would swear that he would pay him on that day without fail. 'And what said you to him?' said I. 'Say to him!' said he, 'I looked him full in the face, and sat me down without speaking a word, being filled with rage and indignation at him; but after a little while he insisted again, and asked me what answer I would make him, at which I smiled, and asked him, if he were in earnest? He grew angry then, and asked me if I laughed at him, and if I thought to laugh him out of his money? I then asked him, if he really did expect I should swear that I would pay him the next week, as I proposed to promise? He told me, yes, he did, and I should swear it, or pay him before he went out of my warehouse.

I wondered, indeed, at the discourse, and at the folly of the merchant, who, I understood afterwards, was a foreigner; and though I thought he had been in jest at first, when he assured me he was not, I was curious to hear the issue, which at first he was loth to go on with, because he knew it would bring about all the rest; but I pressed him to know – so he told me that the merchant carried it to such a height as put him into a furious passion, and, knowing he must break some time or other, he was resolved to put an end to his being insulted in that manner; so at last he rose up in a rage, told the merchant, that as no honest man could take such an oath, unless he had the money by him to pay it, so no honest man could ask such a thing of him; and that, since he must have an answer, his answer was, he would not swear such an oath for him, nor any man living, and if he would not be satisfied without it, he might do his worst – and so turned from him; and knowing the man was a considerable creditor, and might do him a mischief, he resolved to shut up that very night, and did so, carrying all his valuable goods with him into the Mint, and the next day he heard that his angry creditor waylaid him the same afternoon to arrest him, but he was too quick for him; and, as he said, though it almost broke his heart to shut up his shop, yet that being delivered from the insulting temper of his creditor, and the perpetual perplexities of want of money to pay people when they dunned him, and, above all, from the necessity of making solemn promises for trifling sums, and then breaking them again, was to him like a load taken off his back when he was weary, and could stand under it no longer; it was a terror to him, he said, to be continually lying, breaking faith with all mankind, and making promises which he could not perform.

This necessarily brings me to observe here, and it is a little for the ease of the tradesman's mind in such severe cases, that there is a distinction to be made in this case between wilful premeditated lying, and the necessity men may be driven to by their disappointments, and other accidents of their circumstances, to break such promises, as they had made with an honest intention of performing them.

He that breaks a promise, however solemnly made, may be an honest man, but he that makes a promise with a design to break it, or with no resolution of performing it, cannot be so: nay, to carry it farther, he that makes a promise, and does not do his endeavour to perform it, or to put himself into a condition to perform it, cannot be an honest man. A promise once made supposes the person willing to perform it, if it were in his power, and has a binding influence upon the person who made it, so far as his power extends, or that he can within the reach of any reasonable ability perform the conditions; but if it is not in his power to perform it, as in this affair of payment of money is often the case, the man cannot be condemned as dishonest, unless it can be made appear, either

1. That when he made the promise, he knew he should not be able to perform it; or,

2. That he resolved when he made the promise not to perform it, though he should be in a condition to do it. And in both these cases the morality of promising cannot be justified, any more than the immorality of not performing it.

But, on the other hand, the person promising, honestly intending when he made the appointment to perform it if possible, and endeavouring faithfully to be able, but being rendered unable by the disappointment of those on whose promises he depended for the performance of his own; I cannot say that such a tradesman can be charged with lying, or with any immorality in promising, for the breach was not properly his own, but the people's on whom he depended; and this is justified from what I said before, namely, that every promise of that kind supposes the possibility of such a disappointment, even in the very nature of its making; for, if the man were not under a moral incapacity of payment, he would not promise at all, but pay at the time he promised. His promising, then, implies that he has only something future to depend upon, to capacitate him for the payment; that is to say, the appointments of payment by other tradesmen, who owe him (that promises) the money, or the daily supply from the ordinary course of his trade, suppose him a retailer in a shop, and the like; all which circumstances are subject to contingencies and disappointments, and are known to be so by the person to whom the promise is made; and it is with all those contingencies and possibilities of disappointment, that he takes or accepts the tradesman's promise, and forbears him, in hopes that he will be able to perform, knowing, that unless he receives money as above, he cannot.

I must, however, acknowledge, that it is a very mortifying thing to a tradesman, whether we suppose him to be one that values his credit in trade, or his principle as to honest dealing, to be obliged to break his word; and therefore, where men are not too much under the hatches to the creditor, and they can possibly avoid it, a tradesman should not make his promises of payment so positive, but rather conditional, and thereby avoid both the immorality and the discredit of breaking his word; nor will any tradesman, I hope, harden himself in a careless forwardness to promise, without endeavouring or intending to perform, from any thing said in this chapter; for be the excuse for it as good as it will, as to the point of strict honesty, he can have but small regard to his own peace of mind, or to his own credit in trade, who will not avoid it as much as possible.

CHAPTER XVIII

OF THE CUSTOMARY FRAUDS OF TRADE, WHICH HONEST MEN ALLOW THEMSELVES TO PRACTISE, AND PRETEND TO JUSTIFY

As there are trading lies which honest men tell, so there are frauds in trade, which tradesmen daily practise, and which, notwithstanding, they think are consistent with their being honest men.

It is certainly true, that few things in nature are simply unlawful and dishonest, but that all crime is made so by the addition and concurrence of circumstances; and of these I am now to speak: and the first I take notice of, is that of taking and repassing, or putting off, counterfeit or false money.

It must be confessed, that calling in the old money in the time of the late King William was an act particularly glorious to that reign, and in nothing more than this, that it delivered trade from a terrible load, and tradesmen from a vast accumulated weight of daily crime. There was scarce a shopkeeper that had not a considerable quantity or bag full of false and unpassable money; not an apprentice that kept his master's cash, but had an annual loss, which they sometimes were unable to support, and sometimes their parents and friends were called upon for the deficiency.

The consequence was, that every raw youth or unskilful body, that was sent to receive money, was put upon by the cunning tradesmen, and all the bad money they had was tendered in payment among the good, that by ignorance or oversight some might possibly be made to pass; and as these took it, so they were not wanting again in all the artifice and sleight of hand they were masters of, to put it off again; so that, in short, people were made bites and cheats to one another in all their business; and if you went but to buy a pair of gloves, or stockings, or any trifle, at a shop, you went with bad money in one hand, and good money in the other, proffering first the bad coin, to get it off, if possible, and then the good, to make up the deficiency, if the other was rejected.

Thus, people were daily upon the catch to cheat and surprise one another, if they could; and, in short, paid no good money for anything, if they could help it. And how did we triumph, if meeting with some poor raw servant, or ignorant woman, behind a counter, we got off a counterfeit half-crown, or a brass shilling, and brought away their goods (which were worth the said half-crown or shilling, if it had been good) for a half-crown that was perhaps not worth sixpence, or for a shilling not worth a penny: as if this were not all one with picking the shopkeeper's pocket, or robbing his house!

The excuse ordinarily given for this practice was this – namely, that it came to us for good; we took it, and it only went as it came; we did not make it, and the like; as if, because we had been basely cheated by A, we were to be allowed to cheat B; or that because C had robbed our house, that therefore we might go and rob D.

And yet this was constantly practised at that time over the whole nation, and by some of the honestest tradesmen among us, if not by all of them.

When the old money was, as I have said, called in, this cheating trade was put to an end, and the morals of the nation in some measure restored – for, in short, before that, it was almost impossible for a tradesman to be an honest man; but now we begin to fall into it again, and we see the current coin of the kingdom strangely crowded with counterfeit money again, both gold and silver; and especially we have found a great deal of counterfeit foreign money, as particularly Portugal and Spanish gold, such as moydores and Spanish pistoles, which, when we have the misfortune to be put upon with them, the fraud runs high, and dips deep into our pockets, the first being twenty-seven shillings, and the latter seventeen shillings. It is true, the latter being payable only by weight, we are not often troubled with them; but the former going all by tale, great quantities of them have been put off among us. I find, also, there is a great increase of late of counterfeit money of our own coin, especially of shillings, and the quantity increasing, so that, in a few years more, if the wicked artists are not detected, the grievance may be in proportion as great as it was formerly, and perhaps harder to be redressed, because the coin is not likely to be any more called in, as the old smooth money was.

What, then, must be done? And how must we prevent the mischief to conscience and principle which lay so heavy upon the whole nation before? The question is short, and the answer would be as short, and to the purpose, if people would but submit to the little loss that would fall upon them at first, by which they would lessen the weight of it as they go on, as it would never increase to such a formidable height as it was at before, nor would it fall so much upon the poor as it did then.

First, I must lay it down as a stated rule or maxim, in the moral part of the question – that to put off counterfeit base money for good money, knowing it to be counterfeit, is dishonest and knavish.

Nor will it take off from the crime of it, or lessen the dishonesty, to say, 'I took it for good and current money, and it goes as it comes;'

for, as before, my having been cheated does not authorise me to cheat any other person, so neither was it a just or honest thing in that person who put the bad money upon me, if they knew it to be bad; and if it were not honest in them, how can it be so in me? If, then, it came by knavery, it should not go by knavery – that would be, indeed, to say, it goes as it comes, in a literal sense; that is to say, it came by injustice, and I shall make it go so: but that will not do in matters of right and wrong.

The laws of our country, also, are directly against the practice; the law condemns the coin as illegal – that is to say, it is not current money, or, as the lawyers style it, it is not lawful money of England. Now, every bargain or agreement in trade, is in the common and just acceptation, and the language of trade, made for such a price or rate, in the current money of England; and though you may not express it in words at length, it is so understood, as much as if it were set down in writing. If I cheapen any thing at a shop, suppose it the least toy or trifle, I ask them, 'What must you have for it?' The shopkeeper answers – so much; suppose it were a shilling, what is the English but this – one shilling of lawful money of England? And I agree to give that shilling; but instead of it give them a counterfeit piece of lead or tin, washed over, to make it look like a shilling. Do I pay them what I bargained for? Do I give them one shilling of lawful money of England? Do I not put a cheat upon them, and act against justice and mutual agreement?

To say I took this for the lawful money of England, will not add at all, except it be to the fraud; for my being deceived does not at all make it be lawful money: so that, in a word, there can be nothing in that part but increasing the criminal part, and adding one knave more to the number of knaves which the nation was encumbered with before.

The case to me is very clear, namely, that neither by law, justice, nor conscience, can the tradesman put off his bad money after he has taken it, if he once knows it to be false and counterfeit money. That it is against the law is evident, because it is not good and lawful money of England; it cannot be honest, because you do not pay in the coin you agreed for, or perform the bargain you made, or pay in the coin expected of you; and it is not just, because you do not give a valuable consideration for the goods you buy, but really take a tradesman's goods away, and return dross and dirt to him in the room of it.

The medium I have to propose in the room of this, is, that every man who takes a counterfeit piece of money, and knows it to be such, should immediately destroy it – that is to say, destroy it as money, cut it in pieces; or, as I have seen some honest tradesmen do, nail it up against a post, so that it should go no farther. It is true, this is sinking so much upon himself, and supporting the credit of the current coin at his own expense, and he loses the whole piece, and this tradesmen are loth to do: but my answer is very clear, that thus they ought to do, and that sundry public reasons, and several public benefits, would follow to the public, in some of which he might have his share of benefit hereafter, and if he had not, yet he ought to do it.

First, by doing thus, he puts a stop to the fraud – that piece of money is no more made the instrument to deceive others, which otherwise it might do; and though it is true that the loss is only to the last man, that is to say, in the ordinary currency of the money, yet the breach upon conscience and principle is to every owner through whose hands that piece of money has fraudulently passed, that is to say, who have passed it away for good, knowing it to be counterfeit; so that it is a piece of good service to the public to take away the occasion and instrument of so much knavery and deceit.

Secondly, he prevents a worse fraud, which is, the buying and selling such counterfeit money. This was a very wicked, but open trade, in former days, and may in time come to be so again: fellows went about the streets, crying '*Brass money, broken or whole*;' that is to say, they would give good money for bad. It was at first pretended that they were obliged to cut it in pieces, and if you insisted upon it, they would cut it in pieces before your face; but they as often got it without that ceremony, and so made what wicked shifts they could to get it off again, and many times did put it off for current money, after they had bought it for a trifle.

Thirdly, by this fraud, perhaps, the same piece of money might, several years after, come into your hands again, after you had sold it for a trifle, and so you might lose by the same shilling two or three times over, and the like of other people; but if men were obliged to demolish all the counterfeit money they take, and let it go no farther, they they would be sure the fraud could go no farther, nor would the quantity be ever great at a time; for whatever quantity the false coiners should at any time make, it would gradually lessen and sink away, and not a mass of false and counterfeit coin appear together, as was formerly the case, and which lost the nation a vast sum of money to call in.

It has been the opinion of some, that a penalty should be inflicted upon those who offered any counterfeit money in payment; but besides that, there is already a statute against uttering false money, knowing it to be such. If any other or farther law should be made, either to enforce the statute, or to have new penalties added, they would still fall into the same difficulties as in the act.

1. That innocent men would suffer, seeing many tradesmen may take a piece of counterfeit money in tale with other money, and really

and *bona fide* not know it, and so may offer it again as innocently as they at first took it ignorantly; and to bring such into trouble for every false shilling which they might offer to pay away without knowing it, would be to make the law be merely vexatious and tormenting to those against whom it was not intended, and at the same time not to meddle with the subtle crafty offender whom it was intended to punish, and who is really guilty.

2. Such an act would be difficultly executed, because it would still be difficult to know who did knowingly utter false money, and who did not; which is the difficulty, indeed, in the present law – so that, upon the whole, such a law would no way answer the end, nor effectually discover the offender, much less suppress the practice. But I am not upon projects and schemes – it is not the business of this undertaking.

But a general act, obliging all tradesmen to suppress counterfeit money, by refusing to put it off again, after they knew it to be counterfeit, and a general consent of tradesmen to do so; this would be the best way to put a stop to the practice, the morality of which is so justly called in question, and the ill consequences of which to trade are so very well known; nor will any thing but a universal consent of tradesmen, in the honest suppressing of counterfeit money, ever bring it to pass. In the meantime, as to the dishonesty of the practice, however popular it is grown at this time, I think it is out of question; it can have nothing but custom to plead for it, which is so far from an argument, that I think the plea is criminal in itself, and really adds to its being a grievance, and calls loudly for a speedy redress.

Another trading fraud, which, among many others of the like nature, I think worth speaking of, is the various arts made use of by tradesmen to set off their goods to the eye of the ignorant buyer.

I bring this in here, because I really think it is something of kin to putting off counterfeit money; every false gloss put upon our woollen manufactures, by hot-pressing, folding, dressing, tucking, packing, bleaching, &c., what are they but washing over a brass shilling to make it pass for sterling? Every false light, every artificial side-window, sky-light, and trunk-light we see made to show the fine Hollands, lawns, cambrics, &c. to advantage, and to deceive the buyer – what is it but a counterfeit coin to cheat the tradesman's customers? – an *ignis fatuus* to impose upon fools and ignorant people, and make their goods look finer than they are?

But where in trade is there any business entirely free from these frauds? and how shall we speak of them, when we see them so universally made use of? Either they are honest, or they are not. If they are not, why do we, I say, universally make use of them? – if they are honest, why so much art and so much application to manage them, and to make goods appear fairer and finer to the eye than they really are? – which, in its own nature, is evidently a design to cheat, and that in itself is criminal, and can be no other.

And yet there is much to be said for setting goods out to the best advantage too; for in some goods, if they are not well dressed, well pressed, and packed, the goods are not really shown in a true light; many of our woollen manufactures, if brought to market rough and undressed, like a piece of cloth not carried to the fulling or thicking mill, it does not show itself to a just advantage, nay, it does not show what it really is; and therefore such works as may be proper for so far setting it forth to the eye may be necessary. For example:

The cloths, stuffs, serges, druggets, &c., which are brought to market in the west and northern parts of England, and in Norfolk, as they are bought without the dressing and making up, it may be said of them that they are brought to market unfinished, and they are bought there again by the wholesale dealers, or cloth-workers, tuckers, and merchants, and they carry them to their warehouses and workhouses, and there they go through divers operations again, and are finished for the market; nor, indeed, are they fit to be shown till they are so; the stuffs are in the grease, the cloth is in the oil, they are rough and foul, and are not dressed, and consequently not finished; and as our buyers do not understand them till they are so dressed, it is no proper finishing the goods to bring them to market before – they are not, indeed, properly said to be made till that part is done.

Therefore I cannot call all those setting-out of goods to be knavish and false; but when the goods, like a false shilling, are to be set out with fraud and false colours, and made smooth and shining to delude the eye, there, where they are so, it is really a fraud; and though in some cases it extremely differs, yet that does not excuse the rest by any means.

The packers and hot-pressers, tuckers, and cloth-workers, are very necessary people in their trades, and their business is to set goods off to the best advantage; but it may be said, too, that their true and proper business is to make the goods show what really they are, and nothing else. It is true, as above, that in the original dress, as a piece of cloth or drugget, or stuff, comes out of the hand of the maker, it does not show itself as it really is, nor what it should and ought to show: thus far these people are properly called finishers of the manufactures, and their work is not lawful only, but it is a doing justice to the manufacture.

But if, by the exuberances of their art, they set the goods in a false light, give them a false gloss, a finer and smoother surface than really they have: this is like a painted jade, who puts on a false colour upon her tawny skin to deceive and delude her customers, and make her seem the beauty which she has no just claim to the name of.

So far as art is thus used to show these goods to be what they really are not, and deceive the buyer, so far it is a trading fraud, which is an unjustifiable practice in business, and which, like coining of counterfeit money, is making goods to pass for what they really are not; and is done for the advantage of the person who puts them off, and to the loss of the buyer, who is cheated and deceived by the fraud.

The making false lights, sky-lights, trunks, and other contrivances, to make goods look to be what they are not, and to deceive the eye of the buyer, these are all so many brass shillings washed over, in order to deceive the person who is to take them, and cheat him of his money; and so far these false lights are really criminal, they are cheats in trade, and made to deceive the world; to make deformity look like beauty, and to varnish over deficiencies; to make goods which are ordinary in themselves appear fine; to make things which are ill made look well; in a word, they are cheats in themselves, but being legitimated by custom, are become a general practice; the honestest tradesmen have them, and make use of them; the buyer knows of it, and suffers himself to be so imposed upon; and, in a word, if it be a cheat, as no doubt it is, they tell us that yet it is a universal cheat, and nobody trades without it; so custom and usage make it lawful, and there is little to be said but this, *Si populus vult decepi, decipiatur* – if the people will be cheated, let them be cheated, or they shall be cheated.

I come next to the setting out their goods to the buyer by the help of their tongue; and here I must confess our *shop rhetoric* is a strange kind of speech; it is to be understood in a manner by itself; it is to be taken, not in a latitude only, but in such a latitude as indeed requires as many flourishes to excuse it, as it contains flourishes in itself.

The end of it, indeed, is corrupt, and it is also made up of a corrupt composition; it is composed of a mass of rattling flattery to the buyer, and that filled with hypocrisy, compliment, self-praises, falsehood, and, in short, a complication of wickedness; it is a corrupt means to a vicious end: and I cannot see any thing in it but what a wise man laughs at, a good man abhors, and any man of honesty avoids as much as possible.

The shopkeeper ought, indeed, to have a good tongue, but he should not make a common prostitute of his tongue, and employ it to the wicked purpose of abusing and imposing upon all that come to deal with him. There is a modest liberty, which trading licence, like the poetic licence, allows to all the tradesmen of every kind: but tradesmen ought no more to lie behind the counter, than the parsons ought to talk treason in the pulpit.

Let them confine themselves to truth, and say what they will. But it cannot be done; a talking rattling mercer, or draper, or milliner, behind his counter, would be worth nothing if he should confine himself to that mean silly thing called *truth* – they must lie; it is in support of their business, and some think they cannot live without it; but I deny that part, and recommend it, I mean to the tradesmen I am speaking of, to consider what a scandal it is upon trade, to pretend to say that a tradesman cannot live without lying, the contrary to which may be made appear in almost every article.

On the other hand, I must do justice to the tradesmen, and must say, that much of it is owing to the buyers – they begin the work, and give the occasion. It was the saying of a very good shopman once upon this occasion, 'That their customers would not be pleased without lying; and why,' said he, 'did Solomon reprove the buyer? – he said nothing to the shopkeeper – "It is naught, it is naught," says the buyer; "but when he goes away, then he boasteth" (Prov. xx. 14.) The buyer telling us,' adds he, 'that every thing is worse than it is, forces us, in justifying its true value, to tell them it is better than it is.'

It must be confessed, this verbose way of trading is most ridiculous, as well as offensive, both in buyer and seller; and as it adds nothing to the goodness or value of the goods, so, I am sure, it adds nothing to the honesty or good morals of the tradesman, on one side or other, but multiplies trading-lies on every side, and brings a just reproach on the integrity of the dealer, whether he be the buyer or seller.

It was a kind of a step to the cure of this vice in trade, for such it is, that there was an old office erected in the city of London, for searching and viewing all the goods which were sold in bulk, and could not be searched into by the buyer – this was called *garbling*; and the garbler having viewed the goods, and caused all damaged or unsound goods to be taken out, set his seal upon the case or bags which held the rest, and then they were vouched to be marketable, so that when the merchant and the shopkeeper met to deal, there was no room for any words about the goodness of the wares; there was the garbler's seal to vouch that they were marketable and good, and if they were otherwise, the garbler was answerable.

This respected some particular sorts of goods only, and chiefly spices and drugs, and dye-stuffs, and the like. It were well if some other method than that of a rattling tongue could be found out, to ascertain the goodness and value of goods between the shopkeeper and the retail buyer, that such a flux of falsehoods and untruths might be avoided, as we see every day made use of to run up and run down every thing that is bought or sold, and that without any effect too; for, take it one time with another, all the shopkeeper's lying does not make the buyer like the goods at all the better, nor does the buyer's lying make the shopkeeper sell the cheaper.

It would be worth while to consider a little the language that passes between the tradesman and his customer over the counter, and put it into plain homespun English, as the meaning of it really imports. We would not take that usage if it were put into plain words – it would set all the shopkeepers and their customers together by the ears, and we should have fighting and quarrelling, instead of bowing and curtseying, in every shop. Let us hark a little, and hear how it would sound between them. A lady comes into a mercer's shop to buy some silks, or to the laceman's to buy silver laces, or the like; and when she pitches upon a piece which she likes, she begins thus:

Lady. – I like that colour and that figure well enough, but I don't like the silk – there is no substance in it.

Mer. – Indeed, Madam, your ladyship lies – it is a very substantial silk.

Lady. – No, no! you lie indeed, Sir; it is good for nothing; it will do no service.

Mer. – Pray, Madam, feel how heavy it is; you will find it is a lie; the very weight of it may satisfy you that you lie, indeed, Madam.

Lady. – Come, come, show me a better piece; I am sure you have better.

Mer. – Indeed, Madam, your ladyship lies; I may show you more pieces, but I cannot show you a better; there is not a better piece of silk of that sort in London, Madam.

Lady. – Let me see that piece of crimson there.

Mer. – Here it is, Madam.

Lady. – No, that won't do neither; it is not a good colour.

Mer. – Indeed, Madam, you lie; it is as fine a colour as can be dyed.

Lady. – Oh fy! you lie, indeed, Sir; why, it is not in grain.

Mer. – Your ladyship lies, upon my word, Madam; it is in grain, indeed, and as fine as can be dyed.

I might make this dialogue much longer, but here is enough to set the mercer and the lady both in a flame, and to set the shop in an uproar, if it were but spoken out in plain language, as above; and yet what is all the shop-dialect less or more than this? The meaning is plain – it is nothing but *you lie*, and *you lie* – downright Billingsgate, wrapped up in silk and satin, and delivered dressed finely up in better clothes than perhaps it might come dressed in between a carman and a porter.

How ridiculous is all the tongue-padding flutter between Miss Tawdry, the sempstress, and Tattle, my lady's woman, at the change-shop, when the latter comes to buy any trifle! and how many lies, indeed, creep into every part of trade, especially of retail trade, from the meanest to the uppermost part of business! – till, in short, it is grown so scandalous, that I much wonder the shopkeepers themselves do not leave it off, for the mere shame of its simplicity and uselessness.

But habits once got into use are very rarely abated, however ridiculous they are; and the age is come to such a degree of obstinate folly, that nothing is too ridiculous for them, if they please but to make a custom of it.

I am not for making my discourse a satire upon the shopkeepers, or upon their customers: if I were, I could give a long detail of the arts and tricks made use of behind the counter to wheedle and persuade the buyer, and manage the selling part among shopkeepers, and how easily and dexterously they draw in their customers; but this is rather work for a ballad and a song: my business is to tell the complete tradesman how to act a wiser part, to talk to his customers like a man of sense and business, and not like a mountebank and his merry-andrew; to let him see that there is a way of managing behind a counter, that, let the customer be what or how it will, man or woman, impertinent or not impertinent – for sometimes, I must say, the men customers are every jot as impertinent as the women; but, I say, let them be what they will, and how they will, let them make as many words as they will, and urge the shopkeeper how they will, he may behave himself so as to avoid all those impertinences, falsehoods, follish and wicked excursions which I complain of, if he pleases.

It by no means follows, that because the buyer is foolish, the seller must be so too; that because the buyer has a never-ceasing tongue, the seller must rattle as fast as she; that because she tells a hundred lies to run down his goods, he must tell another hundred to run them up; and that because she belies the goods one way, he must do the same the other way.

There is a happy medium in these things. The shopkeeper, far from being rude to his customers on one hand, or sullen and silent on the other, may speak handsomely and modestly, of his goods; what they deserve, and no other; may with truth, and good manners too, set forth his goods as they ought to be set forth; and neither be wanting to the commodity he sells, nor run out into a ridiculous extravagance of words, which have neither truth of fact nor honesty of design in them.

Nor is this middle way of management at all less likely to succeed, if the customers have any share of sense in them, or the goods he shows any merit to recommend them; and I must say, I believe this grave middle way of discoursing to a customer, is generally more effectual, and more to the purpose, and more to the reputation of the shopkeeper, than a storm of words, and a mouthful of common, shop-language, which makes a noise, but has little in it to plead, except to here and there a fool that can no otherwise be prevailed with.

It would be a terrible satire upon the ladies, to say that they will not be pleased or engaged either with good wares or good pennyworths, with reasonable good language, or good manners, but they must have the addition of long harangues, simple, fawning, and flattering language, and a flux of false and foolish words, to set off the goods, and wheedle them in to lay out their money; and that without these they are not to be pleased.

But let the tradesman try the honest part, and stand by that, keeping a stock of fashionable and valuable goods in his shop to show, and I dare say he will run no venture, nor need he fear customers; if any thing calls for the help of noise, and rattling words, it must be mean and sorry, unfashionable, and ordinary goods, together with weak and silly buyers; and let the buyers that chance to read this remember, that whenever they find the shopkeeper begins his noise, and makes his fine speeches, they ought to suppose he (the shopkeeper) has trash to bring out, and believes he has fools to show it to.

CHAPTER XIX

OF FINE SHOPS, AND FINE SHOWS

It is a modern custom, and wholly unknown to our ancestors, who yet understood trade, in proportion to the trade they carried on, as well as we do, to have tradesmen lay out two-thirds of their fortune in fitting up their shops.

By fitting up, I do not mean furnishing their shops with wares and goods to sell – for in that they came up to us in every particular, and perhaps went beyond us too – but in painting and gilding, fine shelves, shutters, boxes, glass-doors, sashes, and the like, in which, they tell us now, it is a small matter to lay out two or three hundred pounds, nay, five hundred pounds, to fit up a pastry-cook's, or a toy-shop.

The first inference to be drawn from this must necessarily be, that this age must have more fools than the last: for certainly fools only are most taken with shows and outsides.

It is true, that a fine show of goods will bring customers; and it is not a new custom, but a very old one, that a new shop, very well furnished, goes a great way to bringing a trade; for the proverb was, and still is, very true, that every body has a penny for a new shop; but that a fine show of shelves and glass-windows should bring customers, that was never made a rule in trade till now.

And yet, even now, I should not except so much against it, if it were not carried on to such an excess, as is too much for a middling tradesman to bear the expense of. In this, therefore, it is made not a grievance only, but really scandalous to trade; for now, a young beginner has such a tax upon him before he begins, that he must sink perhaps a third part, nay, a half part, of his stock, in painting and gilding, wainscoting and glazing, before he begins to trade, nay, before he can open his shop. As they say of building a watermill, two-thirds of the expense lies under the water; and when the poor tradesman comes to furnish his shop, and lay in his stock of goods, he finds a great hole made in his cash to the workmen, and his show of goods, on which the life of his trade depends, is fain to be lessened to make up his show of boards, and glass to lay them in.

Nor is this heavy article to be abated upon any account; for if he does not make a good show, he comes abroad like a mean ordinary fellow, and nobody of fashion comes to his shop; the customers are drawn away by the pictures and painted shelves, though, when they come there, they are not half so well filled as in other places, with goods fit for a trade; and how, indeed, should it be otherwise? the joiners and painters, glaziers and carvers, must have all ready money; the weavers and merchants may give credit; their goods are of so much less moment to the shopkeeper, that they must trust; but the more important show must be finished first, and paid first; and when that has made a deep hole in the tradesman's stock, then the remainder may be spared to furnish the shop with goods, and the merchant must trust for the rest.

It will hardly be believed in ages to come, when our posterity shall be grown wiser by our loss, and, as I may truly say, at our expense, that a pastry-cook's shop, which twenty pounds would effectually furnish at a time, with all needful things for sale, nay, except on an extraordinary show, as on twelfth-day at night for cakes, or upon some great feast, twenty pounds can hardly be laid out at one time in goods for sale, yet that fitting up one of these shops should cost upwards of £300 in the year 1710 – let the year be recorded – the fitting up to consist of the following particulars:–

1. Sash windows, all of looking-glass plates, 12 inches by 16 inches in measure.

2. All the walls of the shop lined up with galley-tiles, and the back shop with galley-tiles in panels, finely painted in forest-work and figures.

3. Two large pier looking-glasses and one chimney glass in the shop, and one very large pier-glass seven feet high in the back shop.

4. Two large branches of candlesticks, one in the shop, and one in the back room.

5. Three great glass lanterns in the shop, and eight small ones.

6. Twenty-five sconces against the wall, with a large pair of silver standing candlesticks in the back room, value £25.

7. Six fine large silver salvers to serve sweetmeats.

8. Twelve large high stands of rings, whereof three silver, to place small dishes for tarts, jellies, &c., at a feast.

9. Painting the ceiling, and gilding the lanterns, the sashes, and the carved work, £55.

These, with some odd things to set forth the shop, and make a show, besides small plate, and besides china basins and cups, amounted to, as I am well informed, above £300.

Add to this the more necessary part, which was:–

1. Building two ovens, about £25.

2. Twenty pounds in stock for pies, cheese-cakes, &c.

So that, in short, here was a trade which might be carried on for about £30 or £40 stock, required £300 expenses to fit up the shop, and make a show to invite customers.

I might give something of a like example of extravagance in fitting up a cutler's shop, *Anglicé* a toyman, which are now come up to such a ridiculous expense, as is hardly to be thought of without the utmost contempt: let any one stop at the Temple, or at Paul's corner, or in many other places.

As to the shops of the more considerable trades, they all bear a proportion of the humour of the times, but do not call for so loud a remark. Leaving, therefore, the just reflection which such things call for, let me bring it home to the young tradesman, to whom I am directing this discourse, and to whom I am desirous to give solid and useful hints for his instruction, I would recommend it to him to avoid all such needless expenses, and rather endeavour to furnish his shop with goods, than to paint and gild it over, to make it fine and gay; let it invite customers rather by the well-filled presses and shelves, and the great choice of rich and fashionable goods, that one customer being well-served may bring another; and let him study to bring his shop into reputation for good choice of wares, and good attendance on his customers; and this shall bring a throng to him much better, and of much better people, than those that go in merely for a gay shop.

Let the shop be decent and handsome, spacious as the place will allow, and let something like the face of a master be always to be seen in it; and, if possible, be always busy, and doing something in it, that may look like being employed: this takes as much with the wiser observers of such things, as any other appearance can do.

I have heard of a young apothecary, who setting up in a part of the town, where he had not much acquaintance, and fearing much whether he should get into business, hired a man acquainted with such business, and made him be every morning between five and six, and often late in the evenings, working very hard at the great mortar; pounding and beating, though he had nothing to do with it, but beating some very needless thing, that all his neighbours might hear it, and find that he was in full employ, being at work early and late, and that consequently he must be a man of vast business, and have a great practice: and the thing was well laid, and took accordingly; for the neighbours, believing he had business, brought business to him; and the reputation of having a trade, made a trade for him.

The observation is just: a show may bring some people to a shop, but it is the fame of business that brings business; and nothing raises the fame of a shop like its being a shop of good trade already; then people go to it, because they think other people go to it, and because they think there is good choice of goods; their gilding and painting may go a little way, but it is the having a shop well filled with goods,[1] having good choice to sell, and selling reasonable – these are the things that bring a trade, and a trade thus brought will stand by you and last; for fame of trade brings trade anywhere.

It is a sign of the barrenness of the people's fancy, when they are so easily taken with shows and outsides of things. Never was such painting and gilding, such sashings and looking-glasses among the shopkeepers, as there is now; and yet trade flourished more in former times by a gread deal that it does now, if we may believe the report of very honest and understanding men. The reason, I think, cannot be to the credit of the present age, nor it it to the discredit of the former; for they carried on their trade with less gaiety, and with less expense, than we do now.[2]

My advice to a young tradesman is to keep the safe middle between these extremes; something the times must be humoured in, because fashion and custom must be followed; but let him consider the depth of his stock, and not lay out half his estate upon fitting up his shop, and then leave but the other half to furnish it; it is much better to have a full shop, than a fine shop; and a hundred pounds in goods will make a much better show than a hundred pounds' worth of painting and carved work; it is good to make a show, but not to be *all show*.

It is true, that painting and adorning a shop seems to intimate, that the tradesman has a large stock to begin with, or else they suggest he

1 [In another place, the author recommends a light stock, as showing a nimble trade. There can be little doubt that he is more reasonable here. A considerable abundance of goods is certainly an attraction to a shop. No doubt, a tradesman with little capital would only be incurring certain ruin having a larger stock than he could readily pay for. He must needs keep a small stock, if he would have a chance at all of doing well in the world. But this does not make it the less an advantage to a tradesman of good capital to keep an abundant and various stock of goods.]

2 [It is really curious to find in this chapter the same contrast drawn between the *old* and the *new* style of fitting up shops, and carrying on business, as would be drawn at the present day by nine out of every ten common observers. The notion that the shops of the past age were plain, while those of the present are gaudy, and that the tradesmen of a past age carried on all their business in a quiet way and with little expense, is as strongly impressed on the minds of the present generation, as it is here seen to have been on those of Defoe's contemporaries, a hundred and twenty years ago, although it is quite impossible that the notion can be just in both cases. The truth probably is, that in Defoe's time, and at all former times, there were conspicuous, but not very numerous, examples of finely decorated shops, which seemed, and really were, very much of a novelty, as well as a rather striking exception from the style in which such places in general were then, and had for many years been furnished. So far, however, from these proving, as Defoe anticipates, a warning to future generations, the general appearance of shops has experienced a vast improvement since those days; and the third-rate class are now probably as fine as the first-rate were at no distant period. At the same time, as in the reign of the first George, we have now also a few shops fitted up in a style of extraordinary and startling elegance, and thus forming that contrast with the general appearance of shops for the last forty years, which makes old people, and many others, talk of all the past as homely and moderate, and all the present as showy and expensive.]

would not make such a show; hence the young shopkeepers are willing to make a great show, and beautify, and paint, and gild, and carve, because they would be thought to have a great stock to begin with; but let me tell you, the reputation of having a great stock is ill purchased, when half your stock is laid out to make the world believe it; that is, in short, reducing yourself to a small stock to have the world believe you have a great one; in which you do no less than barter the real stock for the imaginary, and give away your stock to keep the name of it only.

I take this indeed to be a French humour, or a spice of it turned English; and, indeed, we are famous for this, that when we do mimic the French, we generally do it to our hurt, and over-do the French themselves.

The French nation are eminent for making a fine outside, when perhaps within they want necessaries; and, indeed, a gay shop and a mean stock is something like the Frenchman with his laced ruffles, without a shirt. I cannot but think a well-furnished shop with a moderate outside is much better to a tradesman, than a fine shop and few goods; I am sure it will be much more to his satisfaction, when he casts up his year's account, for his fine shop will weigh but sorrily in his account of profit and loss; it is all a dead article; it is sunk out of his first money, before he makes a shilling profit, and may be some years a-recovering, as trade may go with him.

It is true that all these notions of mine in trade are founded upon the principle of frugality and good husbandry; and this is a principle so disagreeable to the times, and so contrary to the general practice, that we shall find very few people to whom it is agreeable. But let me tell my young tradesmen, that if they must banish frugality and good husbandry, they must at the same time banish all expectation of growing rich by their trade. It is a maxim in commerce, that money gets money, and they that will not frugally lay up their gain, in order to increase their gain, must not expect to gain as they might otherwise do; frugality may be out of fashion among the gentry, but if it comes to be so among tradesmen, we shall soon see that wealthy tradesmen will be hard to find; for they who will not save as well as gain, must expect to go out of trade as lean as they began.

Some people tell us indeed in many cases, especially in trade, that putting a good face upon things goes as far as the real merit of the things themselves; and that a fine, painted, gilded shop, among the rest, has a great influence upon the people, draws customers, and brings trade; and they run a great length in this discourse by satirising on the blindness and folly of mankind, and how the world are to be taken in their own way; and seeing they are to be deluded and imposed upon in such an innocent way, they ought to be so far deluded and imposed upon, alluding to the old proverbial saying, '*Si populus vult decipi, decipiatur*;' that it is no fraud, no crime, and can neither be against conscience, nor prudence; for if they are pleased with a show, why should they not have it? and the like.

This way of talking is indeed plausible; and were the fact true, there might be more in it than I think there is. But I do not grant that the world is thus to be deluded; and that the people do follow this rule in general – I mean, go always to a fine shop to lay out their money. Perhaps, in some cases, it may be so, where the women, and the weakest of the sex too, are chiefly concerned; or where the fops and fools of the age resort; and as to those few, they that are willing to be so imposed upon, let them have it.

But I do not see, that even this extends any farther than to a few toy-shops, and pastry-cooks; and the customers of both these are not of credit sufficient, I think, to weigh in this case: we may as well argue for the fine habits at a puppet-show and a rope-dancing, because they draw the mob about them; but I cannot think, after you go but one degree above these, the thing is of any weight, much less does it bring credit to the tradesman, whatever it may do to the shop.

The credit of a tradesman respects two sorts of people, first, the merchants, or wholesale men, or makers, who sell him his goods, or the customers, who come to his shop to buy.

The first of these are so far from valuing him upon the gay appearance of his shop, that they are often the first that take an offence at it, and suspect his credit upon that account: their opinion upon a tradesman, and his credit with them, is raised quite another way, namely, by his current pay, diligent attendance, and honest figure; the gay shop does not help him at all there, but rather the contrary.

As to the latter, though some customers may at first be drawn by the gay appearance and fine gilding and painting of a shop, yet it is the well sorting a shop with goods, and the selling good pennyworths, that will bring trade, especially after the shop has been open some time: this, and this only, establishes the man and the credit of the shop.

To conclude: the credit raised by the fine show of things is also of a different kind from the substantial reputation of a tradesman; it is rather the credit of the shop, than of the man; and, in a word, it is no more or less than a net spread to catch fools; it is a bait to allure and deceive, and the tradesman generally intends it so. He intends that the customers shall pay for the gilding and painting his shop, and it is the use he really makes of it, namely, that his shop looking like something eminent, he may sell dearer than his neighbours: who, and what kind of fools can so be drawn in, it is easy to describe, but satire is none of our business here.

On the contrary, the customers, who are the substantial dependence of a tradesman's shop, are such as are gained and preserved by good usage, good pennyworths, good wares, and good choice; and a shop that has the reputation of these four, like good wine that needs no bush, needs no painting and gilding, no carved works and ornaments;[3] it requires only a diligent master and a faithful servant, and it will never want a trade.

3 [The author seems here to carry his objections to decoration to an extreme. Good usage, good pennyworths, good wares, and good choice, are doubtless the four cardinal points of business; but a handsome shop also goes a considerable way in attracting customers, and is a principle which no prudent tradesman will despise.]

CHAPTER XX

OF THE TRADESMAN'S KEEPING HIS BOOKS, AND CASTING UP HIS SHOP

It was an ancient and laudable custom with tradesmen in England always to balance their accounts of stock, and of profit and loss, at least once every year; and generally it was done at Christmas, or New-year's tide, when they could always tell whether they went backward or forward, and how their affairs stood in the world; and though this good custom is very much lost among tradesmen at this time, yet there are a great many that do so still, and they generally call it *casting up shop*. To speak the truth, the great occasion of omitting it has been from the many tradesmen, who do not care to look into things, and who, fearing their affairs are not right, care not to know how they go at all, good or bad; and when I see a tradesman that does not cast up once a-year, I conclude that tradesman to be in very bad circumstances, that at least he fears he is so, and by consequence cares not to inquire.

As casting up the shop is the way to know every year whether he goes backward or forward, and is the tradesman's particular satisfaction, so he must cast up his books too, or else it will be very ominous to the tradesman's credit.

Now, in order to doing this effectually once a-year, it is needful the tradesman should keep his books always in order; his day-book duly posted, his cash duly balanced, and all people's accounts always fit for a view. He that delights in his trade will delight in his books; and, as I said that he that will thrive must diligently attend his shop or warehouse, and take up his delight there, so, I say now, he must also diligently keep his books, or else he will never know whether he thrives or no.

Exact keeping his books is one essential part of a tradesman's prosperity. The books are the register of his estate, the index of his stock. All the tradesman has in the world must be found in these three articles, or some of them:–

Goods in the shop;

Money in cash;

Debts abroad.

The shop will at any time show the first of these upon a small stop to cast it up; the cash-chest and bill-box will show the second at demand; and the ledger when posted will show the last; so that a tradesman can at any time, at a week's notice, cast up all these three; and then, examining his accounts, to take the balance, which is a real trying what he is worth in the world.

It cannot be satisfactory to any tradesman to let his books go unsettled, and uncast up, for then he knows nothing of himself, or of his circumstances in the world; the books can tell him at any time what his condition is, and will satisfy him what is the condition of his debts abroad.

In order to his regular keeping his books, several things might be said very useful for the tradesman to consider:

I. Every thing done in the whole circumference of his trade must be set down in a book, except the retail trade; and this is clear, if the goods are not in bulk, then the money is in cash, and so the substance will be always found either there, or somewhere else; for if it is neither in the shop, nor in the cash, nor in the books, it must be stolen and lost.

II. As every thing done must be set down in the books, so it should be done at the very time of it; all goods sold must be entered in the books before they are sent out of the house; goods sent away and not entered, are goods lost; and he that does not keep an exact account of what goes out and comes in, can never swear to his books, or prove his debts, if occasion calls for it.

I am not going to set down rules here for book-keeping, or to teach the tradesman how to do it, but I am showing the necessity and usefulness of doing it at all. That tradesman who keeps no books, may depend upon it he will ere long keep no trade, unless he resolves also to give no credit. He that gives no trust, and takes no trust, either by wholesale or by retail, and keeps his cash all himself, may indeed go on without keeping any books at all; and has nothing to do, when he would know his estate, but to cast up his shop and his cash, and see how much they amount to, and that is his whole and neat estate; for as he owes nothing, so nobody is in debt to him, and all his estate is in his shop; but I suppose the tradesman that trades wholly thus, is not yet born, or if there ever were any such, they are all dead.

A tradesman's books, like a Christian's conscience, should always be kept clean and clear; and he that is not careful of both will give but a sad account of himself either to God or man. It is true, that a great many tradesmen, and especially shopkeepers, understand but little of book-keeping; but it is as true that they all understand something of it, or else they will make but poor work of shopkeeping.

I knew a tradesman that could not write, and yet he supplied the defect with so many ingenious knacks of his own, to secure the account of what people owed him, and was so exact doing it, and then took such care to have but very short accounts with any body, that he brought up his method to be every way an equivalent to writing; and, as I often told him, with half the study and application that those things cost him, he might have learned to write, and keep books too. He made notches upon sticks for all the middling sums, and scored with chalk for lesser things. He had drawers for every particular customer's name, which his memory supplied, for he knew every particular drawer, though he had a great many, as well as if their faces had been painted upon them; he had innumerable figures to signify what he would have written, if he could; and his shelves and boxes always put me in mind of the Egyptian hieroglyphics, and nobody understood them, or any thing of them, but himself.

It was an odd thing to see him, when a country-chap. came up to settle accounts with him; he would go to a drawer directly, among such a number as was amazing: in that drawer was nothing but little pieces of split sticks, like laths, with chalk-marks on them, all as unintelligible as the signs of the zodiac are to an old school-mistress that teaches the horn-book and primer, or as Arabic or Greek is to a ploughman. Every stick had notches on one side for single pounds, on the other side for tens of pounds, and so higher; and the length and breadth also had its signification, and the colour too; for they were painted in some places with one colour, and in some places with anther; by which he knew what goods had been delivered for the money: and his way of casting up was very remarkable, for he knew nothing of figures; but he kept six spoons in a place on purpose, near his counter, which he took out when he had occasion to cast up any sum, and, laying the spoons in a row before him, he counted upon them thus:

One, two, three, and another, one odd spoon, and t'other

By this he told up to six; if he had any occasion to tell any farther, he began again, as we do after the number ten in our ordinary numeration; and by this method, and running them up very quick, he would count any number under thirty-six, which was six spoons of six spoons, and then, by the strength of his head, he could number as many more as he pleased, multiplying them always by sixes, but never higher.

I give this instance to show how far the application of a man's head might go to supply the defect, but principally to show (and it does abundantly show it) what an absolute necessity there is for a tradesman to be very diligent and exact in keeping his books, and what pains those who understand their business will always take to do it.

This tradesman was indeed a country shopkeeper; but he was so considerable a dealer, that he became mayor of the city which he lived in (for it was a city, and that a considerable city too), and his posterity have been very considerable traders in the same city ever since, and they show their great-grandfather's six counting spoons and his hieroglyphics to this day.

After some time, the old tradesman bred up two of his sons to his business, and the young men having learned to write, brought books into the counting-house, things their father had never used before; but the old man kept to his old method for all that, and would cast up a sum, and make up an account with his spoons and his drawers, as soon as they could with their pen and ink, if it were not too full of small articles, and that he had always avoided in his business.

However, as I have said above, this evidently shows the necessity of book-keeping to a tradesman, and the very nature of the thing evidences also that it must be done with the greatest exactness. He that does not keep his books exactly, and so as that he may depend upon them for charging his debtors, had better keep no books at all, but, like my shopkeeper, score and notch every thing; for as books well kept make business regular, easy, and certain, so books neglected turn all into confusion, and leave the tradesman in a wood, which he can never get out of without damage and loss. If ever his dealers know that his books are ill kept, they play upon him, and impose horrid forgeries and falsities upon him: whatever he omits they catch at, and leave it out; whatever they put upon him, he is bound to yield to; so that, in short, as books well kept are the security of the tradesman's estate, and the ascertaining of his debts, so books ill kept will assist every knavish customer or chapman to cheat and deceive him.

Some men keep a due and exact entry or journal of all they sell, or perhaps of all they buy or sell, but are utterly remiss in posting it forward to a ledger; that is to say, to another book, where every parcel is carried to the debtor's particular account. Likewise they keep another book, where they enter all the money they receive, but, as above, never keeping any account for the man; there it stands in the cash-book, and both these books must be ransacked over for the particulars, as well of goods sold, as of the money received, when this customer comes to have his account made up; and as the goods are certainly entered when sold or sent away, and the money is certainly entered when it is received, this they think is sufficient, and all the rest superfluous.

I doubt not such tradesmen often suffer as much by their slothfulness and neglect of book-keeping, as might, especially if their business is considerable, pay for a book-keeper; for what is such a man's case, when his customer, suppose a country dealer, comes to town, which perhaps he does once a-year (as in the custom of other tradesmen), and desires to have his account made up? The London tradesman goes to his books, and first he rummages his day-book back for the whole year, and takes out the foot[1] of all the parcels sent to his chapman, and they make the debtor side of the account; then he takes his cash-book, if it deserves that name, and there he takes out all the sums of money which the chapman has sent up, or bills which he has received, and these make the creditor side of the account; and so the balance is drawn out, and this man thinks himself a mighty good accountant, that he keeps his books exactly; and so perhaps he does, as far as he keeps them at all; that is to say, he never sends a parcel away to his customer, but he enters it down, and never receives a bill from him, but he sets it down when the money is paid; but now take this man and his chap. together, as they are making up this account. The chapman, a sharp clever tradesman, though a countryman, has his pocket-book with him, and in it a copy of his posting-book, so the countrymen call a ledger, where the London tradesman's accounts are copied out; and when the city tradesman has drawn out his account, he takes it to his inn and examines it by his little book, and what is the consequence?

If the city tradesman has omitted any of the bills which the country tradesman has sent him up, he finds it out, and is sure to put him in mind of it. 'Sir,' says he, 'you had a bill from me upon Mr A.G. at such a time, for thirty pounds, and I have your letter that you received the money; but you have omitted it in the account, so that I am not so much in your debt by thirty pounds, as you thought I was.'

'Say you so!' says the city tradesman; 'I cannot think but you must be mistaken.'

'No, no!' says the other, 'I am sure I can't be mistaken, for I have it in my book; besides, I can go to Mr A.G., whom the bill was drawn upon, and there is, to be sure, your own endorsement upon it, and a receipt for the money.'

'Well,' says the citizen, 'I keep my books as exact as any body – I'll look again, and if it be there I shall find it, for I am sure if I had it, it is in my cash-book.'

'Pray do, then,' says the countryman, 'for I am sure I sent it you, and I am sure I can produce the bill, if there be occasion.'

Away goes the tradesman to his books, which he pretends he keeps so exact, and examining them over again, he finds the bill for thirty pounds entered fairly, but in his running the whole year over together, as well he might, he had overlooked it, whereas, if his

1 [The sum at the bottom, or *foot*, of the account.]

cash-book had been duly posted every week, as it ought to have been, this bill had been regularly placed to account.

But now, observe the difference: the bill for thirty pounds being omitted, was no damage to the country tradesman, because he has an account of it in his book of memorandums, and had it regularly posted in his books at home, whatever the other had, and also was able to bring sufficient proof of the payment; so the London tradesman's omission was no hurt to him.

But the case differs materially in the debtor side of the account; for here the tradesman, who with all his boasts of keeping his books exactly, has yet no ledger, which being, as I have said, duly posted, should show every man's account at one view; and being done every week, left it scarce possible to omit any parcel that was once entered in the day-book or journal – I say, the tradesman keeping no ledger, he looks over his day-book for the whole year past, to draw up the debtor side of his customer's account, and there being a great many parcels, truly he overlooks one or two of them, or suppose but one of them, and gives the chapman the account, in which he sums up his debtor side so much, suppose £136,10s.: the chapman examining this by his book, as he did the cash, finds two parcels, one £7, 15s., and the other £9, 13s., omitted; so that by his own book his debtor side was £153, 18s.; but being a cunning sharp tradesman, and withal not exceeding honest, 'Well, well,' says he to himself, 'if Mr G. says it is no more than £136, 10s. what have I to do to contradict him? it is none of my business to keep his books for him; it is time enough for me to reckon for it when he charges me.' So he goes back to him the next day, and settles accounts with him, pays him the balance in good bills which he brought up with him for that purpose, takes a receipt in full of all accounts and demands to such a day of the month, and the next day comes and looks out another parcel of goods, and so begins an account for the next year, like a current chapman, and has the credit or an extraordinary customer that pays well, and clears his accounts every year; which he had not done had he not seen the advantage, and so strained himself to pay, that he might get a receipt in full of all accounts.

It happens some years after that this city tradesman dies, and his executors finding his accounts difficult to make up, there being no books to be found but a day-book and a cash-book, they get some skilful book-keeper to look into them, who immediately sees that the only way to bring the accounts to a head, is to form a ledger out of the other two, and post every body's account into it from the beginning; for though it were a long way back, there is no other remedy.

In doing this, they come to this mistake, among a great many others of the like kind in other chapmen's accounts; upon this they write to the chapman, and tell him they find him debtor to the estate of the deceased in such a sum of money, and desire him to make payment.

The country shopkeeper huffs them, tells them he always made up accounts with Mr. G., the deceased, once a-year, as he did with all his other chapmen, and that he took his receipt in full of all accounts and demands, upon paying the balance to him at such a time; which receipt he has to show; and that he owes him nothing, or but such a sum, being the account of goods bought since.

The executors finding the mistake, and how it happened, endeavour to convince him of it; but it is all one – he wants no convincing, for he knows at bottom how it is; but being a little of a knave himself, or if you please, not a little, he tells them he cannot enter into the accounts so far back – Mr G. always told him he kept his books very exactly, and he trusted to him; and as he has his receipt in full, and it is so long ago, he can say nothing to it.

From hence they come to quarrel, and the executors threaten him with going to law; but he bids them defiance, and insists upon his receipt in full; and besides that, it is perhaps six years ago, and so he tells them he will plead the statute of limitations upon them; and then adds, that he does not do it avoid a just debt, but to avoid being imposed upon, he not understanding books so well as Mr G. pretended to do; and having balanced accounts so long ago with him, he stands by the balance, and has nothing to say to their mistakes, not he. So that, in short, not finding any remedy, they are forced to sit down by the loss; and perhaps in the course of twenty years' trade, Mr G. might lose a great many such parcels in the whole; and had much better have kept a ledger; or if he did not know how to keep a ledger himself, had better have hired a book-keeper to have come once a-week, or once a-month, to have posted his day-book for him.

The like misfortune attends the not balancing his cash, a thing which such book-keepers as Mr G. do not think worth their trouble; nor do they understand the benefit of it. The particulars, indeed, of this article are tedious, and would be too long for a chapter; but certainly they that know any thing of the use of keeping an exact cash-book, know that, without it, a tradesman can never be thoroughly satisfied either of his own not committing mistakes, or of any people cheating him, I mean servants, or sons, or whoever is the first about him.

What I call balancing his cash-book, is, first, the casting up daily, or weekly, or monthly, his receipts and payments, and then seeing what money is left in hand, or, as the usual expression of the tradesman is, what money is in cash; secondly, the examining his money, telling it over, and seeing how much he has in his chest or bags, and then seeing if it agrees with the balance of his book, that what is, and what should be, correspond.

And here let me give tradesmen a caution or two.

1. Never sit down satisfied with an error in the cash; that is to say, with a difference between the money really in the cash, and the balance in the book; for if they do not agree, there must be a mistake somewhere, and while there is a mistake in the cash, the tradesman cannot, at least he ought not to be, easy. He that can be easy with a mistake in his cash, may be easy with a gang of thieves in his house; for if his money does not come right, he must have paid something that is not set down, and that is to be supposed as bad as if it were lost; or he must have somebody about him that can find the way to his money besides himself, that is to say, somebody that should not come to it; and if so, what is the difference between that and having a gang of thieves about him? – for every one that takes money out of his cash without his leave, and without letting him know it, is so far a thief to him: and he can never pretend to balance his cash, nor, indeed, know any thing of his affairs, that does not know which way his money goes.

2. A tradesman endeavouring to balance his cash, should no more be satisfied if he finds a mistake in his cash one way, than another – that is to say, if he finds more in cash than by the balance of his cash-book ought to be there, than if he finds less, or wanting in cash. I know many, who, when they find it thus, sit down satisfied, and say, 'Well, there is an error, and I don't know where it lies; but come, it is an error on the right hand; I have more cash in hand than I should have, that is all, so I am well enough; let it go; I shall find it some time or other.' But the tradesman ought to consider that he is quite in the dark; and as he does not really know where it lies, so, for ought he knows, the error may really be to his loss very considerably – and the case is very plain, that it is as dangerous to be over, as it would be to be under; he should, therefore, never give it over till he has found it out, and brought it to rights. For example:

If there appears to be more money in the cash than there is by the balance in the cash-book, this must follow – namely, that some parcel of money must have been received, which is not entered in the book; now, till the tradesman knows what sum of money this is, that is thus not entered, how can he tell but the mistake may be quite the other way, and the cash be really wrong to his loss? Thus,

My cash-book being cast up for the last month, I find, by the foot of the leaf, there is cash remaining in hand to balance £176, 10s. 6d.

To see if all things are right, I go and tell my money over, and there, to my surprise, I find £194, 10s. 6d. in cash, so that I have £18 there more than I should have. Now, far from being pleased that I have more money by me than I should have, my inquiry is plain, 'How comes this to pass?'

Perhaps I puzzle my head a great while about it, but not being able to find out, I sit down easy and satisfied, and say, 'Well, I don't much concern myself about it; it is better to be so than £18 missing; I cannot tell where it lies, but let it lie where it will, here is the money to make up the mistake when it appears.'

But how foolish is this! how ill-grounded the satisfaction! and how weak am I to argue thus, and please myself with the delusion! For some months after, it appears, perhaps, that whereas there was £38 entered, received of Mr B.K., the figure 3 was mistaken, and set down for a figure of 5, for the sum received was £58; so that, instead of having £18 more in cash than there ought to be, I have 40s. wanting in my cash, which my son or my apprentice stole from me when they put in the money, and made the mistake of the figures to puzzle the book, that it might be some time before it should be discovered.

Upon the whole, take it as a rule, the tradesman ought to be as unsatisfied when he finds a mistake to his gain in his cash, as when he finds it to his loss; and it is every whit as dangerous, nay, it is the more suspicious, because it seems to be laid as a bait for him to stop his mouth, and to prevent further inquiries; and it is on that account that I leave this caution upon record, that the tradesman may be duly alarmed.

The keeping a cash-book is one of the nicest parts of a tradesman's business, because there is always the bag and the book to be brought together, and if they do not exactly speak the same language, even to a farthing, there must be some omission; and how big or how little that omission may be, who knows, or how shall it be known, but by casting and recasting up, telling, and telling over and over again, the money?

If there is but twenty shillings over in the money, the question is, 'How came it there?' It must be received somewhere, and of somebody, more than is entered; and how can the cash-keeper, be he master or servant, know but more was received with it, which is not, and should have been, entered, and so the loss may be the other way? It is true, in telling money there may have been a mistake, and he that received a sum of money may have received twenty shillings too much, or five pounds too much – and such a mistake I have known to be made in the paying and receiving of money – and a man's cash has been more perplexed, and his mind more distracted about it, than the five pounds have been worth, because he could not find it out, till some accident has discovered it;[2] and the reason is, because not

2 [This reminds the editor of an amusing anecdote he has heard, illustrative of the diseased accuracy, as it may be called, of a certain existing London merchant. On reckoning up his household book one year, he found that he had expended one penny more than was accounted for, and there was accordingly an error to that extent in his

knowing which way it could come there, he could not know but some omission might be made to his loss another way, as in the case above mentioned.

I knew, indeed, a strong waterman, who drove a very considerable trade, but, being an illiterate tradesman, never balanced his cash-book for many years, nor scarce posted his other books, and, indeed, hardly understood how to do it; but knowing his trade was exceedingly profitable, and keeping his money all himself, he was easy, and grew rich apace, in spite of the most unjustifiable, and, indeed, the most intolerable, negligence; but lest this should be pleaded as an exception to my general rule, and to invalidate the argument, give me leave to add, that, though this man grew rich in spite of indolence, and a neglect of his book, yet, when he died, two things appeared, which no tradesman in his wits would desire should be said of him.

I. The servants falling out, and maliciously accusing one another, had, as it appeared by the affidavits of several of them, wronged him of several considerable sums of money, which they received, and never brought into the books; and others, of sums which they brought into the books, but never brought into the cash; and others, of sums which they took ready money in the shop, and never set down, either the goods in the day-book, or the money into the cash-book; and it was thought, though he was so rich as not to feel it, that is, not to his hurt, yet that he lost three or four hundred pounds a-year in that manner, for the two or three last years of his life; but his widow and son, who came after him, having the discovery made to them, took better measures afterwards.

II. He never did, or could know, what he was worth, for the accounts in his books were never made up; nor when he came to die, could his executors make up any man's account, so as to be able to prove the particulars, and make a just demand of their debt, but found a prodigious number of small sums of money paid by the debtors, as by receipts in their books and on their files, some by himself, and some by his man, which were never brought to account, or brought into cash; and his man's answer being still, that he gave all to the master, they could not tell how to charge him by the master's account, because several sums, which the master himself received, were omitted being entered in the same manner, so that all was confusion and neglect; and though the man died rich, it was in spite of that management that would have made any but himself have died poor.

reckoning. The very idea of an error, however trifling the amount, gave him great uneasiness, and he set himself with the greatest anxiety to discover, if possible, the occasion. He employed the by-hours of weeks in the vain attempt; but at length, having one day to cross Waterloo Bridge, where there is a pontage of a penny for foot passengers, he all at once, to his inconceivable joy, recollected having there disbursed the coin in question about a twelvemonth before.]

Exact book-keeping is to me the effect of a man whose heart is in his business, and who intends to thrive. He that cares not whether his books are kept well or no, is in my opinion one that does not much care whether he thrives or no; or else, being in desperate circumstances, knows it, and that he cannot, or does not thrive, and so matters not which way it goes.

It is true, the neglect of the books is private and secret, and is seldom known to any body but the tradesman himself, at least till he comes to break, and be a bankrupt, and then you frequently hear them exclaim against him, upon that very account. 'Break!' says one of the assignees; 'how should he but break? – why, he kept no books; you never saw books kept in such a scandalous manner in your life; why, he has not posted his cash-book, for I know not how many months; nor posted his day-book and journal at all, except here and there an account that he perhaps wanted to know the balance of; and as for balancing his cash, I don't see any thing of that done, I know not how long. Why, this fellow could never tell how he went on, or how things stood with him: I wonder he did not break a long time ago.'

Now, the man's case was this: he knew how to keep his books well enough, perhaps, and could write well enough; and if you look into his five or six first years of trade, you find all his accounts well kept, the journal duly posted, the cash monthly balanced; but the poor man found after that, that things went wrong, that he went backwards, and that all went down-hill, and he hated to look into his books. As a profligate never looks into his conscience, because he can see nothing there but what terrifies and affrights him, makes him uneasy and melancholy, so a sinking tradesman cares not to look into his books, because the prospect there is dark and melancholy. 'What signify the accounts to me?' says he; 'I can see nothing in the books but debts that I cannot pay, and debtors that will never pay; I can see nothing there but how I have trusted my estate away like a fool, and how I am to be ruined for my easiness, and being a sot:' and this makes him throw them away, and hardly post things enough to make up when folks call to pay; or if he does post such accounts as he has money to receive from, that's all, and the rest lie at random, till, as I say, the assignees come to reproach him with his negligence.

Whereas, in truth, the man understood his books well enough, but had no heart to look in them, no courage to balance them, because of the afflicting prospect of them.

But let me here advise tradesmen to keep a perfect acquaintance with their books, though things are bad and discouraging; it keeps them in full knowledge of what they are doing, and how they really stand; and it brings them sometimes to the just reflections on their circumstances which they ought to make; so to stop in time, as I hinted before, and not let things run too far before they are surprised and torn to pieces by violence.

And, at the worst, even a declining tradesman should not let his books be neglected; if his creditors find them punctually kept to the last, it will be a credit to him, and they would see he was a man fit for business; and I have known when that very thing has recommended a tradesman so much to his creditors, that after the ruin of his fortunes, some or other of them have taken him into business, as into partnership, or into employment, only because they knew him to be qualified for business, and for keeping books in particular.

But if we should admonish the tradesman to an exact and regular care of his books, even in his declining fortunes, much more should it be his care in his beginning, and before any disaster has befallen him. I doubt not, that many a tradesman has miscarried by the mistakes and neglect of his books; for the losses that men suffer on that account are not easily set down; but I recommend it to a tradesman to take exact care of his books, as I would to every man to take care of his diet and temperate living, in order to their health; for though, according to some, we cannot, by all our care and caution, lengthen out life, but that every one must and shall live their appointed time,[3] yet, by temperance and regular conduct, we may make that life more comfortable, more agreeable, and pleasant, by its being more healthy and hearty; so, though the exactest book-keeping cannot be said to make a tradesman thrive, or that he shall stand the longer in his business, because his profit and loss do not depend upon his books, or the goodness of his debts depend upon the debtor's accounts being well posted, yet this must be said, that the well keeping of his books may be the occasion of his trade being carried on with the more ease and pleasure, and the more satisfaction, by having numberless quarrels, and contentions, and law-suits, which are the plagues of a tradesman's life, prevented and avoided; which, on the contrary, often torment a tradesman, and make his whole business be uneasy to him for want of being able to make a regular proof of things by his books.

A tradesman without his books, in case of a law-suit for a debt, is like a married woman without her certifcate. How many times has a woman

3 [The correct doctrine is, we *may* not, by our utmost care and diligence, avoid the causes of an early and premature death; but he who acts according to the rules which promote health, and avoids all things which tend to endanger it, has a much better chance of living to the natural period appointed for human life than he who acts otherwise – besides, as stated in the text, making his life more agreeable. The author's illustration would be more properly drawn if we were to say, 'The tradesman, by keeping exact accounts, may not succeed in contending against certain unfavourable circumstances, no more than the man who lives according to the just rules of nature may thereby succeed in eviting other evils that tend to cut short life; but as the temperate man is most likely to be healthy, so is the tradesman, who keeps exact accounts, most likely to thrive in business.']

been cast, and her cause not only lost, but her reputation and character exposed, for want of being able to prove her marriage, though she has been really and honestly married, and has merited a good character all her days? And so in trade, many a debt has been lost, many an account been perplexed by the debtor, many a sum of money been recovered, and actually paid over again, especially after the tradesman has been dead, for want of his keeping his books carefully and exactly when he was alive; by which negligence, if he has not been ruined when he was living, his widow and children have been ruined after his decease; though, had justice been done, he had left them in good circumstances, and with sufficient to support them.

And this brings me to another principal reason why a tradesman should not only keep books, but be very regular and exact in keeping them in order, that is to say, duly posted, and all his affairs exactly and duly entered in his books; and this is, that if he should be surprised by sudden or unexpected sickness, or death, as many are, and as all may be, his accounts may not be left intricate and unsettled, and his affairs thereby be perplexed.

Next to being prepared for death, with respect to Heaven and his soul, a tradesman should be always in a state of preparation for death, with respect to his books; it is in vain that he calls for a scrivener or lawyer, and makes a will, when he finds a sudden summons sent him for the grave, and calls his friends about him to divide and settle his estate; if his business is in confusion below stairs, his books out of order, and his accounts unsettled, to what purpose does he give his estate among his relations, when nobody knows where to find it?

As, then, the minister exhorts us to take care of our souls, and make our peace with Heaven, while we are in a state of health, and while life has no threatening enemies about it, no diseases, no fevers attending; so let me second that advice to the tradesman always to keep his books in such a posture, that if he should be snatched away by death, his distressed widow and fatherless family may know what is left for them, and may know where to look for it. He may depend upon it, that what he owes to any one they will come fast enough for, and his widow and executrix will be pulled to pieces for it, if she cannot and does not speedily pay it. Why, then, should he not put her in a condition to have justice done her and her children, and to know how and of whom to seek for his just debts, that she may be able to pay others, and secure the remainder for herself and her children? I must confess, a tradesman not to leave his books in order when he dies, argues him to be either.

1. A very bad Christian, who had few or no thoughts of death upon him, or that considered nothing of its frequent coming unexpected and sudden without warning; or,

2. A very unnatural relation, without the affections of a father, or a husband, or even of a friend, that should rather leave what he had to be swallowed up by strangers, than leave his family and friends in a condition to find, and to recover it.

Again, it is the same case as in matters religious, with respect to the doing this in time, and while health and strength remain. For, as we say very well, and with great reason, that the work of eternity should not be left to the last moments; that a death-bed is no place, and a sick languishing body no condition, and the last breath no time, for repentance; so I may add, neither are these the place, the condition, nor the time, to make up our accounts. There is no posting the books on a death-bed, or balancing the cash-book in a high fever. Can the tradesman tell you where his effects lie, and to whom he has lent or trusted sums of money, or large quantities of goods, when he is delirious and light-headed? All these things must be done in time, and the tradesman should take care that his books should always do this for him, and then he has nothing to do but make his will, and dispose of what he has; and for the rest he refers them to his books, to know where every thing is to be had.

CHAPTER XXI

OF THE TRADESMAN LETTING HIS WIFE BE ACQUAINTED WITH HIS BUSINESS

It must be acknowledged, that as this chapter seems to be written in favour of the women, it also seems to be an officious, thankless benefaction to the wives; for that, as the tradesman's ladies now manage, they are above the favour, and put no value upon it. On the contrary, the women, generally speaking, trouble not their heads about it, scorn to be seen in the counting house, much less behind the counter; despise the knowledge of their husbands' business, and act as if they were ashamed of being tradesmen's wives, and never intended to be tradesmen's widows.

If this chosen ignorance of theirs comes some time or other to be their loss, and they find the disadvantage of it too late, they may read their fault in their punishment, and wish too late they had acted the humbler part, and not thought it below them to inform themselves of what it is so much their interest to know. This pride is, indeed, the great misfortune of tradesmen's wives; for, as they lived as if they were above being owned for the tradesman's wife, so, when he dies, they live to be the shame of the tradesman's widow. They knew nothing how he got his estate when he was alive, and they know nothing where to find it when he is dead. This drives them into the hands of lawyers, attorneys, and solicitors, to get in their effects; who, when they have got it, often run away with it, and leave the poor widow in a more disconsolate and perplexed condition than she was in before.

It is true, indeed, that this is the women's fault in one respect, and too often it is so in many, since the common spirit is, as I observed, so much above the tradesman's condition; but since it is not so with every body, let me state the case a little for the use of those who still have ther senses about them; and whose pride is not got so much above their reason, as to let them choose to be tradesmen's beggars, rather than tradesmen's widows.

When the tradesman dies, it is to be expected that what estate or effects he leaves, is, generally speaking, dispersed about in many hands; his widow, if she is left executrix, has the trouble of getting things together as well as she can; if she is not left executrix, she has not the trouble indeed, but then it is looked upon that she is dishonoured in not having the trust; when she comes to look into her affairs, she is more or less perplexed and embarrassed, as she has not or has acquainted herself, or been made acquainted, with her husband's affairs in his lifetime.

If she has been one of those gay delicate ladies, that valuing herself upon her being a gentlewoman, and that thought it a step below herself, when she married this mechanic thing called a tradesman, and consequently scorned to come near his shop, or warehouse, and by consequence acquainting herself with any of his affairs,[1] or so much as where his effects lay, which are to be her fortune for the future – I say, if this has been her case, her folly calls for pity now, as her pride did for contempt before; for as she was foolish in the first, she may be miserable in the last part of it; for now she falls into a sea of trouble, she has the satisfaction of knowing that her husband has died, as the tradesmen call it, well to pass, and that she is left well enough; but she has at the same time the mortification of knowing nothing how to get it in, or in what hands it lies. The only relief she has is her husband's books, and she is happy in that, but just in proportion to the care he took in keeping them; even when she finds the names of debtors, she knows not who they are, or where they dwell, who are good, and who are bad; the only remedy she has here, if her husband had ever a servant, or apprentice, who was so near out of his time as to be acquainted with the customers, and with the books, then she is forced to be beholden to him to settle the accounts for her, and endeavour to get in the debts; in return for which she is forced to give him his time and freedom, and let him into the trade, make him master of all the business in the world, and it may be at last, with all her pride, has to take him for a husband; and when her friends upbraid her with it, that she should marry her apprentice boy, when it may be she was old enough to be his mother, her answer is, 'Why, what could I do? I see I must have been ruined else; I had nothing but what lay abroad in debts, scattered about the world, and nobody but he knew how to get them in. What could I do? If I had not done it, I must have been a beggar.' And so, it may be, *she is* at last too, if the boy of a husband proves a brute to her, as many do, and as in such unequal matches indeed most such people do.

1 [Most of the wives of tradesmen above a certain rather humble condition would now smile at the idea of their being expected to attend their husbands' shops, in order to form an intimate acquaintance with their affairs. Doubtless, however, in the days of Defoe, when the capitals of tradesmen were less, when provision for widows by insurance upon lives was not practised, and when the comparative simplicity of the modes of conducting business admitted it, a female in that situation would only be exercising a prudent caution, and doing nothing in the least inconsistent with the delicacy of her sex, in obeying the rules laid down in the text.]

Thus, that pride which once set her above a kind, diligent, tender husband, and made her scorn to stoop to acquaint herself with his affairs, by which, had she done it, she had been tolerably qualified to get in her debts, dispose of her shop-goods, and bring her estate together – the same pride sinks her into the necessity of cringing to a scoundrel, and taking her servant to be her master.

This I mention for the caution of those ladies who stoop to marry men of business, and yet despise the business they are maintained by; that marry the tradesman, but scorn the trade. If madam thinks fit to stoop to the man, she ought never to think herself above owning his employment; and as she may upon occasion of his death be left to value herself upon it, and to have at least her fortune and her children's to gather up out of it, she ought not to profess herself so unacquainted with it as not to be able to look into it when necessity obliges her.

It is a terrible disaster to any woman to be so far above her own circumstances, that she should not qualify herself to make the best of things that are left her, or to preserve herself from being cheated, and being imposed upon. In former times, tradesmen's widows valued themselves upon the shop and trade, or the warehouse and trade, that were left them; and at least, if they did not carry on the trade in their own names, they would keep it up till they put it off to advantage; and often I have known a widow get from £300 to £500 for the good-will, as it is called, of the shop and trade, if she did not think fit to carry on the trade; if she did, the case turned the other way, namely, that if the widow did not put off the shop, the shop would put off the widow; and I may venture to say, that where there is one widow that keeps on the trade now, after a husband's decease, there were ten, if not twenty, that did it then.

But now the ladies are above it, and disdain it so much, that they choose rather to go without the prospect of a second marriage, in virtue of the trade, than to stoop to the mechanic low step of carrying on a trade; and they have their reward, for they do go without it; and whereas they might in former times match infinitely to their advantage by that method, now they throw themselves away, and the trade too.[2]

But this is not the case which I particularly aim at in this chapter. If the women will act weakly and foolishly, and throw away the

2 [The number of widows, or at least females, carrying on trade in England, is still very considerable. In Scotland, it is a comparatively rare case. A native of the northern part of the island is apt to be strongly impressed with this fact, when, in the large manufacturing towns of England, he sees female names in so many cases inscribed upon the waggons used in the transport of goods. The complaint in the text, that females have, to such an extent, ceased to carry on the business of their deceased husbands, is probably, like many other complaints of the same kind already pointed out, merely a piece of querulousness on the part of our author, or the result of a very common mental deception.]

advantages that he puts into their hands, be that to them, and it is their business to take care of that; but I would have them have the opportunity put into their hands, and that they may make the best of it if they please; if they will not, the fault is their own. But to this end, I say, I would have every tradesman make his wife so much acquainted with his trade, and so much mistress of the managing part of it, that she might be able to carry it on if she pleased, in case of his death; if she does not please, that is another case; or if she will not acquaint herself with it, that also is another case, and she must let it alone; but he should put it into her power, or give her the offer of it.

First, he should do it for her own sake, namely, as before, that she may make her advantage of it, either for disposing herself and the shop together, as is said above, or for the more readily disposing the goods, and getting in the debts, without dishonouring herself, as I have observed, and marrying her 'prentice boy, in order to take care of the effects – that is to say, ruining herself to prevent her being ruined.

Secondly, he should do it for his children's sake, if he has any, that if the wife have any knowledge of the business, and has a son to breed up to it, though he be not yet of age to take it up, she may keep the trade for him, and introduce him into it, that so he may take the trouble off her hands, and she may have the satisfaction of preserving the father's trade for the benefit of his son, though left too young to enter upon it at first.

Thus I have known many a widow that would have thought it otherwise below her, has engaged herself in her husbands's business, and carried it on, purely to bring her eldest son up to it, and has preserved it for him, and which has been an estate to him, whereas otherwise it must have been lost, and he would have had the world to seek for a new business.

This is a thing which every honest affectionate mother would, or at least should, be so willing to do for a son, that she, I think, who would not, ought not to marry a tradesman at all; but if she would think herself above so important a trust for her own children, she should likewise think herself above having children by a tradesman, and marry somebody whose children she would act the mother for.

But every widow is not so unnatural, and I am willing to suppose the tradesman I am writing to shall be better married, and, therefore, I give over speaking to the woman's side, and I will suppose the tradesman's wife not to be above her quality, and willing to be made acquainted with her husband's affairs, as well as to be helpful to him, if she can, as to be in a condition to be helpful to herself and her family, if she comes to have occasion. But, then, the difficulty often lies on the other side the question, and the tradesman cares not to lay open his business to, or acquaint his wife with it; and many circumstances of the tradesman draw him into this snare; for I must call it a snare both to him and to her.

I. The tradesman is foolishly vain of making his wife a gentlewoman, and, forsooth, he will have her sit above in the parlour, and receive visits, and drink tea, and entertain her neighbours, or take a coach and go abroad; but as to the business, she shall not stoop to touch it; he has apprentices and journeymen, and there is no need of it.

II. Some trades, indeed, are not proper for the women to meddle in, or custom has made it so, that it would be ridiculous for the women to appear in their shops; that is, such as linen and woollen drapers, mercers, booksellers, goldsmiths, and all sorts of dealers by commission, and the like – custom, I say, has made these trades so effectually shut out the women, that, what with custom, and the women's generally thinking it below them, we never, or rarely, see any women in those shops or warehouses.

III. Or if the trade is proper, and the wife willing, the husband declines it, and shuts her out – and this is the thing I complain of as an unjustice upon the woman. But our tradesmen, forsooth, think it an undervaluing to them and to their business to have their wives seen in their shops – that is to say, that, because other trades do not admit them, therefore they will not have their trades or shops thought less masculine or less considerable than others, and they will not have their wives be seen in their shops.

IV. But there are two sorts of husbands more who decline acquainting their wives with their business; and those are, (1.) Those who are unkind, haughty, and imperious, who will not trust their wives, because they will not make them useful, that they may not value themselves upon it, and make themselves, as it were, equal to their husbands. A weak, foolish, and absurd suggestion! as if the wife were at all exalted by it, which, indeed, is just the contrary, for the woman is rather humbled and made a servant by it: or, (2.) The other sort are those who are afraid their wives should be let into the grand secret of all – namely, to know that they are bankrupt, and undone, and worth nothing.

All these considerations are foolish or fraudulent, and in every one of them the husband is in the wrong – nay, they all argue very strongly for the wife's being, in a due degree, let into the knowledge of their business; but the last, indeed, especially that she may be put into a posture to save him from ruin, if it be possible, or to carry on some business without him, if he is forced to fail, and fly; as many have been, when the creditors have encouraged the wife to carry on a trade for the support of her family and children, when he perhaps may never show his head again.

But let the man's case be what it will, I think he can never call it a hard shift to let his wife into an acquaintance with his business, if she desires it, and is fit for it; and especially in case of mortality, that she may not be left helpless and friendless with her children when her husband is gone, and when, perhaps, her circumstances may require it.

I am not for a man setting his wife at the head of his business, and placing himself under her like a journeyman, like a certain china-seller, not far from the East India House, who, if any customers came into the shop that made a mean, sorry figure, would leave them to her husband to manage and attend them; but if they looked like quality, and people of fashion, would come up to her husband, when he was showing them his goods, putting him by with a 'Hold your tongue, Tom, and let me talk.' I say, it is not this kind, or part, that I would have the tradesman's wife let into, but such, and so much, of the trade only as may be proper for her, not ridiculous, in the eye of the world, and may make her assisting and helpful, not governing to him, and, which is the main thing I am at, such as should qualify her to keep up the business for herself and children, if her husband should be taken away, and she be left destitute in the world, as many are.

Thus much, I think, it is hard a wife should not know, and no honest tradesman ought to refuse it; and above all, it is a great pity the wives of tradesmen, who so often are reduced to great inconvenience for want of it, should so far withstand their own felicity, as to refuse to be thus made acquainted with their business, by which weak and foolish pride they expose themselves, as I have observed, to the misfortune of throwing the business away, when they may come to want it, and when the keeping it up might be the restoring of their family, and providing for their children.

For, not to compliment tradesmen too much, their wives are not all ladies, nor are their children all born to be gentlemen. Trade, on the contrary, is subject to contingencies; some begin poor, and end rich; others, and those very many, begin rich, and end poor: and there are innumerable circumstances which may attend a tradesman's family, which may make it absolutely necessary to preserve the trade for his children, if possible; the doing which may keep them from misery, and raise them all in the world, and the want of it, on the other hand, sinks and suppresses them. For example:–

A tradesman has begun the world about six or seven years; he has, by his industry and good understanding in business, just got into a flourishing trade, by which he clears five or six hundred pounds a-year; and if it should please God to spare his life for twenty years or more, he would certainly be a rich man, and get a good estate; but on a sudden, and in the middle of all his prosperity, he is snatched away by a sudden fit of sickness, and his widow is left in a desolate despairing condition, having five children, and big with another; but the eldest of these is not above six years old, and, though he is a boy, yet he is utterly incapable to be concerned in the business; so the trade which (had his father lived to bring him up in his shop or warehouse) would have been an estate to him, is like to be lost, and perhaps go all away to the eldest apprentice, who, however, wants two years of his time. Now, what is to be done for this unhappy family?

'Done!' says the widow; 'why, I will never let the trade fall so, that should be the making of my son, and in the meantime be the maintenance of all my children.'

'Why, what can you do, child?' says her father, or other friends; 'you know nothing of it. Mr ——— did not acquaint you with his business.'

'That is true,' says the widow; 'he did not, because I was a fool, and did not care to look much into it, and that was my fault. Mr ——— did not press me to it, because he was afraid I might think he intended to put me upon it; but he often used to say, that if he should drop off before his boys were fit to come into the shop, it would be a sad loss to them – that the trade would make gentlemen of a couple of them, and it would be great pity it should go away from them.'

'But what does that signify now, child?' adds the father; 'you see it is so; and how can it be helped?'

'Why,' says the widow, 'I used to ask him if he thought I could carry it on for them, if such a thing should happen?'

'And what answer did he make?' says the father.

'He shook his head,' replied the widow, 'and answered, "Yes, I might, if I had good servants, and if I would look a little into it beforehand."'

'Why,' says the father, 'he talked as if he had foreseen his end.'

'I think he did foresee it,' says she, 'for he was often talking thus.'

'And why did you not take the hint then,' says her father, 'and acquaint yourself a little with things, that you might have been prepared for such an unhappy circumstance, whatever might happen?'

'Why, so I did,' says the widow, 'and have done for above two years past; he used to show me his letters, and his books, and I know where he bought every thing; and I know a little of goods too, when they are good, and when bad, and the prices; also I know all the country-people he dealt with, and have seen most of them, and talked with them. Mr —— used to bring them up to dinner sometimes, and he would prompt my being acquainted with them, and would sometimes talk of his business with them at table, on purpose that I might hear it; and I know a little how to sell, too, for I have stood by him sometimes, and seen the customers and him chaffer with one another.'

'And did your husband like that you did so?' says the father.

'Yes,' says she, 'he loved to see me do it, and often told me he did so; and told me, that if he were dead, he believed I might carry on the trade as well as he.'

'But he did not believe so, I doubt,' says the father.

'I do not know as to that, but I sold goods several times to some customers, when he has been out of the way.'

'And was he pleased with it when he came home? Did you do it to his mind?'

'Nay, I have served a customer sometimes when he has been in the warehouse, and he would go away to his counting-house on purpose, and say, "I'll leave you and my wife to make the bargain," and I have pleased the customer and him too.'

'Well,' says the father, 'do you think you could carry on the trade?'

'I believe I could, if I had but an honest fellow of a journeyman for a year or two to write in the books, and go abroad among customers.'

'Well, you have two apprentices; one of them begins to understand things very much, and seems to be a diligent lad.'

'He comes forward, indeed, and will be very useful, if he does not grow too forward, upon a supposition that I shall want him too much: but it will be necessary to have a man to be above him for a while.'

'Well,' says the father, 'we will see to get you such a one.'

In short, they got her a man to assist to keep the books, go to Exchange, and do the business abroad, and the widow carried on the business with great application and success, till her eldest son grew up, and was first taken into the shop as an apprentice to his mother; the eldest apprentice served her faithfully, and was her journeyman four years after his time was out; then she took him in partner to one-fourth of the trade, and when her son came of age, she gave the apprentice one of her daughters, and enlarged his share to a third, gave her own son another third, and kept a third for herself to support the family.

Thus the whole trade was preserved, and the son and son-in-law grew rich in it, and the widow, who grew as skilful in the business as her husband was before her, advanced the fortunes of all the rest of her children very considerably.

This was an example of the husband's making the wife (but a little) acquainted with his business; and if this had not been the case, the trade had been lost, and the family left just to divide what the father left; which, as they were seven of them, mother and all, would not have been considerable enough to have raised them above just the degree of having bread to eat, and none to spare.

I hardly need give any examples where tradesmen die, leaving flourishing businesses, and good trades, but leaving their wives ignorant and destitute, neither understanding their business, nor knowing how to learn, having been too proud to stoop to it when they had husbands, and not courage or heart to do it when they have none. The town is so full of such as these, that this book can scarce fall into the hands of any readers but who will be able to name them among their own acquaintance.

These indolent, lofty ladies have generally the mortification to see their husbands' trades catched up by apprentices or journeymen in the shop, or by other shopkeepers in the neighbourhood, and of the same business, that might have enriched them, and descended to their children; to see their bread carried away by strangers, and other families flourishing on the spoils of their fortunes.

And this brings me to speak of those ladies, who, though they do, perhaps, for want of better offers, stoop to wed a trade, as we call it, and take up with a mechanic; yet all the while they are the tradesmen's wives, they endeavour to preserve the distinction of their fancied character; carry themselves as if they thought they were still above their station, and that, though they were unhappily yoked with a tradesman, they would still keep up the dignity of their birth, and be called gentlewomen; and in order to this, would behave like such all the way, whatever rank they were levelled with by the misfortune of their circumstances.

This is a very unhappy, and, indeed, a most unseasonable kind of pride; and if I might presume to add a word here by way of caution to such ladies, it should be to consider, before they marry tradesmen, the great disadvantages they lay themselves under, in submitting to be a tradesman's wife, but not putting themselves in a condition to take the benefit, as well as the inconvenience of it; for while they are above the circumstances of the tradesman's wife, they are deprived of all the remedy against the miseries of a tradesman's widow; and if the man dies, and leaves them little or nothing but the trade to carry on and maintain them, they, being unacquainted with that, are undone.

A lady that stoops to marry a tradesman, should consider the usage of England among the gentry and persons of distinction, where the case is thus: if a lady, who has a title of honour, suppose it be a countess, or if she were a duchess, it is all one – if, I say, she stoop to marry a private gentleman, she ceases to rank for the future as a countess, or duchess, but must be content to be, for the time to come, what her husband can entitle her to, and no other; and, excepting the courtesy of the people calling her my Lady Duchess, or the Countess, she is no more than plain Mrs such a one, meaning the name of her husband, and no other.

Thus, if a baronet's widow marry a tradesman in London, she is no more my lady, but plain Mrs ——, the draper's wife, &c. The application of the thing is thus: if the lady think fit to marry a mechanic, say a glover, or a cutler, or whatever it is, she should remember she is a glover's wife from that time, and no more; and to keep up her dignity, when fortune has levelled her circumstances, is but a piece of unseasonable pageantry, and will do her no service at all. The thing she is to inquire is, what she must do if Mr ——, the glover, or cutler, should die? whether she can carry on the trade afterwards, or whether she can live without it? If she find she cannot live without it, it is her prudence to consider in time, and so to acquaint herself with the trade, that she may be able to do it when she comes to it.

I do confess, there is nothing more ridiculous than the double pride of the ladies of this age, with respect to marrying what they call below their birth. Some ladies of good families, though but of mean fortune, are so stiff upon the point of honour, that they refuse to marry tradesmen, nay, even merchants, though vastly above them in wealth and fortune, only because they are tradesmen, or, as they are pleased to call them, though improperly, mechanics; and though perhaps they have not above £500 or £1000 to their portion, scorn the man for his rank, who does but turn round, and has his choice of wives, perhaps, with two, or three, or four thousand pounds, before their faces.

The gentlemen of quality, we see, act upon quite another foot, and, I may say, with much more judgment, seeing nothing is more frequent than when any noble family are loaded with titles and honour rather than fortune, they come down into the city, and choose wives among the merchants' and tradesmen's daughters to raise their families; and I am mistaken, if at this time we have not several duchesses, countesses, and ladies of rank, who are the daughters of citizens and tradesmen, as the Duchess of Bedford, of A ——e, of Wharton, and others; the Countess of Exeter, of Onslow, and many more, too many to name, where it is thought no dishonour at all for those persons to have matched into rich families, though not ennobled; and we have seen many trading families lay the foundation of nobility by their wealth and opulence – as Mr Child, for example, afterwards Sir Josiah Child, whose posterity by his two daughters are now Dukes of Beaufort and of Bedford, and his grandson Lord Viscount Castlemain, and yet he himself began a tradesman, and in circumstances very mean.

But this stiffness of the ladies, in refusing to marry tradesmen, though it is weak in itself, is not near so weak as the folly of those who first do stoop to marry thus, and yet think to maintain the dignity of their birth in spite of the meanness of their fortune, and so, carrying themselves above that station in which Providence has placed them, disable themselves from receiving the benefit which their condition offers them, upon any subsequent changes of their life.

This extraordinary stiffness, I have known, has brought many a well-bred gentlewoman to misery and the utmost distress, whereas, had they been able to have stooped to the subsequent circumstances of life, which Providence also thought fit to make their lot, they might have lived comfortably and plentifully all their days.

It is certainly every lady's prudence to bring her spirit down to her condition; and if she thinks fit, or it is any how her lot to marry a tradesman, which many ladies of good families have found it for their advantage to do – I say, if it be her lot, she should take care she does not make that a curse to her, which would be her blessing, by despising her own condition, and putting herself into a posture not to enjoy it.

In all this, I am to be understood to mean that unhappy temper, which I find so much among the tradesman's wives at this time, of being above taking any notice of their husband's affairs, as if nothing were before them but a constant settled state of prosperity, and it were impossible for them to taste any other fortune; whereas, that very hour they embark with a tradesman, they ought to remember that they are entering a state of life full of accidents and hazards, and that innumerable families, in as good circumstances as theirs, fall every day into disasters and misfortunes, and that a tradesman's condition is liable to more casualties than any other life whatever.

How many widows of tradesmen, nay, and wives of broken and ruined tradesmen, do we daily see recover themselves and their shattered families, when the man has been either snatched away by death, or demolished by misfortunes, and has been forced to fly to the East or West Indies, and forsake his family in search of bread?

Women, when once they give themselves leave to stoop to their own circumstances, and think fit to rouse up themselves to their own relief, are not so helpless and shiftless creatures as some would make them appear in the world; and we see whole families in trade frequently recovered by their industry: but, then, they are such women as can stoop to it, and can lay aside the particular pride of their first years; and who, without looking back to what they have been, can be content to look into what Providence has brought them to be, and what they must infallibly be, if they do not vigorously apply to the affairs which offer, and fall into the business which their husbands leave them the introduction to, and do not level their minds to their condition. It may, indeed, be hard to do this at first, but necessity is a spur to industry, and will make things easy where they seem difficult; and this necessity will humble the minds of those whom nothing else could make to stoop; and where it does not, it is a defect of the understanding, as well as of prudence, and must reflect upon the senses as well as the morals of the person.

CHAPTER XXII

OF THE DIGNITY OF TRADE IN ENGLAND MORE THAN IN OTHER COUNTRIES

It is said of England, by way of distinction, and we all value ourselves upon it, that it is a trading country; and King Charles II., who was perhaps that prince of all the kings that ever reigned in England, that best understood the country and the people that he governed, used to say, 'That the tradesmen were the only gentry in England.' His majesty spoke it merrily, but it had a happy signification in it, such as was peculiar to the bright genius of that prince, who, though he was not the best governor, was the best acquainted with the world of all the princes of his age, if not of all the men in it; and, though it be a digression, give me leave, after having quoted the king, to add three short observations of my own, in favour of England, and of the people and trade of it, and yet without the least partiality to our own country.

I. We are not only a trading country, but the greatest trading country in the world.

II. Our climate is the most agreeable climate in the world to live in.

III. Our Englishmen are the stoutest and best men (I mean what we call men of their hands) in the world.

These are great things to advance in our own favour, and yet to pretend not to be partial too; and, therefore, I shall give my reasons, which I think support my opinion, and they shall be as short as the heads themselves, that I may not go too much off from my subject.

1. We are the greatest trading country in the world, because we have the greatest exportation of the growth and product of our land, and of the manufacture and labour of our people; and the greatest importation and consumption of the growth, product, and manufactures of other countries from abroad, of any nation in the world.[1]

2. Our climate is the best and most agreeable, because a man can be more out of doors in England than in other countries. This was King

1 [We have here a pleasing trait of the superior sagacity of Defoe, in as far as it was a prevalent notion down to his time, and even later (nor is it, perhaps, altogether extinguished yet), that the prosperity of a country was marked by its excess of exports over imports. Defoe justly ranks the amount of importation on a level with that of exportation, as indicative of the well-being of the country.]

Charles II.'s reason for it, and I cannot name it, without doing justice to his majesty in it.

3. Our men are the stoutest and best, because, strip them naked from the waist upwards, and give them no weapons at all but their hands and heels, and turn them into a room, or stage, and lock them in with the like number of other men of any nation, man for man, and they shall beat the best men you shall find in the world.

From this digression, which I hope will not be disagreeable, as it is not very tedious, I come back to my first observation, that England is a trading country, and two things I offer from that head.

First, our tradesmen are not, as in other countries, the meanest of our people.

Secondly, some of the greatest and best, and most flourishing families, among not the gentry only, but even the nobility, have been raised from trade, owe their beginning, their wealth, and their estates, to trade; and, I may add,

Thirdly, those families are not at all ashamed of their original, and, indeed, have no occasion to be ashamed of it.

It is true, that in England we have a numerous and an illustrious nobility and gentry; and it is true, also, that not so many of those families have raised themselves by the sword as in other nations, though we have not been without men of fame in the field too.

But trade and learning have been the two chief steps by which our gentlemen have raised their relations, and have built their fortunes; and from which they have ascended up to the prodigious height, both in wealth and number, which we see them now risen to.

As so many of our noble and wealthy families are raised by, and derive from trade, so it is true, and, indeed, it cannot well be otherwise, that many of the younger branches of our gentry, and even of the nobility itself, have descended again into the spring from whence they flowed, and have become tradesmen; and thence it is, that, as I said above, our tradesmen in England are not, as it generally is in other countries, always of the meanest of our people.

Indeed, I might have added here, that trade itself in England is not, as it generally is in other countries, the meanest thing the men can turn their hand to; but, on the contrary, trade is the readiest way for men to raise their fortunes and families; and, therefore, it is a field for men of figure and of good families to enter upon.

N.B. By trade we must be understood to include navigation, and foreign discoveries, because they are, generally speaking, all promoted and carried on by trade, and even by tradesmen, as well as merchants; and the tradesmen are at this time as much concerned in shipping (as owners) as the merchants; only the latter may be said to be the chief employers of the shipping.

Having thus done a particular piece of justice to ourselves, in the value we put upon trade and tradesmen in England, it reflects very much upon the understanding of those refined heads, who pretend to depreciate that part of the nation, which is so infinitely superior in number and in wealth to the families who call themselves gentry, or quality, and so infinitely more numerous.

As to the wealth of the nation, that undoubtedly lies chiefly among the trading part of the people; and though there are a great many families raised within few years, in the late war, by great employments, and by great actions abroad, to the honour of the English gentry; yet how many more families among the tradesmen have been raised to immense estates, even during the same time, by the attending circumstances of the war, such as the clothing, the paying, the victualling and furnishing, &c., both army and navy! And by whom have the prodigious taxes been paid, the loans supplied, and money advanced upon all occasions? By whom are the banks and companies carried on? – and on whom are the customs and excises levied? Have not the trade and tradesmen born the burden of the war? – and do they not still pay four millions a-year interest for the public debts? On whom are the funds levied, and by whom the public credit supported? Is not trade the inexhausted fund of all funds, and upon which all the rest depend?

As is the trade, so in proportion are the tradesmen; and how wealthy are tradesmen in almost all the several parts of England, as well as in London! How ordinary is it to see a tradesman go off the stage, even but from mere shopkeeping, with from ten to forty thousand pounds' estate, to divide among his family! – when, on the contrary, take the gentry in England from one end to the other, except a few here and there, what with excessive high living, which is of late grown so much into a disease, and the other ordinary circumstances of families, we find few families of the lower gentry, that is to say, from six or seven hundred a-year downwards, but they are in debt and in necessitous circumstances, and a great many of greater estates also.

On the other hand, let any one who is acquainted with England, look but abroad into the several counties, especially near London, or within fifty miles of it. How are the ancient families worn out by time and family misfortunes, and the estates possessed by a new race of tradesmen, grown up into families of gentry, and established by the immense wealth, gained, as I may say, behind the counter, that is, in the shop, the warehouse, and the counting-house! How are the sons of tradesmen ranked among the prime of the gentry! How are the daughters of tradesmen at this time adorned with the ducal coronets, and seen riding in the coaches of the best of our nobility! Nay, many of our trading gentlemen at this time refuse to be ennobled, scorn being knighted, and content themselves with being known to be rated among the richest commoners in the nation. And it must be acknowledged, that, whatever they be as to court-breeding and to manners, they, generally speaking, come behind none of the gentry in knowledge of the world.

At this very day we see the son of Sir Thomas Scawen matched into the ducal family of Bedford, and the son of Sir James Bateman into the princely house of Marlborough, both whose ancestors, within the memory of the writer of these sheets, were tradesmen in London; the first Sir William Scawen's apprentice, and the latter's grandfather a porter upon or near London Bridge.

How many noble seats, superior to the palaces of sovereign princes (in some countries) do we see erected within few miles of this city by tradesmen, or the sons of tradesmen, while the seats and castles of the ancient gentry, like their families, look worn out, and fallen into decay. Witness the noble house of Sir John Eyles, himself a merchant, at Giddy-hall near Rumford; Sir Gregory Page on Blackheath, the son of a brewer; Sir Nathaniel Mead near Wealgreen, his father a linen-draper, with many others too long to repeat; and, to crown all, the Lord Castlemains at Wanstead, his father Sir Josiah Child, originally a tradesman.

It was a smart, but just repartee, of a London tradesman, when a gentleman, who had a good estate too, rudely reproached him in company, and bade him hold his tongue, for he was no gentleman. 'No, Sir,' says he, 'but I can buy a gentleman, and therefore I claim a liberty to speak among gentlemen.'

Again, in how superior a port or figure (as we now call it) do our tradesmen live, to what the middling gentry either do or can support! An ordinary tradesman now, not in the city only, but in the country, shall spend more money by the year, than a gentleman of four or five hundred pounds a-year can do, and shall increase and lay up every year too, whereas the gentleman shall at the best stand stock still, just where he began, nay, perhaps decline; and as for the lower gentry, from a hundred pounds a-year to three hundred, or thereabouts, though they are often as proud and high in their appearance as the other – as to them, I say, a shoemaker in London shall keep a better house, spend more money, clothe his family better, and yet grow rich too. It is evident where the difference lies; *an estate's a pond, but a trade's a spring*: the first, if it keeps full, and the water wholesome, by the ordinary supplies and drains from the neighbouring grounds, it is well, and it is all that is expected; but the other is an inexhausted current, which not only fills the pond, and keeps it full, but is continually running over, and fills all the lower ponds and places about it.

This being the case in England, and our trade being so vastly great, it is no wonder that the tradesmen in England fill the lists of our nobility and gentry; no wonder that the gentlemen of the best families marry tradesmen's daughters, and put their younger sons apprentices to tradesmen; and how often do these younger sons come to buy the elder son's estates, and restore the family, when the elder, and head of the house, proving rakish and extravagant, has wasted his patrimony, and is obliged to make out the blessing of Israel's family, where the younger son bought the birthright, and the elder was doomed to serve him.

Trade is so far here from being inconsistent with a gentleman, that, in short, trade in England makes gentlemen, and has peopled this nation with gentlemen; for after a generation or two the tradesmen's children, or at least their grand-children, come to be as good gentlemen, statesmen, parliament-men, privy-counsellors, judges, bishops, and noblemen, as those of the highest birth and the most ancient families, and nothing too high for them. Thus the late Earl of Haversham was originally a merchant; the late Secretary Craggs was the son of a barber; the present Lord Castlemain's father was a tradesman; the great-grandfather of the present Duke of Bedford the same; and so of several others. Nor do we find any defect either in the genius or capacities of the posterity of tradesmen, arising from any remains of mechanic blood, which it is pretended should influence them, but all the gallantry of spirit, greatness of soul, and all the generous principles, that can be found in any of the ancient families, whose blood is the most untainted, as they call it, with the low mixtures of a mechanic race, are found in these; and, as is said before, they generally go beyond them in knowledge of the world, which is the best education.

We see the tradesmen of England, as they grow wealthy, coming every day to the Herald's Office, to search for the coats-of-arms of their ancestors, in order to paint them upon their coaches, and engrave them upon their plate, embroider them upon their furniture, or carve them upon the pediments of their new houses; and how often do we see them trace the registers of their families up to the prime nobility, or the most ancient gentry of the kingdom!

In this search we find them often qualified to raise new families, if they do not descend from old; as was said of a certain tradesman of London that if he could not find the ancient race of gentlemen from which he came, he would begin a new race, who should be as good gentlemen as any that went before them. They tell us a story of the old Lord Craven, who was afterwards created Earl of Craven by King Charles II., that, being upbraided with his being of an upstart nobility, by the famous Aubery, Earl of Oxford, who was himself of the very ancient family of the Veres, Earls of Oxford, the Lord Craven told him, he (Craven) would cap pedigrees with him (Oxford) for a wager. The Earl of Oxford laughed at the challenge, and began reckoning up his famous ancestors, who had been Earls of Oxford for a hundred years past, and knights for some hundreds of years more; but when my Lord Craven began, he read over his family thus:– 'I am William Lord Craven; my father was Lord Mayor of London, and my grandfather was the Lord knows who; wherefore I think my pedigree as good as yours, my lord.' The story was merry enough, but is to my purpose exactly; for let the grandfather be who he would, his father, Sir William Craven, who was Lord Mayor of London, was a wholesale grocer, and raised the family by trade, and yet nobody doubts but that the family of Craven is at this day as truly noble, in all the beauties which adorn noble birth and blood, as can be desired of any family, however ancient, or anciently noble.

In Italy, and especially at Venice, we see every day the sons of merchants, and other trades, who grow in wealth and estates, and can advance for the service of their country a considerable sum of money, namely, 60,000 to 100,000 dollars, are accepted to honour by the senate, and translated into the list of the nobility, without any regard to the antiquities of their families, or the nobility of blood; and in all ages the best kings and sovereign princes have thought fit to reward the extraordinary merit of their subjects with titles of honour, and to rank men among their nobility, who have deserved it by good and great actions, whether their birth and the antiquity of their families entitled them to it or not.

Thus in the late wars between England and France, how was our army full of excellent officers, who went from the shop, and from behind the counter, into the camp, and who distinguished themselves there by their merit and gallant behaviour. And several such came to command regiments, and even to be general officers, and to gain as much reputation in the service as any; as Colonel Pierce, Wood, Richards, and several others that might be named.

All this confirms what I have said before, namely, that trade in England neither is nor ought to be levelled with what it is in other countries; nor the tradesmen depreciated as they are abroad, and as some of our gentry would pretend to do in England; but that, as many of our best families rose from trade, so many branches of the best families in England, under the nobility, have stooped so low as to be put apprentices to tradesmen in London, and to set up and follow those trades when they have come out of their times, and have thought it no dishonour to their blood.

To bring this once more home to the ladies, who are so scandalised at that mean step, which they call it, of marrying a tradesman – it may be told them for their humiliation, that, however they think fit to act, sometimes those tradesmen come of better families than their own; and oftentimes, when they have refused them to their loss, those very tradesmen have married ladies of superior fortune to them, and have raised families of their own, who in one generation have been superior to those nice ladies both in dignity and estate, and have, to their great mortification, been ranked above them upon all public occasions.

The word tradesman in England does not sound so harsh as it does in other countries; and to say *a gentleman-tradesman*, is not so much nonsense as some people would persuade us to reckon it: and, indeed, as trade is now flourishing in England, and increasing, and the wealth of our tradesmen is already so great, it is very probable a few years will show us still a greater race of trade-bred gentlemen, than ever England yet had.

The very name of an English tradesman will, and does already obtain in the world; and as our soldiers by the late war gained the reputation of being some of the best troops in the world, and our seamen are at this day, and very justly too, esteemed the best sailors in the world, so the English tradesmen may in a few years be allowed to rank with the best gentlemen in Europe; and as the prophet Isaiah said of the merchants of Tyre, that 'her traffickers were the honourable of the earth,' (Isaiah, xxiii. 8.)

In the meantime, it is evident their wealth at this time out-does that of the like rank of any nation in Europe; and as their number is prodigious, so is their commerce; for the inland commerce of England – and it is of those tradesmen, or traffickers, that I am now speaking in particular – is certainly the greatest of its kind of any in the world; nor is it possible there should ever be any like it, the consumption of all sorts of goods, both of our own manufacture, and of foreign growth, being so exceeding great.

If the English nation were to be nearly inquired into, and its present opulence and greatness duly weighed, it would appear, that, as the figure it now makes in Europe is greater than it ever made before – take it either in King Edward III.'s reign, or in Queen Elizabeth's, which were the two chief points of time when the English fame was in its highest extent – I say, if its present greatness were to be duly weighed, there is no comparison in its wealth, the number of its people, the value of its lands, the greatness of the estates of its private inhabitants; and, in consequence of all this, its real strength is infinitely beyond whatever it was before, and if it were needful, I could fill up this work with a very agreeable and useful inquiry into the particulars.

But I content myself with turning it to the case in hand, for the truth of fact is not to be disputed – I say, I turn it to the case in hand thus: whence comes it to be so? – how is it produced? War has not done it;

no, nor so much as helped or assisted to it; it is not by any martial exploits; we have made no conquests abroad, added no new kingdoms to the British empire, reduced no neighbouring nations, or extended the possession of our monarchs into the properties of others; we have grained nothing by war and encroachment; we are butted and bounded just where we were in Queen Elizabeth's time; the Dutch, the Flemings, the French, are in view of us just as they were then. We have subjected no new provinces or people to our government; and, with few or no exceptions, we are almost for dominion where King Edward I. left us; nay, we have lost all the dominions which our ancient kings for some hundreds of years held in France – such as the rich and powerful provinces of Normandy, Poictou, Gascoigne, Bretagne, and Acquitaine; and instead of being enriched by war and victory, on the contrary we have been torn in pieces by civil wars and rebellions, as well in Ireland as in England, and that several times, to the ruin of our richest families, and the slaughter of our nobility and gentry, nay, to the destruction even of monarchy itself, and this many years at a time, as in the long bloody wars between the houses of Lancaster and York, the many rebellions of the Irish, as well in Queen Elizabeth's time, as in King Charles I.'s time, and the fatal massacre, and almost extirpation of the English name in that kingdom; and at last, the late rebellion in England, in which the monarch fell a sacrifice to the fury of the people, and monarchy itself gave way to tyranny and usurpation, for almost twenty years.

These things prove abundantly that the rising greatness of the British nation is not owing to war and conquests, to enlarging its dominion by the sword, or subjecting the people of other countries to our power; but it is all owing to trade, to the increase of our commerce at home, and the extending it abroad.

It is owing to trade, that new discoveries have been made in lands unknown, and new settlements and plantations made, new colonies placed, and new governments formed in the uninhabited islands, and the uncultivated continent of America; and those plantings and settlements have again enlarged and increased the trade, and thereby the wealth and power of the nation by whom they were discovered and planted. We have not increased our power, or the number of our subjects, by subduing the nations which possessed those countries, and incorporating them into our own, but have entirely planted our colonies, and peopled the countries with our own subjects, natives of this island; and, excepting the negroes, which we transport from Africa to America, as slaves to work in the sugar and tobacco plantations, all our colonies, as well in the islands as on the continent of America, are entirely peopled from Great Britain and Ireland, and chiefly the former; the natives having either removed farther up into the country, or by their own folly and treachery raising war against us, been destroyed and cut off.

As trade alone has peopled those countries, so trading with them has raised them also to a prodigy of wealth and opulence; and we see now the ordinary planters at Jamaica and Barbadoes rise to immense estates, riding in their coaches and six, especially at Jamaica, with twenty or thirty negroes on foot running before them whenever they please to appear in public.

As trade has thus extended our colonies abroad, so it has, except those colonies, kept our people at home, where they are multiplied to that prodigious degree, and do still continue to multiply in such a manner, that if it goes on so, time may come that all the lands in England will do little more than serve for gardens for them, and to feed their cows; and their corn and cattle be supplied from Scotland and Ireland.

What is the reason that we see numbers of French, and of Scots, and of Germans, in all the foreign nations in Europe, and especially filling up their armies and courts, and that you see few or no English there?

What is the reason, that when we want to raise armies, or to man navies in England, we are obliged to press the seamen, and to make laws and empower the justices of the peace, and magistrates of towns, to force men to go for soldiers, and enter into the service, or allure them by giving bounty-money, as an encouragement to men to list themselves? – whereas the people of other nations, and even the Scots and Irish, travel abroad, and run into all the neighbour nations, to seek service, and to be admitted into their pay.

What is it but trade? – the increase of business at home, and the employment of the poor in the business and manufactures of this kingdom, by which the poor get so good wages, and live so well, that they will not list for soldiers; and have so good pay in the merchants' service, that they will not serve on board the ships of war, unless they are forced to do it?

What is the reason, that, in order to supply our colonies and plantations with people, besides the encouragement given in those colonies to all people that will come there to plant and to settle, we are obliged to send away thither all our petty offenders, and all the criminals that we think fit to spare from the gallows, besides what we formerly called the kidnapping trade? – that is to say, the arts made use of to wheedle and draw away young vagrant and indigent people, and people of desperate fortunes, to sell themselves – that is, bind themselves for servants, the numbers of which are very great.

It is poverty fills armies, mans navies, and peoples colonies. In vain the drums beat for soldiers, and the king's captains invite seamen to serve in the armies for fivepence a-day, and in the royal navy for twenty-three shillings per month, in a country where the ordinary labourer can have nine shillings a-week for his labour, and the manufacturers earn from twelve to sixteen shillings a-week for their work, and while trade gives thirty shillings per month wages to the seamen on board merchant ships. Men will always stay or go, as the pay gives them encouragement; and this is the reason why it has been so much more difficult to raise and recruit armies in England, than it has been in Scotland and Ireland, France and Germany.

The same trade that keeps our people at home, is the cause of the well living of the people here; for as frugality is not the national virtue of England, so the people that get much spend much; and as they work hard, so they live well, eat and drink well, clothe warm, and lodge soft – in a word, the working manufacturing people of England eat the fat, and drink the sweet, live better, and fare better, than the working poor of any other nation in Europe; they make better wages of their work, and spend more of the money upon their backs and bellies, than in any other country. This expense of the poor, as it causes a prodigious consumption both of the provisions, and of the manufactures of our country at home, so two things are undeniably the consequence of that part.

1. The consumption of provisions increases the rent and value of the lands, and this raises the gentlemen's estates, and that again increases the employment of people, and consequently the numbers of them, as well those who are employed in the husbandry of land, breeding and feeding of cattle, &c., as of servants in the gentlemen's families, who, as their estates increase in value, so they increase their families and equipages.

2. As the people get greater wages, so they, I mean the same poorer part of the people, clothe better, and furnish better, and this increases the consumption of the very manufactures they make; then that comsumption increases the quantity made, and this creates what we call inland trade, by which innumerable families are employed, and the increase of the people maintained, and by which increase of trade and people the present growing prosperity of this nation is produced.

The whole glory and greatness of England, then, being thus raised by trade, it must be unaccountable folly and ignorance in us to lessen that one article in our own esteem, which is the only fountain from whence we all, take us as a nation, are raised, and by which we are enriched and maintained. The Scripture says, speaking of the riches and glory of the city of Tyre – which was, indeed, at that time, the great port or emporium of the world for foreign commerce, from whence all the silks and fine manufactures of Persia and India were exported all over the western world – 'That her merchants were princes;' and, in another place, 'By thy traffic thou hast increased thy riches.' (Ezek. xxviii. 5.) Certain it is, that our traffic has increased our riches; and it is also certain, that the flourishing of our manufactures is the foundation of all our traffic, as well our merchandise as our inland trade.

The inland trade of England is a thing not easily described; it would, in a word, take up a whole book by itself; it is the foundation of all our wealth and greatness; it is the support of all our foreign trade, and of our manufacturing, and, as I have hitherto written, of the tradesmen who carry it on. I shall proceed with a brief discourse of the trade itself.

CHAPTER XXIII

OF THE INLAND TRADE OF ENGLAND, ITS MAGNITUDE, AND THE GREAT ADVANTAGE IT IS TO THE NATION IN GENERAL

I have, in a few words, described what I mean by the inland trade of England, in the introduction to this work. It is the circulation of commerce among ourselves.

I. For the carrying on our manufactures of several kinds in the several counties where they are made, and the employing the several sorts of people and trades needful for the said manufactures.

II. For the raising and vending provisions of all kinds for the supply of the vast numbers of people who are employed every where by the said manufactures.

III. For the importing and bringing in from abroad all kinds of foreign growth and manufactures which we want.

IV. For the carrying about and dispersing, as well our own growth and manufactures as the foreign imported growth and manufactures of other nations, to the retailer, and by them to the last consumer, which is the utmost end of all trade; and this, in every part, to the utmost corner of the island of Great Britain and Ireland.

This I call inland trade, and these circulators of goods, and retailers of them to the last consumer, are those whom we are to understand by the word tradesmen, in all the parts of this work; for (as I observed in the beginning) the ploughmen and farmers who labour at home, and the merchant who imports our merchandise from abroad, are not at all meant or included, and whatever I have been saying, except where they have been mentioned in particular, and at length.

This inland trade is in itself at this time the wonder of all the world of trade, nor is there any thing like it now in the world, much less that exceeds it, or perhaps ever will be, except only what itself may grow up to in the ages to come; for, as I have said on all occasions, it is still growing and increasing.

By this prodigy of a trade, all the vast importation from our own colonies is circulated and dispersed to the remotest corner of the island, whereby the consumption is become so great, and by which those colonies are so increased, and are become so populous and so wealthy as I have already observed of them. This importation consists chiefly of sugars and tobacco, of which the consumption in Great Britain is scarcely to be conceived of, besides the consumption of cotton, indigo, rice, ginger, pimento or Jamaica pepper, cocoa or chocolate, rum and molasses, train-oil, salt-fish, whale-fin, all sorts of furs, abundance of valuable drugs, pitch, tar, turpentine, deals, masts, and timber, and many other things of smaller value; all which, besides the employing a very great number of ships and English seamen, occasion again a very great exportation of our own manufactures of all sorts to those colonies; which being circulated again for consumption there, that circulation is to be accounted a branch of home or inland trade, as those colonies are on all such occasions esteemed as a branch of part of ourselves, and of the British government in the world.

This trade to our West Indies and American colonies, is very considerable, as it employs so many ships and sailors, and so much of the growth of those colonies is again exported by us to other parts of the world, over and above what is consumed among us at home; and, also, as all those goods, and a great deal of money in specie, is returned hither for and in balance of our own manufactures and merchandises exported thither – on these accounts some have insisted that more real wealth is brought into Great Britain every year from those colonies, than is brought from the Spanish West Indies to old Spain, notwithstanding the extent of their dominion is above twenty times as much, and notwithstanding the vast quantity of gold and silver which they bring from the mines of Mexico, and the mountains of Potosi.[1]

Whether these people say true or no, is not my business to inquire here; though, if I may give my opinion, I must acknowledge that I believe they do; but be it so or not, it is certain that it is an infinitely extended trade, and daily increasing; and much of it, if not all, is and ought to be esteemed as an inland trade, because, as above, it is a circulation among ourselves.

As the manufactures of England, particularly those of wool (cotton wool included), and of silk, are the greatest, and amount to the greatest value of any single manufacture in Europe,[2] so they not only employ more people, but those people gain the most money, that is to say, have the best wages for their work of any people in the world; and yet, which is peculiar to England, the English manufactures are, allowing for their goodness, the cheapest at market of any in the world, too. Even France itself, after all the pains they are at to get our

1 [The amount of trade produced by the British colonies is still great; but it has been ascertained that it is not profitable to the nation at large, as much more is paid from the public purse for the military protection required by the colonies, than returns to individuals through the medium of business.]

2 [The cotton manufacture has now the prominence which, in Defoe's time, was due to those of wool and silk.]

wool, and all the expense they have been at to imitate our manufactures, by getting over our workmen, and giving them even greater wages than they had here, have yet made so little proficiency in it, and are so far from outselling us in foreign markets, that they still, in spite of the strictest prohibitions, send hither, and to Holland and Germany, for English broad-cloths, druggets, duroys, flannels, serges, and several other sorts of our goods, to supply their own. Nor can they clothe themselves to their satisfaction with their own goods; but if any French gentleman of quality comes over hither from France, he is sure to bring no more coats with him than backs, but immediately to make him new clothes as soon as he arrives, and to carry as many new suits home with him at his return, as he can get leave to bring ashore when he comes there – a demonstration that our manufacture exceeds theirs, after all their boasts of it, both in goodness and in cheapness, even by their own confession. But I am not now to enter upon the particular manufactures, but the general trade in the manufacture; this particular being a trade of such a magnitude, it is to be observed for our purpose, that the greatness of it consists of two parts:–

1. The consumption of it at home, including our own plantations and factories.

2. The exportation of it to foreign parts, exclusive of the said plantations and factories.

It is the first of these which is the subject of my present discourse, because the tradesmen to whom, and for whose instruction these chapters are designed, are the people principally concerned in the making all these manufactures, and wholly and solely concerned in dispersing and circulating them for the home consumption; and this, with some additions, as explained above, I call *inland trade*.

The home-consumption of our own goods, as it is very great, so it has one particular circumstance attending it, which exceedingly increases it as a trade, and that is, that besides the numbers of people which it employs in the raising the materials, and making the goods themselves as a manufacture – I say, besides all this, there are multitudes of people employed, cattle maintained, with waggons and carts for the service on shore, barges and boats for carriage in the rivers, and ships and barks for carrying by sea, and all for the circulating these manufactures from one place to another, for the consumption of them among the people.

So that, in short, the circulation of the goods is a business not equal, indeed, but bearing a very great proportion to the trade itself.

This is owing to another particular circumstance of our manufacture, and perhaps is not so remarkably the case of any other manufacture or country in Europe, namely, that though all our manufactures are used and called for by almost all the people, and that in every part of the whole British dominion, yet they are made and wrought in their several distinct and respective countries in Britain, and some of them at the remotest distance from one another, hardly any two manufactures being made in one place. For example:

The broad-cloth and druggets in Wilts, Gloucester, and Worcestershire; serges in Devon and Somersetshire; narrow-cloths in Yorkshire and Staffordshire; kerseys, cottons, half-thicks, duffields, plains, and coarser things, in Lancashire and Westmoreland; shalloons in the counties of Northampton, Berks, Oxford, Southampton, and York; women's-stuffs in Norfolk; linsey-woolseys, &c., at Kidderminster; dimmeties and cotton-wares at Manchester; flannels at Salisbury, and in Wales; tammeys at Coventry; and the like. It is the same, in some respects, with our provisions, especially for the supply of the city of London, and also of several other parts: for example, when I speak of provisions, I mean such as are not made use of in the county where they are made and produced. For example:

Butter, in firkins, in Suffolk and Yorkshire; cheese from Cheshire, Wiltshire, Warwickshire, and Gloucestershire; herrings, cured red, from Yarmouth in Norfolk; coals, for fuel, from Northumberland and Durham; malt from the counties of Hertford, Essex, Kent, Bucks, Oxford, Berks, &c.

And thus of many other things which are the proper produce of one part of the country only, but are from thence dispersed for the ordinary use of the people into many, or perhaps into all the other counties of England, to the infinite advantage of our inland commerce, and employing a vast number of people and cattle; and consequently those people and cattle increasing the consumption of provisions and forage, and the improvement of lands; so true it is, and so visible, that trade increases people, and people increase trade.

This carriage of goods in England from those places is chiefly managed by horses and waggons; the number of which is not to be guessed at, nor is there any rule or art that can be thought of, by which any just calculation can be made of it, and therefore I shall not enter upon any particular of it at this time; it is sufficient to say, what I believe to be true, namely, that it is equal to the whole trade of some nations, and the rather because of the great improvement of land, which proceeds from the employing so many thousands of horses as are furnished for this part of business.

In other countries, and indeed, in most countries in Europe, all their inland trade, such as it is, is carried on by the convenience of navigation, either by coastings on the sea, or by river-navigation. It is true, our coasting trade is exceedingly great, and employs a prodigious number of ships, as well from all the shores of England to London, as from one port to another.

But as to our river-navigation, it is not equal to it, though in some places it is very great too; but we have but a very few navigable rivers in England, compared with those of other countries; nor are many of those rivers we have navigable to any considerable length from the sea. The most considerable rivers in England for navigation are as follows:– The Thames, the Trent, the Severn, the Wye, the Ouse, the Humber, the Air, and the Calder. These are navigable a considerable way, and receive several other navigable rivers into them; but except these there are very few rivers in England which are navigable much above the first town of note within their mouth.

Most of our other greatest and most navigable rivers are navigable but a very little way in; as the northern Ouse but to York, the Orwell but to Ipswich, the Yare but to Norwich; the Tyne itself but a very little above Newcastle, not in all above twelve miles; the Tweed not at all above Berwick; the great Avon but to Bristol; the Exe but to Exeter; and the Dee but to Chester: in a word, our river-navigation is not to be named for carriage, with the vast bulk of carriage by pack-horses and by waggons; nor must the carriage by pedlars on their backs be omitted.[3]

This carriage is the medium of our inland trade, and, as I said, is a branch of the trade itself. This great carriage is occasioned by the situation of our produce and manufactures. For example – the Taunton and Exeter serges, perpetuanas, and duroys, come chiefly by land; the clothing, such as the broad-cloth and druggets from Wilts, Gloucester, Worcester, and Shropshire, comes all by land-carriage to London, and goes down again by land-carriages to all parts of England; the Yorkshire clothing trade, the Manchester and Coventry trades, all by land, not to London only, but to all parts of England, by horse-packs – the Manchester men being, saving their wealth, a kind of pedlars, who carry their goods themselves to the country shopkeepers every where, as do now the Yorkshire and Coventry manufacturers also.

Now, in all these manufactures, however remote from one another, every town in England uses something, not only of one or other, but of all the rest. Every sort of goods is wanted every where; and where they make one sort of goods, and sell them all over England, they at the same time want other goods from almost every other part. For example:

Norwich makes chiefly woollen stuffs and camblets, and these are sold all over England; but then Norwich buys broad-cloth from Wilts and Worcestershire, serges and sagathies from Devon and

3 [It is scarcely necessary to remind the reader, that the canal navigation of England has come into existence since the date of this work – the railway communication is but of yesterday.]

Somersetshire, narrow cloth from Yorkshire, flannel from Wales, coal from Newcastle, and the like; and so it is, *mutatis mutandis*, of most of the other parts.

The circulating of these goods in this manner, is the life of our inland trade, and increases the numbers of our people, by keeping them employed at home; and, indeed, of late they are prodigiously multiplied; and they again increase our trade, as shall be mentioned in its place.

As the demand for all sorts of English goods is thus great, and they are thus extended in every part of the island, so the tradesmen are dispersed and spread over every part also; that is to say, in every town, great or little, we find shopkeepers, wholesale or retail, who are concerned in this circulation, and hand forward the goods to the last consumer. From London, the goods go chiefly to the great towns, and from those again to the smaller markets, and from those to the meanest villages; so that all the manufactures of England, and most of them also of foreign countries, are to be found in the meanest village, and in the remotest corner of the whole island of Britain, and are to be bought, as it were, at every body's door.

This shows not the extent of our manufactures only, but the usefulness of them, and how they are so necessary to mankind that our own people cannot be without them, and every sort of them, and cannot make one thing serve for another; but as they sell their own, so they buy from others, and every body here trades with every body: this it is that gives the whole manufacture so universal a circulation, and makes it so immensely great in England. What it is abroad, is not so much to our present purpose.

Again, the magnitude of the city of London adds very considerably to the greatness of the inland trade; for as this city is the centre of our trade, so all the manufactures are brought hither, and from hence circulated again to all the country, as they are particularly called for. But that is not all; the magnitude of the city influences the whole nation also in the article of provisions, and something is raised in every county in England, however remote, for the supply of London; nay, all the best of every produce is brought hither; so that all the people, and all the lands in England, seem to be at work for, or employed by, or on the account of, this overgrown city.

This makes the trade increase prodigiously, even as the city itself increases; and we all know the city is very greatly increased within few years past. Again, as the whole nation is employed to feed and clothe this city, so here is the money, by which all the people in the whole nation seem to be supported and maintained.

I have endeavoured to make some calculation of the number of shopkeepers in this kingdom, but I find it is not to be done – we may as well count the stars; not that they are equal in number neither, but it is as impossible, unless any one person corresponded so as to have them numbered in every town or parish throughout the kingdom. I doubt not they are some hundreds of thousands, but there is no making an estimate – the number is in a manner infinite. It is as impossible likewise to make any guess at the bulk of their trade, and how much they return yearly; nor, if we could, would it give any foundation for any just calculation of the value of goods in general, because all our goods circulate so much, and go so often through so many hands before they come to the consumer. This so often passing every sort of goods through so many hands, before it comes into the hands of the last consumer, is that which makes our trade be so immensely great. For example, if there is made in England for our home-consumption the value of £100,000 worth of any particular goods, say, for example, that it be so many pieces of serge or cloth, and if this goes through ten tradesmen's hands, before it comes to the last consumer, then there is £1,000,000 returned in trade for that £100,000 worth of goods; and so of all the sorts of goods we trade in.

Again, as I said above, all our manufactures are so useful to, and depend on, one another so much in trade, that the sale of one necessarily causes the demand of the other in all parts. For example, suppose the poorest countryman wants to be clothed, or suppose it be a gentleman wants to clothe one of his servants, whether a footman in a livery, or suppose it be any servant in ordinary apparel, yet he shall in some part employ almost every one of the manufacturing counties of England, for making up one ordinary suit of clothes. For example:

If his coat be of woollen-cloth, he has that from Yorkshire; the lining is shalloon from Berkshire; the waistcoat is of callamanco from Norwich; the breeches of a strong drugget from Devizes, Wiltshire; the stockings being of yarn from Westmoreland; the hat is a felt from Leicester; the gloves of leather from Somersetshire; the shoes from Northampton; the buttons from Macclesfield in Cheshire, or, if they are of metal, they come from Birmingham, or Warwickshire; his garters from Manchester; his shirt of home-made linen of Lancashire, or Scotland.

If it be thus of every poor man's clothing, or of a servant, what must it be of the master, and of the rest of the family? And in this particular the case is the same, let the family live where they will; so that all these manufactures must be found in all the remotest towns and counties in England, be it where you will.

Again, take the furnishing of our houses, it is the same in proportion, and according to the figure and quality of the person. Suppose, then, it be a middling tradesman that is going to live in some market-town, and to open his shop there; suppose him not to deal in the manufacture, but in groceries, and such sort of wares as the country grocers sell.

This man, however, must clothe himself and his wife, and must furnish his house: let us see, then, to how many counties and towns, among our manufactures, must he send for his needful supply. Nor is the quantity concerned in it; let him furnish himself as frugally as he pleases, yet he must have something of every necessary thing; and we will suppose for the present purpose the man lived in Sussex, where very few, if any, manufactures are carried on; suppose he lived at Horsham, which is a market-town in or near the middle of the county.

For his clothing of himself – for we must allow him to have a new suit of clothes when he begins the world – take them to be just as above; for as to the quality or quantity, it is much the same; only, that instead of buying the cloth from Yorkshire, perhaps he has it a little finer than the poor man above, and so his comes out of Wiltshire, and his stockings are, it may be, of worsted, not of yarn, and so they come from Nottingham, not Westmoreland; but this does not at all alter the case.

Come we next to his wife; and she being a good honest townsman's daughter, is not dressed over fine, yet she must have something decent, being newly married too, especially as times go, when the burghers' wives of Horsham, or any other town, go as fine as they do in other places: allow her, then, to have a silk gown, with all the necessaries belonging to a middling tolerable appearance, yet you shall find all the nation more or less concerned in clothing this country grocer's wife, and furnishing his house, and yet nothing at all extravagant. For example:

Her gown, a plain English mantua-silk, manufactured in Spitalfields; her petticoat the same; her binding, a piece of chequered-stuff, made at Bristol and Norwich; her under-petticoat, a piece of black callamanco, made at Norwith – quilted at home, if she be a good housewife, but the quilting of cotton from Manchester, or cotton-wool from abroad; her inner-petticoats, flannel and swanskin, from Salisbury and Wales; her stockings from Tewksbury, if ordinary, from Leicester, if woven; her lace and edgings from Stony Stratford the first, and Great Marlow the last; her muslin from foreign trade, as likewise her linen, being something finer than the man's, may perhaps be a guilick-Holland; her wrapper, or morning-gown, a piece of Irish linen, printed at London; her black hood, a thin English lustring; her gloves, lamb's-skin, from Berwick and Northumberland, or Scotland; her ribands, being but very few, from Coventry, or London; her riding-hood, of English worsted-camblet, made at Norwich.

Come next to the furniture of their house. It is scarce credible, to how many counties of England, and how remote, the furniture of but a mean house must send them, and how many people are every where employed about it; nay, and the meaner the furniture, the more people and places employed. For example:

The hangings, suppose them to be ordinary linsey-woolsey, are made at Kidderminster, dyed in the country, and painted, or watered, at London; the chairs, if of cane, are made at London; the ordinary matted chairs, perhaps in the place where they live; tables, chests of drawers, &c., made at London; as also looking-glass; bedding, &c., the curtains, suppose of serge from Taunton and Exeter, or of camblets, from Norwich, or the same with the hangings, as above; the ticking comes from the west country, Somerset and Dorsetshire; the feathers also from the same country; the blankets from Whitney in Oxfordshire; the rugs from Westmoreland and Yorkshire; the sheets, of good linen, from Ireland; kitchen utensils and chimney-furniture, almost all the brass and iron from Birmingham and Sheffield; earthen-ware from Stafford, Nottingham, and Kent; glass ware from Sturbridge in Worcestershire, and London.

I give this list to explain what I said before, namely, that there is no particular place in England, where all the manufactures are made, but every county or place has its peculiar sort, or particular manufacture, in which the people are wholly employed; and for all the rest that is wanted, they fetch them from other parts.[4]

But, then, as what is thus wanted by every particular person, or family, is but in small quantities, and they would not be able to send for it to the country or town where it is to be bought, there are shopkeepers in every village, or at least in every considerable market-town, where the particulars are to be bought, and who find it worth their while to furnish themselves with quantities of all the particular goods, be they made where and as far off as they will; and at these shops the people who want them are easily supplied.

Nor do even these shopkeepers go or send to all the several counties where those goods are made – that is to say, to this part for the cloth, or to that for the lining; to another for the buttons, and to another for the thread; but they again correspond with the wholesale dealers in London, where there are particular shops or warehouses for all these; and they not only furnish the country shopkeepers, but give them large credit, and sell them great quantities of goods, by which they

4 [Since Defoe's time, little alteration has taken place in the locality of a number of manufactures in England; but, in the interval, an entire change has been effected in Scotland, which now possesses various manufactures of importance in the commercial economy of the nation. We need only allude to the cambrics, gauzes, and silks of Paisley; the cottons and other goods of Glasgow; the plaidings of Stirlingshire; the stockings of Hawick; the printing-paper of Mid-Lothian; the carpets and bonnets of Kilmarnock; the iron of Muirkirk and Carron; the linens of Fife and Dundee; and the shawls of Edinburgh.]

again are enabled to trust the tailors who make the clothes, or even their neighbours who wear them; and the manufacturers in the several counties do the like by those wholesale dealers who supply the country shops.

Through so many hands do all the necessary things pass for the clothing a poor plain countryman, though he lived as far as Berwick-upon-Tweed; and this occasions, as I have said, a general circulation of trade, both to and from London, from and to all the parts of England, so that every manufacture is sold and removed five or six times, and perhaps more, before it comes at the last consumer.

This method of trade brings another article in, which also is the great foundation of the increase of commerce, and the prodigious magnitude of our inland trade is much owing to it; and that is giving credit, by which every tradesman is enabled to trade for a great deal more than he otherwise could do. By this method a shopkeeper is able to stock his shop, or warehouses, with two or three times as much goods in value, as he has stock of his own to begin the world with, and by that means is able to trust out his goods to others, and give them time, and so under one another – nay, I may say, many a tradesman begins the world with borrowed stocks, or with no stock at all, but that of credit, and yet carries on a trade for several hundreds, nay, for several thousands, of pounds a-year.

By this means the trade in general is infinitely increased – nay, the stock of the kingdom in trade is doubled, or trebled, or more, and there is infinitely more business carried on, than the real stock could be able to manage, if no credit were to be given; for credit in this particular is a stock, and that not an imaginary, but a real stock; for the tradesman, that perhaps begins but with five hundred, or one thousand pounds' stock, shall be able to furnish or stock his shop with four times the sum in the value of goods; and as he gives credit again, and trusts other tradesmen under him, so he launches out into a trade of great magnitude; and yet, if he is a prudent manager of his business, he finds himself able to answer his payments, and so continually supply himself with goods, keeping up the reputation of his dealings, and the credit of his shop, though his stock be not a fifth, nay, sometimes not a tenth part, in proportion to the returns that he makes by the year: so that credit is the foundation on which the trade of England is made so considerable.

Nor is it enough to say, that people must and will have goods, and that the consumption is the same; it is evident that consumption is not the same; and in those nations where they give no credit, or not so much as here, the trade is small in proportion, as I shall show in its place.

CHAPTER XXIV

OF CREDIT IN TRADE, AND HOW A TRADESMAN OUGHT TO VALUE AND IMPROVE IT: HOW EASILY LOST, AND HOW HARD IT IS TO BE RECOVERED

Credit is, or ought to be, the tradesman's *mistress*; but I must tell him too, he must not think of ever casting her off, for if once he loses her, she hardly ever returns; and yet she has one quality, in which she differs from most of the ladies who go by that name – if you court her, she is gone; if you manage so wisely as to make her believe you really do not want her, she follows and courts you. But, by the way, no tradesman can be in so good circumstances as to say he does not want, that is, does not stand in need of credit.

Credit, next to real stock, is the foundation, the life and soul, of business in a private tradesman; it is his prosperity; it is his support in the substance of his whole trade; even in public matters, it is the strengh and fund of a nation. We felt, in the late wars, the consequence of both the extremes – namely, of wanting and of enjoying a complete fund of credit.

Credit makes war, and makes peace; raises armies, fits out navies, fights battles, besieges towns; and, in a word, it is more justly called the sinews of war than the money itself,[1] because it can do all these things without money – nay, it will bring in money to be subservient, though it be independent.

Credit makes the soldier fight without pay, the armies march without provisions, and it makes tradesmen keep open shop without stock. The force of credit is not to be described by words; it is an impregnable fortification, either for a nation, or for a single man in business; and he that has credit is invulnerable, whether he has money or no; nay, it will make money, and, which is yet more, it will make money without an intrinsic, without the *materia medica* (as the doctors have it); it adds a value, and supports whatever value it adds, to the meanest substance; it makes paper pass for money, and fills the Exchequer and the banks with as many millions as it pleases, upon demand.

1 [How strikingly was this proved in the last war, when the British government obtained credit for no less than six hundred millions to conduct warlike operations, and by these means was ultimately victorious.]

As I said in last chapter, it increases commerce; so, I may add, it makes trade, and makes the whole kingdom trade for many millions more than the national specie can amount to.

It may be true, as some allege, that we cannot drive a trade for more goods than we have to trade with, but then it is as true, that it is by the help of credit that we can increase the quantity, and that more goods are made to trade with than would otherwise be; more goods are brought to market than they could otherwise sell; and even in the last consumption, how many thousands of families wear out their clothes before they pay for them, and eat their dinner upon tick with the butcher! Nay, how many thousands who could not buy any clothes, if they were to pay for them in ready money, yet buy them at a venture upon their credit, and pay for them as they can!

Trade is anticipated by credit, and it grows by the anticipation; for men often buy clothes before they pay for them, because they want clothes before they can spare the money; and these are so many in number, that really they add a great stroke to the bulk of our inland trade. How many families have we in England that live upon credit, even to the tune of two or three years' rent of their revenue, before it comes in! – so that they must be said to *eat the calf in the cow's belly*. This encroachment they make upon the stock in trade; and even this very article may state the case: I doubt not but at this time the land owes to the trade some millions sterling; that is to say, the gentlemen owe to the tradesmen so much money, which, at long run, the rents of their lands must pay.

The tradesmen having, then, trusted the landed men with so much, where must they have it but by giving credit also to one another? Trusting their goods and money into trade, one launching out into the hands of another, and forbearing payment till the lands make it good out of their produce, that is to say, out of their rents.

The trade is not limited; the produce of lands may be and is restrained. Trade cannot exceed the bounds of the goods it can sell; but while trade can increase its stock of cash by credit, it can increase its stock of goods for sale, and then it has nothing to do but to find a market to sell at; and this we have done in all parts of the world, still by the force of our stocks being so increased.

Thus, credit raising stock at home, that stock enables us to give credit abroad; and thus the quantity of goods which we make, and which is infinitely increased at home, enables us to find or force a vent abroad. This is apparent, our home trade having so far increased our manufacture, that England may be said to be able almost to clothe the whole world; and in our carrying on the foreign trade wholly upon the English stocks, giving credit to almost all the nations of the world; for it is evident, our stocks lie at this time upon credit in the warehouses of the merchants in Spain and Portugal, Holland and Germany, Italy and Turkey; nay, in New Spain and Brazil.

The exceeding quantity of goods thus raised in England cannot be supposed to be the mere product of the solid wealth and stocks of the English people; we do not pretend to it; the joining those stocks to the value of goods, always appearing in England in the hands of the manufacturers, tradesmen, and merchants, and to the wealth which appears in shipping, in stock upon land, and in the current coin of the nation, would amount to such a prodigy of stock, as not all Europe could pretend to.

But all this is owing to the prodigious thing called credit, the extent of which in the British trade is as hard to be valued, as the benefit of it to England is really not to be described. It must be likewise said, to the honour of our English tradesman, that they understand how to manage the credit they both give and take, better than any other tradesmen in the world; indeed, they have a greater opportunity to improve it, and make use of it, and therefore may be supposed to be more ready in making the best of their credit, than any other nations are.

Hence it is that we frequently find tradesmen carrying on a prodigious trade with but a middling stock of their own, the rest being all managed by the force of their credit; for example, I have known a man in a private warehouse in London trade for forty thousand pounds a-year sterling, and carry on such a return for many years together, and not have one thousand pounds' stock of his own, or not more – all the rest has been carried on upon credit, being the stocks of other men running continually through his hands; and this is not practised now and then, as a great rarity, but is very frequent in trade, and may be seen every day, as what in its degree runs through the whole body of the tradesmen in England.[2]

Every tradesman both gives and takes credit, and the new mode of setting it up over their shop and warehouse doors, in capital letters, *No trust by retail*, is a presumption in trade; and though it may have been attempted in some trades, was never yet brought to any perfection; and most of those trades, who were the forwardest to set it up, have been obliged to take it down again, or act contrary to it in their business, or see some very good customers go away from them to other shops, who, though they have not brought money with them, have yet good foundations to make any tradesmen trust them, and who do at proper times make payments punctual enough.

2 [The author's praises of credit must be received with caution. If his descriptions of the credit system of his own day are true, an improvement has since taken place, as business neither is nor can be now carried on to such an extent upon credit – a circumstance that redounds to the advantage of all parties.]

On the contrary, instead of giving no trust by retail, we see very considerable families who buy nothing but on trust; even bread, beer, butter, cheese, beef, and mutton, wine, groceries, &c., being the things which even with the meanest families are generally sold for ready money. Thus I have known a family, whose revenue has been some thousands a-year, pay their butcher, and baker, and grocer, and cheesemonger, by a hundred pounds at a time, and be generally a hundred more in each of their debts, and yet the tradesmen have thought it well worth while to trust them, and their pay has in the end been very honest and good.

This is what I say brings land so much in debt to trade, and obliges the tradesman to take credit of one another; and yet they do not lose by it neither, for the tradesmen find it in the price, and they take care to make such families pay warmly for the credit, in the rate of their goods; nor can it be expected it should be otherwise, for unless the profit answered it, the tradesman could not afford to be so long without his money.

This credit takes its beginning in our manufactures, even at the very first of the operation, for the master manufacturer himself begins it. Take a country clothier, or bay-maker, or what other maker of goods you please, provided he be one that puts out the goods to the making; it is true that the poor spinners and weavers cannot trust; the first spin for their bread, and the last not only weave for their bread, but they have several workmen and boys under them, who are very poor, and if they should want their pay on Saturday night, must want their dinner on Sunday; and perhaps would be in danger of starving with their families, by the next Saturday.

But though the clothier cannot have credit for spinning and weaving, he buys his wool at the stapler's or fellmonger's, and he gets two or three months' credit for that; he buys his oil and soap of the country shopkeeper, or has it sent down from his factor at London, and he gets longer credit for that, and the like of all other things; so that a clothier of any considerable business, when he comes to die, shall appear to be £4000 or £5000 in debt.

But, then, look into his books, and you shall find his factor at Blackwell Hall, who sells his cloths, or the warehouse-keeper who sells his duroys and druggets, or both together, have £2000 worth of goods in hand left unsold, and has trusted out to drapers, and mercers, and merchants, to the value of £4000 more; and look into his workhouse at home, namely, his wool-lofts, his combing-shop, his yarn-chamber, and the like, and there you will find it – in wool unspun, and in yarn spun, and in wool at the spinners', and in yarn at and in the looms at the weavers'; in rape-oil, gallipoli oil, and perhaps soap, &c., in his warehouses, and in cloths at the fulling-mill, and in his rowing-shops, finished and unfinished, £4000 worth of goods more; so that, though this clothier owed £5000 at his death, he has nevertheless died in good circumstances, and has £5000 estate clear to go among his children, all his debts paid and discharged. However, it is evident, that at the very beginning of this manufacturer's trade, his £5000 stock is made £10,000, by the help of his credit, and he trades for three times as much in the year; so that £5000 stock makes £10,000 stock and credit, and that together makes £30,000 a-year returned in trade.

When you come from him to the warehouse-keeper in London, there you double and treble upon it, to an unknown degree; for the London wholesale man shall at his death appear to have credit among the country clothiers for £10,000 or £15,000, nay, to £20,000, and yet have kept up an unspotted credit all his days.

When he is dead, and his executors or widow come to look into things, they are frightened with the very appearance of such a weight of debts, and begin to doubt how his estate will come out at the end of it. But when they come to cast up his books and his warehouse, they find,

In debts abroad, perhaps £30,000
In goods in his warehouse, ... £12,000

So that, in a word, the man has died immensely rich; that is to say, worth between £20,000 and £30,000, only that, having been a long standard in trade, and having a large stock, he drove a very great business, perhaps to the tune of £60,000 or £70,000 a-year; so that, of all the £30,000 owing, there may be very little of it delivered above four to six months, and the debtors being many of them considerable merchants, and good paymasters, there is no difficulty in getting in money enough to clear all his own debts; and the widow and children being left well, are not in such haste for the rest but that it comes in time enough to make them easy; and at length it all comes in, or with but a little loss.

As it is thus in great things, it is the same in proportion with small; so that in all the trade of England, you may reckon two-thirds of it carried on upon credit; in which reckoning I suppose I speak much within compass, for in some trades there is four parts of five carried on so, and in some more.

All these things serve to show the infinite value of which credit is to the tradesman, as well as to trade itself; and it is for this reason I have closed my instructions with this part of the discourse. Credit is the choicest jewel the tradesman is trusted with; it is better than money many ways; if a man has £10,000 in money, he may certainly trade for £10,000, and if he has no credit, he cannot trade for a shilling more.

But how often have we seen men, by the mere strength of their credit, trade for ten thousand pounds a-year, and have not one groat of real stock of their own left in the world! Nay, I can say it of my own knowledge, that I have known a tradesman trade for ten thousand pounds a-year, and carry it on with full credit to the last gasp, then die, and break both at once; that is to say, die unsuspected, and yet, when his estate has been cast up, appear to be five thousand pounds worse than nothing in the world: how he kept up his credit, and made good his payments so long, is indeed the mystery, and makes good what I said before, namely, that as none trade so much upon credit in the world, so none know so well how to improve and manage credit to their real advantage, as the English tradesmen do; and we have many examples of it, among our bankers especially, of which I have not room to enter at this time into the discourse, though it would afford a great many diverting particulars.[3]

I have mentioned on several occasions in this work, how nice and how dainty a dame this credit is, how soon she is affronted and disobliged, and how hard to be recovered, when once distasted and fled; particularly in the story of the tradesman who told his friends in a public coffee-house that he was broke, and should shut up his shop the next day. I have hinted how chary we ought to be of one another's credit, and that we should take care as much of our neighbour tradesman's credit as we would of his life, or as we would of firing his house, and, consequently, the whole street.

Let me close all with a word to the tradesman himself, that if it be so valuable to him, and his friends should be all so chary of injuring his reputation, certainly he should be very chary of it himself. The tradesman that is not as tender of his credit as he is of his eyes, or of his wife and children, neither deserves credit, nor will long be master of it.

As credit is a coy mistress, and will not easily be courted, so she is a mighty nice touchy lady, and is soon affronted; if she is ill used, she flies at once, and it is a very doubtful thing whether ever you gain her favour again.

Some may ask me here, 'How comes it to pass, since she is so nice and touchy a lady, that so many clowns court and carry her, and so many fools keep her so long?' My answer is, that those clowns have yet good breeding enough to treat her civilly; he must be a fool indeed that will give way to have his credit injured, and sit still and be quiet – that will not bustle and use his utmost industry to vindicate his own reputation, and preserve his credit.

But the main question for a tradesman in this case, and which I have not spoken of yet, is, 'What is the man to do to preserve his credit? What are the methods that a young tradesman is to take, to gain a

3 [Defoe speaks of such cases as if there were something laudable in them, whereas it is obviously for the interest of all honest traders, that no such men should be allowed to carry on business.]

good share of credit in his beginning, and to preserve and maintain it when it is gained?'[4]

Every tradesman's credit is supposed to be good at first. He that begins without credit, is an unhappy wretch of a tradesman indeed, and may be said to be broke even before he sets up; for what can a man do, who by any misfortune in his conduct during his apprenticeship, or by some ill character upon him so early, begins with a blast upon his credit? My advice to such a young man would be, not to set up at all; or if he did, to stay for some time, till by some better behaviour, either as a journeyman, or as an assistant in some other man's shop or warehouse, he had recovered himself; or else to go and set up in some other place or town remote from that where he has been bred; for he must have a great assurance that can flatter himself to set up, and believe he shall recover a lost reputation.

But take a young tradesman as setting up with the ordinary stock, that is to say, a negative character, namely, that he has done nothing to hurt his character, nothing to prejudice his behaviour, and to give people a suspicion of him: what, then, is the first principle on which to build a tradesman's reputation? and what is it he is to do?

The answer is short. Two things raise credit in trade, and, I may say, they are the only things required; there are some necessary addenda, but these are the fundamentals.

1. Industry.
2. Honesty.

I have dwelt upon the first; the last I have but a few words to say to, but they will be very significant; indeed, that head requires no comment, no explanations or enlargements: nothing can support credit, be it public or private, but honesty; a punctual dealing, a general probity in every transaction. He that once breaks through his honesty, violates his credit – once denominate a man a knave, and you need not forbid any man to trust him.

Even in the public it appears to be the same thing. Let any man view the public credit in its present flourishing circumstances, and compare it with the latter end of the years of King Charles II. after the Exchequer had been shut up, parliamentary appropriations misapplied, and, in a word, the public faith broken; who would

4 [Defoe almost appears in this place to lay capital out of the question, and to represent credit as all in all. Credit is a matter of great consequence; but we must not attempt to carry on business by its means alone. It should only be considered as an aid to capital. Those who, without capital, endeavour to set up in business by means of credit, or, when capital is exhausted, attempt to struggle on by means of credit alone, will, in general, only have a life of anxiety and dispeace for their pains.]

lend? Seven or eight per cent. was given for anticipations in King William's time, though no new fraud had been offered, only because the old debts were unpaid; and how hard was it to get any one to lend money at all!

But, after by a long series of just and punctual dealing, the Parliament making good all the deficient funds, and paying even those debts for which no provision was made, and the like, how is the credit restored, the public faith made sacred again, and how money flows into the Exchequer without calling for, and that at three or four per cent. interest, even from foreign countries as well as from our own people! They that have credit can never want money; and this credit is to be raised by no other method, whether by private tradesmen, or public bodies of men, by nations and governments, but by a general probity and an honest punctual dealing.

The reason of this case is as plain as the assertion; the cause is in itself; no man lends his money but with an expectation of receiving it again with the interest. If the borrower pays it punctually without hesitations and defalcations, without difficulties, and, above all, without compulsion, what is the consequence? – he is called an honest man, he has the reputation of a punctual fair dealer. And what then? – why, then, he may borrow again whenever he will, he may take up money and goods, or anything, upon his bare words, or note; when another man must give bondsmen, or *mainprize*, that is, a pawn or pledge for security, and hardly be trusted to neither. This is credit.

It is not the quality of the person would give credit to his dealing; not kings, princes, emperors, it is all one; nay, a private shopkeeper shall borrow money much easier than a prince, if the credit of the tradesman has the reputation of being an honest man. Not the crown itself can give credit to the head that wears it, if once he that wears it comes but to mortgage his honour in the matter of payment of money.

Who would have lent King Charles II. fifty pounds on the credit of his word or bond, after the shutting up the Exchequer? The royal word was made a jest of, and the character of the king was esteemed a fluttering trifle, which no man would venture upon, much less venture his money upon.

In King William's time the case was much the same at first; though the king had not broken his credit then with any man, yet how did they break their faith with the whole world, by the deficiency of the funds, the giving high and ruinous interest to men almost as greedy as vultures, the causing the government to pay great and extravagant rates for what they bought, and great premiums for what they borrowed – these were the injuries to the public for want of credit; nor was it in the power of the whole nation to remedy it; on the contrary, they made it still grow worse and worse, till, as above, the parliament recovered it. And how was it done? Not but by the same method a private person must do the same, namely, by doing justly, and fairly, and honestly, by every body.

Thus credit began to revive, and to enlarge itself again; and usury, which had, as it were, eaten up mankind in business, declined, and so things came to their right way again.

The case is the same with a tradesman; if he shuffles in payment, bargains at one time, and pays at another, breaks his word and his honour in the road of his business, he is gone; no man will take his bills, no man will trust him.

The conclusion is open and clear: the tradesman cannot be too careful of his credit, he cannot buy it too dear, or be too careful to preserve it: it is in vain to maintain it by false and loose doing business; by breaking faith, refusing to perform agreements, and such shuffling things as those; the greatest monarch in Europe could not so preserve his credit.

Nothing but probity will support credit; just, and fair, and honourable dealings give credit, and nothing but the same just, and fair, and honourable dealings will preserve it.

CHAPTER XXV

OF THE TRADESMAN'S PUNCTUAL PAYING HIS BILLS AND PROMISSORY NOTES UNDER HIS HAND, AND THE CREDIT HE GAINS BY IT

As I said that credit is maintained by just and honourable dealing, so that just dealing depends very much upon the tradesman's punctual payment of money in all the several demands that are upon him. The ordinary demands of money upon a tradesman are –

I. Promises of money for goods bought at time.

II. Bills drawn upon him; which, generally speaking, are from the country, that is to say, from some places remote from where he lives. Or,

III. Promissory notes under his hand, which are passed oftentimes upon buying goods: bought also at time, as in the first head.

IV. Bonds bearing interest, given chiefly for money borrowed at running interest.

1. Promises of money for goods bought at time. This indeed is the loosest article in a tradesman's payments; and it is true that a tradesman's credit is maintained upon the easiest terms in this case of any other that belongs to trade; for in this case not one man in twenty keeps to his time; and so easy are tradesmen to one another, that in general it is not much expected, but he that pays tolerably well, and without dunning, is a good man, and in credit; shall be trusted any where, and keeps up a character in his business: sometimes he pays sooner, sometimes later, and is accounted so good a customer, that though he owes a great deal, yet he shall be trusted any where, and is as lofty and touchy if his credit be called in question, as if he paid all ready money.

And, indeed, these men shall often buy their goods as cheap upon the credit of their ordinary pay, as another man shall that brings his money in his hand; and it is reasonable it should be so, for the ready-money man comes and buys a parcel here and a parcel there, and comes but seldom, but the other comes every day, that is to say, as often as he wants goods, buys considerably, perhaps deals for two or three thousand pounds a-year with you, and the like, and pays currently too. Such a customer ought indeed to be sold as cheap to, as the other chance customer for his ready money. In this manner of trade, I say, credit is maintained upon the easiest terms of any other, and yet here the tradesman must have a great care to keep it up too; for though it be the easiest article to keep up credit in, yet even in this article the tradesman may lose his credit, and then he is undone at once; and this is by growing (what in the language of trade is called) long-winded, putting off and putting off continually, till he will bear dunning; then his credit falls, his dealer that trusted him perhaps a thousand pounds previously, that esteemed him as good as ready money, now grows sick of him, declines him, cares not whether he deals with him or no, and at last refuses to trust him any longer. Then his credit is quite sunk and gone, and in a little after that his trade is ruined and the tradesman too; for he must be a very extraordinary tradesman that can open his shop after he has outlived his credit: let him look which way he will, all is lost, nobody cares to deal with him, and, which is still worse, nobody will trust him.

2. Bills drawn upon him from the country, that is to say, from some places remote from where he now dwells: it is but a little while ago since those bills were the loosest things in trade, for as they could not be protested, so they would not (in all their heats) always sue for them, but rather return them to the person from whom they received them.

In the meantime, let the occasion be what it will, the tradesman ought on all occasions to pay these notes without a public recalling and returning them, and without hesitation of any kind whatsoever. He that lets his bills lie long unpaid, must not expect to keep his credit much after them.

Besides, the late law for noting and protesting inland bills, alters the case very much. Bills now accepted, are protested in form, and, if not punctually paid, are either returned immediately, or the person on whom they are drawn is liable to be sued at law; either of which is at best a blow to the credit of the acceptor.

A tradesman may, without hurt to his reputation, refuse to accept a bill, for then, when the notary comes he gives his reasons, namely, that he refuses to accept the bill for want of advice, or for want of effects in his hands for account of the drawer, or that he has not given orders to draw upon him; in all which cases the non-acceptance touches the credit of the drawer; for in trade it is always esteemed a dishonourable thing to draw upon any man that has not effects in his hands to answer the bill; or to draw without order, or to draw and not give advice of it; because it looks like a forwardness to take the remitter's money without giving him a sufficient demand for it, where he expects and ought to have it.

A tradesman comes to me in London, and desires me to give him a bill payable at Bristol, for he is going to the fair there, and being to buy goods there, he wants money at Bristol to pay for them. If I give him a bill, he pays me down the money upon receipt of it, depending upon my credit for the acceptance of the bill. If I draw this bill where I have no reason to draw it, where I have no demand, or no effects to answer it, or if I give my correspondent no advice of it, I abuse the remitter, that is, the man whose money I take, and this reflects upon my credit that am the drawer, and the next time this tradesman wants money at Bristol fair, he will not come to me. 'No,' says he, 'his last bills were not accepted.' Or, if he does come to me, then he demands that he should not pay his money till he has advice that my bills are accepted.

But, on the other hand, if bills are right drawn, and advice duly given, and the person has effects in his hands, then, if he refuses the bill, he says to the notary he does not accept the bill, but gives no reason for it, only that he says absolutely, 'I will not accept it – you may take that for an answer;' or he adds, 'I refuse to accept it, for reasons best known to myself.' This is sometimes done, but this does not leave the person's credit who refuses, so clear as the other, though perhaps it may not so directly reflect upon him; but it leaves the case a little dubious and uncertain, and men will be apt to write back to the person who sent the bill to inquire what the drawer says to it, and what account he gives, or what character he has upon his tongue for the person drawn upon.

As the punctual paying of bills when accepted, is a main article in the credit of the acceptor, so a tradesman should be very cautious in permitting men to draw upon him where he has not effects, or does not give order; for though, as I said, it ought not to affect his reputation not to accept a bill where it ought not to be drawn, yet a tradesman that is nice of his own character does not love to be always or often refusing to accept bills, or to have bills drawn upon him where he has no reason to accept them, and therefore he will be very positive in forbidding such drawing; and if, notwithstanding that, the importunities of the country tradesman oblige him to draw, the person drawn upon will give smart and rough answers to such bills; as particularly, 'I refuse to accept this bill, because I have no effects of the drawer's to answer it.' Or thus, 'I refuse to accept this bill, because I not only gave no orders to draw, but gave positive orders not to draw.' Or thus, 'I neither will accept this bill, nor any other this man shall draw;' and the like. This thoroughly clears the credit of the acceptor, and reflects grossly on the drawer.

And yet, I say, even in this case a tradesman does not care to be drawn upon, and be obliged to see bills presented for acceptance, and for payment, where he has given orders not to draw, and where he has no effects to answer.

It is the great error of our country manufacturers, in many, if not in most, parts of England at this time, that as soon as they can finish their goods, they hurry them up to London to their factor, and as soon as the goods are gone, immediately follow them with their bills for the money, without waiting to hear whether the goods are come to a market, are sold, or in demand, and whether they are likely to sell quickly or not; thus they load the factor's warehouse with their goods before they are wanted, and load the factor with their bills, before it is possible that he can have gotten cash in his hand to pay them.

This is, first, a direct borrowing money of their factor; and it is borrowing, as it were, whether the factor will lend or no, and sometimes whether he can or no. The factor, if he be a man of money, and answers their bills, fails not to make them pay for advancing; or sells the goods to loss to answer the bills, which is making them pay dear for the loan; or refuses their bills, and so baulks both their business and their credit.

But if the factor, willing to oblige his employers, and knowing he shall otherwise lose their commission, accepts the bills on the credit of the goods, and then, not being able to sell the goods in time, is also made unable to pay the bills when due – this reflects upon his credit, though the fault is indeed in the drawer whose effects are not come in; and this has ruined many an honest factor.

First, it has hurt him by drawing large sums out of his cash, for the supply of the needy manufacturer, who is his employer, and has thereby made him unable to pay his other bills currently, even of such men's drafts who had perhaps good reason to draw.

Secondly, it keeps the factor always bare of money, and wounds his reputation, so that he pays those very bills with discredit, which in justice to himself he ought not to pay at all, and the borrower has the money, at the expense of the credit of the lender; whereas, indeed, the reproach ought to be to him that borrows, not to him that lends – to him that draws where there are no effects to warrant his draft, not to him that pays where he does not owe.

But the damage lies on the circumstances of accepting the bill, for the factor lends his employer the money the hour he accepts the bill, and the blow to his credit is for not paying when accepted. When the bill is accepted, the acceptor is debtor to the person to whom the bill is payable, or in his right to every indorser; for a bill of exchange is in this case different from a bond, namely, that the right of action is transferable by indorsement, and every indorser has a right to sue the acceptor in his own name, and can transfer that right to another; whereas in a bond, though it be given to me by assignment, I must sue in the name of the first person to whom the bond is payable, and he may at any time discharge the bond, notwithstanding my assignment.

Tradesmen, then, especially such as are factors,[1] are unaccountably to blame to accept bills for their employers before their goods are sold, and the money received, or within reach: if the employers cannot wait, the reproach should lie on them, not on the factor; and, indeed, the manufacturers all over England are greatly wrong in that part of their business; for, not considering the difference between a time of demand and a time of glut, a quick or a dead market, they go on in the same course of making, and, without slackening their hands as to quantity, crowd up their goods, as if it were enough to them that the factor had them, and that they were to be reckoned as sold when they were in his hands: but would the factor truly represent to them the state of the market – that there are great quantities of goods in hand unsold, and no present demand, desiring them to slack their hands a little in making; and at the same time back their directions in a plain and positive way, though with respect too, by telling them they could accept no more bills till the goods were sold. This would bring the trade into a better regulation, and the makers would stop their hands when the market stopped; and when the merchant ceased to buy, the manufacturers would cease to make, and, consequently, would not crowd or clog the market with goods, or wrong their factors with bills.

But this would require a large discourse, and the manufacturers' objections should be answered, namely, that they cannot stop, that they have their particular sets of workmen and spinners, whom they are obliged to keep employed, or, if they should dismiss them, they could not have them again when a demand for goods came, and the markets revived, and that, besides, the poor would starve.

These objections are easy to be answered, though that is not my present business; but thus far it is to my purpose – it is the factor's business to keep himself within compass: if the goods cannot be sold, the maker must stay till they can; if the poor must be employed, the manufacturer is right to keep them at work if he can; but if he cannot, without oppressing the factor, then he makes the factor employ them, not himself; and I do not see the factor has any obligation upon him to consider the spinners and weavers, especially not at the expense of his own credit, and his family's safety.

Upon the whole, all tradesmen that trade thus, whether by commission from the country, or upon their own accounts, should make it the standing order of their business not to suffer themselves to be overdrawn by their employers, so as to straiten themselves in their cash, and make them unable to pay their bills when accepted.

1 [By factors, Defoe seems to mean the class of persons whom we now name commission-agents.]

It is also to be observed, that when a tradesman once comes to suffer himself to be thus overdrawn, and sinks his credit in kindness to his employer, he buys his employment so dear as all his employer can do for him can never repay the price.

And even while he is thus serving his employer, he more and more wounds himself; for suppose he does (with difficulty) raise money, and, after some dunning, does pay the bills, yet he loses in the very doing it, for he never pays them with credit, but suffers in reputation by every day's delay. In a word, a tradesman that buys upon credit, that is to say, in a course of credit, such as I have described before, may let the merchant or the warehouse-keeper call two or three times, and may put him off without much damage to his credit; and if he makes them stay one time, he makes it up again another, and recovers in one good payment what he lost in two or three bad ones.

But in bills of exchange or promissory notes, it is quite another thing; and he that values his reputation in trade should never let a bill come twice for payment, or a note under his hand stay a day after it is due, that is to say, after the three days of *grace*, as it is called. Those three days, indeed, are granted to all bills of exchange, not by law, but by the custom of trade: it is hard to tell how this custom prevailed, or when it began, but it is one of those many instances which may be given, where custom of trade is equal to an established law; and it is so much a law now in itself, that no bill is protested now, till those three days are expired; nor is a bill of exchange esteemed due till the third day; no man offers to demand it, nor will any goldsmith, or even the bank itself, pay a foreign bill sooner. But that by the way.

Bills of exchange being thus sacred in trade, and inland bills being (by the late law for protesting them, and giving interest and damage upon them) made, as near as can be, equally sacred, nothing can be of more moment to a tradesman than to pay them always punctually and honourably.

Let no critic cavil at the word *honourably*, as it relates to trade: punctual payment is the honour of trade, and there is a word always used among merchants which justifies my using it in this place; and that is, when a merchant draws a bill from abroad upon his friend at London, his correspondent in London answering his letter, and approving his drawing upon him, adds, that he shall be sure to *honour* his bill when it appears; that is to say, to accept it.

Likewise, when the drawer gives advice of his having drawn such a bill upon him, he gives an account of the sum drawn, the name of the person it is payable to, the time it is drawn at, that is, the time given for payment, and he adds thus – 'I doubt not your giving my bill due honour;' that is, of accepting it, and paying it when it is due.

This term is also used in another case in foreign trade only, namely – a merchant abroad (say it be at Lisbon, or Bourdeaux) draws a bill of £300 sterling upon his correspondent at London: the correspondent happens to be dead, or is broke, or by some other accident the bill is not accepted; another merchant on the Exchange hearing of it, and knowing, and perhaps corresponding with, the merchant abroad who drew the bill, and loth his credit should suffer by the bill going back protested, accepts it, and pays it for him. This is called accepting it for the honour of the drawer; and he writes so upon the bill when he accepts it, which entitles him to re-draw the same with interest upon the drawer in Lisbon or Bourdeaux, as above.

This is, indeed, a case peculiar to foreign commerce, and is not often practised in home trade, and among shopkeepers, though sometimes I have known it practised here too: but I name it on two accounts, first – to legitimate the word honourable, which I had used, and which has its due propriety in matters of trade, though not in the same acceptation as it generally receives in common affairs; and, secondly, to let the tradesman see how deeply the honour, that is, the credit of trade, is concerned in the punctual payment of bills of exchange, and the like of promissory notes; for in point of credit there is no difference, though in matter of form there is.

There are a great many variations in the drawing bills from foreign countries, according as the customs and usages of merchants direct, and according as the coins and rates of exchange differ, and according as the same terms are differently understood in several places; as the word *usance*, and *two usance*, which is a term for the number of days given for payment, after the date of the bill; and though this is a thing particularly relating to merchants, and to foreign commerce, yet as the nature of bills of exchange is pretty general, and that sometimes an inland tradesman, especially in seaport towns, may be obliged to take foreign accepted bills in payment for their goods; or if they have money to spare (as sometimes it is an inland tradesman's good luck to have), may be asked to discount such bills – I say, on this account, and that they may know the value of a foreign bill when they see it, and how far it has to run, before it has to be demanded, I think it not foreign to the case before me, to give them the following account:–

1. As to the times of payment of foreign bills of exchange, and the terms of art ordinarily used by merchants in drawing, and expressed in the said bills: the times of payment are, as above, either–

(1.) At sight; which is to be understood, not the day it is presented, but three days (called days of grace) after the bill is accepted: (2.) usance: (3.) two usance.[2]

Usance between London and all the towns in the States Generals' dominions, and also in the provinces now called the Austrian Netherlands [Belgium], is one month. And two usance is two months; reckoning not from the acceptance of the bill, but from the date of it. Usance between London and Hamburgh is two months, Venice is three months; and double usance, or two usance, is double that time. Usance payable at Florence or Leghorn, is two months; but from thence payable at London, usance is three months. Usance from London to Rouen or Paris, is one month; but they generally draw at a certain number of days, usually twenty-one days' sight. Usance from London to Seville, is two months; as likewise between London and Lisbon, and Oporto, to or from. Usance from Genoa to Rome is payable at Rome ten days after sight. Usance between Antwerp and Genoa, Naples or Messina, is two months, whether to or from. Usance from Antwerp or Amsterdam, payable at Venice, is two months, payable in bank.

There are abundance of niceties in the accepting and paying of bills of exchange, especially foreign bills, which I think needless to enter upon here; but this I think I should not omit, namely –

That if a man pays a bill of exchange before it is due, though he had accepted it, if the man to whom it was payable proves a bankrupt after he has received the money, and yet before the bill becomes due, the person who voluntarily paid the money before it was due, shall be liable to pay it again to the remitter; for as the remitter delivered his money to the drawer, in order to have it paid again to such person as he should order, it is, and ought to be, in his power to divert the payment by altering the bill, and make it payable to any other person whom he thinks fit, during all the time between the acceptance and the day of payment.

This has been controverted, I know, in some cases, but I have always found, that by the most experienced merchants, and especially in places of the greatest business abroad, it was always given in favour of the remitter, namely, that the right of guiding the payment is in him, all the time the bill is running; and no bill can or ought to be paid before it is due, without the declared assent of the remitter, signified under his hand, and attested by a public notary.

2 [All bills and promissory notes, inland or foreign, payable in this country, are allowed three days of grace beyond the actual period expressed upon them; thus, a bill drawn at thirty days after date, is payable only on the thirty-third day. If bills be not presented for payment on the last day of grace, they cannot be protested, and consitute only an evidence of the debt for legal recovery. If the last day of grace be a Sunday, the bill is presentible on the Saturday previous.]

There are, I say, abundance of niceties in the matter of foreign exchanges, and in the manner of drawing, accepting, and protesting bills; but as I am now speaking with, and have confined my discourse in this work to, the inland tradesmen of England, I think it would be as unprofitable to them to meddle with this, as it would be difficult to them to understand it.[3]

I return, therefore, to the subject in hand, as well as to the people to whom I have all along directed my discourse.

Though the inland tradesmen do not, and need not, acquaint themselves with the manner of foreign exchanges, yet there is a great deal of business done by exchange among ourselves, and at home, and in which our inland trade is chiefly concerned; and as this is the reason why I speak so much, and repeat it so often to the tradesman for whose instruction I am writing, that he should maintain the credit of his bills, so it may not be amiss to give the tradesman some directions concerning such bills.

He is to consider, that, in general, bills pass through a number of hands, by indorsation from one to another, and that if the bill comes

3 [In consequence of the great extension of commerce since the time of Defoe, a short explanation of the principle and practice of drawing foreign bills of exchange now seems necessary. Foreign bills of exchange are used, in order to avoid the necessity of transmitting actual money from one country to another. A merchant, for instance, in Nova Scotia, is owing £100 to a manufacturer in Glasgow: he seeks out some one who is a creditor to that amount to some person in Britain; we shall say he finds a captain in the army who wishes to draw £100 from his agent in London. To this captain the Nova Scotia merchant pays £100, and gets his order or bill on the London agent, which bill he sends to the manufacturer in Glasgow, and the manufacturer transmits the bill to London for payment; any banker, indeed, will give him the money for it, deducting a small commission. Thus two debts are liquidated, without the transmission of a farthing in money. The demand for bills in foreign countries to send to Great Britain, has the effect of raising them to a premium, which is called the rate of exchange, and is a burden which falls on the purchaser of the bill. Foreign bills of exchange drawn on parties in Great Britain, have expressed upon them the number of days after sight at which they are to be payable. Thus, a merchant on receiving a foreign bill drawn at 'thirty days after sight,' hastens to get it 'sighted,' or shown to the party on whom it is drawn, and that party accepts it, at the same time marking the date of doing so. The bill is then complete and negociable, and is presented for payment to the acceptor at the end of the time specified, allowing the usual three days of grace. Should the bill not be accepted on being 'sighted,' it is a dishonoured bill, and is returned with a legal protest to the foreign correspondent. To avert, as far as possible, the loss of foreign bills by shipwreck, a set of three bills is drawn for each transaction, called first, second, and third, of the same tenor. For example: 'Thirty days after sight pay this my first bill of exchange, for the sum of £100 sterling; second and third of the same tenor being unpaid.' This first bill is first sent, and by next conveyance the second is sent. Should the first arrive safely, the second, on making its appearance, is destroyed. The third is retained by the foreign correspondent till he hear whether the former two have arrived at their destination, and is sent only if they have been lost. On receiving whichever comes first, it is the duty of the receiver to communicate intelligence of the fact to the sender.]

to be protested afterwards and returned, it goes back again through all those hands with this mark of the tradesman's disgrace upon it, namely, that it has been accepted, but that the man who accepted it is not able to pay it, than which nothing can expose the tradesman more.

He is to consider that the grand characteristic of a tradesman, and by which his credit is rated, is this of paying his bills well or ill. If any man goes to the neighbours or dealers of a tradesman to inquire of his credit, or his fame in business, which is often done upon almost every extraordinary occasion, the first question is, 'How does he pay his bills?' As when we go to a master or mistress to inquire the character of a maid-servant, one of the first questions generally is of her probity, 'Is she honest?' so here, if you would be able to judge of the man, your first question is, 'What for a paymaster is he? How does he pay his bills?' – strongly intimating, and, indeed, very reasonably, that if he has any credit, or any regard to his credit, he will be sure to pay his bills well; and if he does not pay his bills well, he cannot be sound at bottom, because he would never suffer a slur there, if it were possible for him to avoid it. On the other hand, if a tradesman pays his bills punctually, let whatever other slur be upon his reputation, his credit will hold good. I knew a man in the city, who upon all occasions of business issued promissory notes, or notes under his hand, at such or such time, and it was for an immense sum of money that he gave out such notes; so that they became frequent in trade, and at length people began to carry them about to discount, which lessened the gentleman so much, though he was really a man of substance, that his bills went at last at twenty per cent. discount or more; and yet this man maintained his credit by this, that though he would always take as much time as he could get in these notes, yet when they came due they were always punctually paid to a day; no man came twice for his money.

This was a trying case, for though upon the multitude of his notes that were out, and by reason of the large discount given upon them, his credit at first suffered exceedingly, and men began to talk very dubiously of him, yet upon the punctual discharge of them when due, it began presently to be taken notice of, and said openly how well he paid his notes; upon which presently the rate of his discount fell, and in a short time all his notes were at *par*; so that punctual payment, in spite of rumour, and of a rumour not so ill grounded as rumours generally are, prevailed and established the credit of the person, who was indeed rich at bottom, but might have found it hard enough to have stood it, if, as his bills had a high discount upon them, they had been ill paid too. All which confirms what I have hitherto alleged, namely, of how much concern it is for a tradesman to pay his bills and promissory notes very punctually.

I might argue here how much it is his interest to do so, and how it enables him to coin as many bills as he pleases – in short, a man whose notes are currently paid, and the credit of whose bills is established by their being punctually paid, has an infinite advantage in trade; he is a bank to himself; he can buy what bargains he pleases; no advantage in business offers but he can grasp at it, for his notes are current as another man's cash; if he buys at time in the country, he has nothing to do but to order them to draw for the money when it is due, and he gains all the time given in the bills into the bargain.

If he knows what he buys, and how to put it off, he buys a thousand pounds' worth of goods at once, sells them for less time than he buys at, and pays them with their own money. I might swell this discourse to a volume by itself, to set out the particular profit that such a man may make of his credit, and how he can raise what sums he will, by buying goods, and by ordering the people whom he is to pay in the country, to draw bills on him. Nor is it any loss to those he buys of, for as all the remitters of money know his bills, and they are currently paid, they never scruple delivering their money upon his bills, so that the countryman or manufacturer is effectually supplied, and the time given in the bill is the property of the current dealer on whom they are drawn.

But, then, let me add a caution here for the best of tradesmen not to neglect – namely, as the tradesman should take care to pay his bills and notes currently, so, that he may do it, he must be careful what notes he issues out, and how he suffers others to draw on him. He that is careful of his reputation in business, will also be cautious not to let any man he deals with over draw him, or draw upon him before the money drawn for his due. And as to notes promissory, or under his hand, he is careful not to give out such notes but on good occasions, and where he has the effects in his hand to answer them; this keeps his cash whole, and preserves his ability of performing and punctually paying when the notes become due; and the want of this caution has ruined the reputation of a tradesman many times, when he might otherwise have preserved himself in as good credit and condition as other men.

All these cautions are made thus needful on account of that one useful maxim, that the tradesman's *all* depends upon his punctual complying with the payment of his bills.